INDIAN SOCIETY AND THE SECULAR

Indian Society and the Secular

Essays

Romila Thapar

Three Essays
COLLECTIVE

First Edition November 2016

ISBN 978-93-83968-16-9

B-957 Palam Vihar, GURGAON (Haryana) 122 017 India
Tel: 91-124 236 9023, +91 98681 26587, +91 98683 44843
info@threeessays.com Website: www.threeessays.com
Printed and bound at Chaman Offset Printers, New Delhi

Contents

RELIGION AND CONTEMPORARY POLITICS

Preface

The essays and lectures in this collection date to the last twenty years and revolve around various aspects of the perception of secularism by Indian society. One could ask as to how the concept of secularism became so central to contemporary India. It is viewed by secular opinion as essential, but others wishing to use religion as a political tool, regard secularism as that which has to be contested and denied. The main point of these essays is to show that secularism is not just a slogan to be bandied about on various occasions as it frequently is in our times. It has a distinct meaning that has to be understood. It does imply a fundamental change in our mind-set with the introduction of a reasoned way of seeing how we function as a society and set right the mal-functioning.

As a concept it has not yet been firmly rooted in the functioning of our democracy. We often speak of India being a secular democracy, but is it actually so? This question is particularly pertinent to events that have taken place and decisions taken by those that have governed, in the last three decades.

My argument is that the definition given to secularism during the national movement and just after is not a sufficient definition. It was then spoken of as meaning the co-existence of all religions. We prided ourselves on having always been a people that were tolerant and non-violent and therefore co-existence was sufficient. This was a necessary definition for anti-colonial nationalism and to contest the aspirations of Hindu and Muslim religious 'nationalisms' working towards the establishing of a Muslim and a Hindu nation. But history shows otherwise. There were no jihads and crusades over religion. But nevertheless there was intolerance, manifested not only in religious contestations, but much more in another aspect of social life, namely the extreme intolerance in excluding large groups of people from basic humanism by calling them polluting. Every religion in India discriminated against such groups.

What this shows is that the co-existence of all religions is not an adequate definition of secularism. Human rights and equal status as citizens have also to be guaranteed in a secular society. The definition of secularism has to incorporate the idea that the state has to keep an equal distance from all religious organisations and institutions, as has been argued by various people. But a state can only call itself secular when it can ensure that every citizen has access to basic human rights such as food, health care, education, employment and social justice. The recent lynching of Dalits, Adivasis, Muslims and Christians, and raping of women, does not allow Indian society to be called secular by any stretch of the imagination.

Secularism, therefore, does not refer only to the role of religion in society, although this role has to be analysed in detail. A distinction can be made between the practice of religion as a personal system of belief and faith that everyone is entitled to, and the control exercised by religious organisations on social activity through the institutions that they run and which they use to exercise power over society. Whereas the practice of worship and exercise of belief is not questioned, provided it does not impinge on or harm other members of society, the role of religious institutions controlling civil laws has to be re-evaluated. Governance is invested in those duly elected and those manning various wings of the administration of the country. Governance through the lynching by vigilantes is not the definition of a democracy.

Those that have a political agenda not conducive to secularising society can easily whip up a disfigured or distorted history. We frequently hear the statement that Hindus in India have suffered a thousand years of slavery and oppression under Muslim rule. I am constantly amazed at this statement as it implies a deliberate shutting out of Indian history during the entire second millennium AD. It reflects a complete unfamiliarity with the history of India. Yet it is responsible people who make such statements. One suspects that they do know better and therefore the remarks are deliberately political and intended to create hostilities. It is also strange to hear caste Hindus speak of their victimisation at the hands of Muslim rulers, when there is a history of the victimisation of Adivasis and Dalits for twenty-five hundred years. It is a victimisation that cannot be easily brushed aside as it created a mind-set that is present to this day. One wonders who is victimising whom?

The history of the last thousand years is immensely rich in terms of the forms of thought and worship that emerged within Hinduism and partly through historical change and partly as a consequence of other belief systems. Some major works in Sanskrit were written during this time. *Dharmashastras* took up discussions on new issues such as the laws of inheritance among upper caste Hindus. There were new articulations of belief and worship through the Bhakti devotional sects composed in regional languages. These enriched the Hindu religion as well as the regional languages. The *Ramayana* for instance was rendered into regional languages, and their authors did not regard themselves as enslaved people. It was in these languages again that there were magnificent compositions by Hindu and Muslim devotees worshipping Krishna or Shiva. Brahmana and Jaina scholars were associated with the Mughal court and received patronage from the rulers to help translate Sanskrit works into Persian. Dhrupada, the foundation of Hindustani Classical music, grew out of these traditions at the courts of the Sultans and the Mughals. This was also the period that saw the emergence of Carnatic music through the compositions of the three great masters. Much of what is practiced as Hinduism today goes back to this period.

In terms of heritage, the one heritage that we hesitate to recognise because we are so bent on declaring ourselves to be entirely spiritually oriented, is the great tradition that we have of rational thought. It is argued that secularism is alien to the Indian tradition because Indians are too religiously inclined. But a serious study of Indian philosophy going back to the time of the *Upanishads* and the Buddha, reveals that there were many streams of thought – which is not surprising – and that these ranged from idealism to materialism. Subsequent to the Buddhist and Jaina teaching there were intense discussions between brahmana and non-brahmana scholars (Buddhist and Jaina) on issues concerning logic and rational thought, and these are known from Gupta times in the mid-first millennium AD. Such discussions continued into the medieval period and a fourteenth century compendium on the various schools of philosophy starts with a chapter on the Charvaka/Lokayata materialism, not because it was the most important but because this stream of thinking continued to be widely discussed. I have therefore argued that it is possible to link, not secularism which is a modern concept, but ideas conducive to a secular way of thinking from some of these earlier philosophies.

We also need to be aware of the historical context of the ideas that are held to be authoritative by various political groups today. Our identity as Indians and the ideas that we hold about our past were conditioned by the colonial interpretation of Indian history. I have discussed this in the paper included here from a seminar at the Library of Congress, held in 2004. The two theories that are basic to the views of extremist religious nationalism are rooted in the nineteenth century interpretations of colonial writers.

One was what came to be called the two-nation theory first put forward by James Mill in the early nineteenth century, where he argued that the history of India consisted of the two Hindu and Muslim nations that lived in a state of constant antagonism. The British had to hold the peace between them. His periodisation of Indian history into Hindu, Muslim and British periods, is still used in public discussion although it has been discarded in academic historical writing. This kind of colonial thinking stoked Muslim and Hindu communalism and gave rise to the politics and organisation of the Muslim League and the Hindu Mahasabha.

The other theory was the one propagated by various colonial scholars, pre-eminently Max Müller, and this was the Theory of Aryan Race. The foundations of Indian civilisation were traced to the *Vedas* and their Aryan authors. The Aryans were projected as culturally superior and racially pure and the theory discounted the presence of non-Aryans and their contribution to that culture. The Hindu identity was traced back to the Aryans and this process is continuing with the Aryans being taken further and further back in time. This identity is then used to justify the theory that Hindus have primacy as citizens of modern India.

It is important to recognise that political organisations, claiming to be devoted to Indian culture, and presenting the indigenous history of India unpolluted by western ideas, actually draw their ideas from colonial scholarship. These are not indigenous ideas but come from colonial readings supporting colonial policy in India. They continue to support the same policy even in the garb of religious nationalism. This is not altogether surprising since these two religious nationalisms were not anti-colonial but were pitted against each other. They were loyal to colonial scholarship and in some instances to colonial authority. This is one reason why history today has become a contested area, because the scholarship in history over the past fifty years has seriously questioned colonial interpretations and replaced them with more pertinent and precise explanations of the past. These explanations conflict with the ideas of religious nationalism, considered untenable by historians. Historians have now moved onto new ways of trying to crack old chestnuts.

An example of this is the kind of research that is now being done in the field of genetics and the use of DNA to provide clues as to the identity of populations in India in the past. At one level this has again been reduced to trying to track the Aryans, without coming to terms with the fact that 'Aryan' is not a biological fact, it is a linguistic entity. The label is named after the language, and not after the people as a race. A variety of people could have spoken Indo-Aryan, and the speakers of Indo-Aryan are particular about the correctness of the language. This leads to asking different questions from the DNA analysis from those that have been asked in the recent past. Tracking the mixing of populations along a timeline could provide worthwhile information, provided it is done with a strict control over the data and the method of analysis. Such control cannot be guaranteed in every laboratory. The presence of Aryan speakers has also to be viewed as cultural amalgamation and change, rather than the imposition of a language across the sub-continent.

The kind of history that is now being researched and analysed has moved a long way away from either the colonial reconstructions or even the nationalist history of the mid-twentieth century. The borders between civilisations are slowly dissolving and we are discovering that civilisations are indeed porous. This requires re-evaluating the concept of civilisation, and moving away from the notion of civilisational blocks identified by territory, a single religion and a single language. Now that we know that even the culture of the elite has absorbed aspects of non-elite cultures, the understanding of a multiplicity of cultures becomes more appropriate rather than a single dominant civilisation. The question is what is the concept of a civilisation to be replaced with, if it is replaced? There has been much written recently on World Systems and perhaps these ideas need to be more closely investigated.

I have tried to show in these essays that the concept of secularism is far broader and more inclusive than what we have thought it to be in our times. If at one level it relates to religious articulation then at another it incorporates ideas of history as reflecting the past that we have inherited. Since historical research is constantly bringing up new ideas and theories, these also have an impact on the understanding of the process of secularising society.

Romila Thapar
JNU, New Delhi

29 July 2016

The Role of Religion in Political Conflicts[1]

Any attempt to understand religious conflict in contemporary India must first comprehend the forms and functions of indigenous religions in India, which were different from those that we assume on the basis of the Semitic religions. I trace these differences by looking at the nature of pre-modern religions in India, and particularly those aspects that are central to the contemporary debates. But I would also like to argue that the conflict is only tangentially religious, for its motivation lies in reactions to other essentials of Indian life as well. Because of this there is at the same time a large element of political mobilisation in the guise of religion.

The indigenous religions of India were multiple and distinctive. Prior to the coming of Islam they would have been listed as Vedic Brahmanism; the Shramana religions which included Buddhism and Jainism; Shaiva devotionalism and Vaishnava Bhagavatism or what is sometimes called Puranic Hinduism; Shaktism; and apart from these whose literature is well established, many cults of a wide range of people gener-

---

1   Lecture delivered at the conference organised by the Department of
     Theology, University of Uppsala, March 1995.

ally from the lower rungs of society. Each of these established forms were distinctive although there was a marginal overlap. Each sect whose imprint survives, experienced dominance and decline in various parts of the sub-continent at different times. It would indeed be difficult to argue that any one of these constituted either a majority or a minority community – the kind of social and political construction that has drawn on religion during the last two centuries.

Historically, the religion of the Indus civilisation is the earliest, but its reconstruction remains speculative at the moment given the sparseness of data. The subsequent Vedic Brahmanism of the first millennium BC focused on the performance of the sacrificial ritual, the *yajna*, which soon became the preserve of the brahmanas, who claimed to be intermediaries between the patron of the sacrifice and the deities being propitiated. Ritual chants were imbued with a magical power and had to be correctly pronounced so as to avert accidents. In the competition for status between the priest and the clan chief, the superiority of the priest was asserted through a ritual stratification of society. Social differentiation, actually based on access to resources, was reinforced through the notion of ritual purity and pollution. Eventually those at the lowest level were regarded as untouchable. This was not a religion of the Book, nor was it a proselytising faith, since caste status was crucial to its practice and caste was determined by birth. These remained constant characteristics in what we call Hinduism. Gradually, when clan-based societies gave way to monarchies and states and the growth of cities, then new religions emerged.[2]

The religions of the Shramanas, such as Buddhism and Jainism, coincide with these changes.[3] They questioned the

---

2   Romila Thapar, *From Lineage to State*, Delhi, 1984.
3   Romila Thapar, 'Ethics, Religion and Social Protest in the First Millenium BC in Northern India' in Romila Thapar, *Ancient Indian Social History: Some Interpretations*, New Delhi, 1978, pp. 40-62.

efficacy of the sacrificial ritual and therefore the status of the brahmana. The focus shifted from the worship of many deities to the centrality of social ethics, referred to as observing the dharma. This as a Brahmanical concept referred to sacred duty. The early Buddhists had no place for deity, which is why Durkheim queried Buddhism being called a religion. The theory of transmigration and rebirth became axiomatic to the moral code – as you act in this birth, so you shall be born in the next. They each established orders of renouncers, monks who constituted the Sangha, which was the highest religious authority with its own hierarchy and administration, and whose proclamations were binding. Renunciation was seen as the ideal path in the attainment of *nirvana*, the termination of the cycle of births. But renunciation was not open to all, and the ethical code and form of worship for the laity had perforce to be different.

The Shramanic religions had little in common with Vedic Brahmanism. The teachings of the founders were recorded and the history of the Sangha maintained, so as to locate changes in rules and breakaway sects, not to mention the relationship with political authority when the Sangha became powerful. Both, the monks and the lay followers, could be of any caste, though clearly upper castes were initially preferred for reasons of status and financial support.

Visitors to early India, therefore, often described its religion as consisting of Brahmanism and Shramanism. Megesthenes makes this distinction in the fourth century BC; the Mauryan king Ashoka refers to it a century later; the grammarian Patanjali speaks of the animosity between the two; and even as late as the eleventh century, Alberuni refers to the brahmana and the *sammaniyya*.[4] But by this time, within each of these there had been changes.

____

4   Strabo 15.1.39; Arrian, *Indica*, 11; J. Bloch, *Les Inscriptions d' Asoka*,

Brahmanism would probably have declined with the fading out of clans, but the rituals of empowerment were retained in the emergent monarchies. Kings performed the Vedic sacrifices and on such occasions the brahmanas received handsome grants of land. Some royal families such as the Iksvakus were known not to take chances, performing Vedic sacrifices and making equally impressive donations to the Buddhists.[5]

But aside from this, a more significant departure was one that introduced new forms of Hindu belief and worship. With Shaiva devotionalism and Vaishnava Bhagavatism, directing worship towards Shiva or Vishnu as focal deities, and a move away from Vedic ritual to a personalised, devotional cult, the emphasis shifted to the relationship between the individual and the deity. This was, in part, the influence of the Shramanic religions, and in part the articulation of a large number of groups who had been excluded by the Vedic ritual, but who had their own deities and form of worship.

The survival of Brahmanism was, then, dependent on its appropriating the forms of worship of various castes, which we today recognise as manifestations of devotionalism. This was done by incorporating their mythology and rituals of worship and by taking over the narratives of deities and popular heroes and "sanskritising" them: that is, translating them into high culture. Some brahmanas, therefore, acquired a different function from that of performing Vedic sacrifices. These brahmanas chose to become the priests and mentors of new theistic sects, involving deities different from the major ones of the Vedic pantheon or new manifestations of earlier deities. Thus Indra, Varuna and Mitra, the classic deities of the Indo-Aryan texts, faded into the background with the foreground-

---

Paris, 1950, pp. 87, 99, 112; S. D. Joshi (ed.), *Patanjali Vyakarna Mahabhasya*, Poona, 1968, II.4.9; I.476; E. Sachau, *Alberuni's India*, Delhi, 1964 (reprint), 21.

5   D. C. Sircar, *Select Inscriptions*, Vol. I., Calcutta, 1965, pp. 228 ff.

ing of Shiva and Vishnu. Equally significant, the Vedic sacrificial ritual was performed on fewer occasions, and worship in the form of *puja*, distinctly different from the Vedic sacrificial ritual, became increasingly popular. This change is more frequently referred to as Puranic Hinduism. Attempts at systematising these manifold religious expressions is reflected in the many *Puranas*, which were composed from about the fourth century A.D. onwards, each dedicated to a deity and purporting to be the text of the sect worshipping that deity.

The role of the priest was strengthened with the introduction of the worship of images around the Christian era. However, among some sects and forms of worship, particularly at the lower social levels, the priest did not need to be a brahmana. The brahmanas, therefore, could be in a situation where they had to negotiate with a local cult or sect, providing it with a location and status in the Puranic hierarchy of deities and rituals. This depended largely on the caste and resources of those who were members of the sect. The religion of some of the lowest castes could well be entirely excluded, whereas others better off could be accommodated.

The rise of Shaktism or Tantrism further demonstrates this process. What are believed to have been a number of substratum cults, focusing on the power of goddesses and notions of fertility, commonly found in various parts of South Asia, began to surface from the early centuries of the Christian era. Within a few centuries this became an important aspect of religious expression. Its legitimacy as a significant feature of Indian religion is evident from the fact that it not only permeated a range of religious belief and ritual, but it also received the patronage of ruling families and elite groups.

Since the individual's relationship with deity was central, it was open to people to choose a deity and to worship the deity in a manner of their choice. However, the form of worship and eschatology was frequently conditioned by what was thought appropriate by the caste to which the individual belonged. For example, even a belief as widespread as that of metempsychosis and rebirth, regarded by many as characteristic of Hinduism, was not universally accepted. Those who died the death of a hero were said to go to heaven, where they live to eternity in the company of accomplished celestial maidens. Of the heroes of the *Mahabharata*, the eldest refuses to enter heaven until he is permitted to take his faithful dog with him.

Royal patronage continued a policy where support was extended to more than one religious sect, by the same ruler or by his successors, either for personal reasons or for reasons of public policy. It is difficult, therefore, to speak of there having been a "state religion" in early India. The open-endedness of Puranic Hinduism also provided a convenient entry-point for Hellenistic and central Asian dynasties ruling in northern India, and seeking identity with local cultures.

The imprint of Buddhism and Jainism on devotional worship can perhaps be seen not only from the obvious similarities, but also from the fears that took the form of confrontations.[6] With the establishment, particularly of Shaiva sects, incidents of religious intolerance become apparent. Hostility between the Shaivas and the Buddhists and Jainas is recorded. Buddhist monasteries were destroyed and Buddhist monks killed in Kashmir and in eastern India. The Jainas were attacked in Tamilnadu and Karnataka in the south. Each accused the other of propagating a false religion and the term *pashanda* was used, which has been translated as "heretic", although this is not the most apposite translation. But the conflict was conditioned by factors other than religion alone. There was competition for courtly patronage and the largesse of kings and of wealthy merchants. There was further competition among the

---

6   Romila Thapar, *Cultural Transactions and Early India*, Delhi, 1993.

literati for controlling administration and the implicit powers of such control. But these were localised conflicts and persecutions. There were neither Inquisitions nor Crusades nor Jihads – Holy Wars. The more severe intolerance of Indian society lay not in religion, as in Christianity and Islam, but in insisting on the social degradation of those ranked as the untouchables and lower castes, a degradation paralleled in many ancient and some not-so-ancient societies, which flourished on the backs of slaves.

In my description of Hinduism I have suggested that it was not a religion with a linear development, but instead is better seen as a mosaic of religious articulations and organisations that relate to each other at some level, but are also distinct. Above all, there are juxtaposed strands, with a continuing existence and history in themselves as well. Also evident among these strands is a rich presence of philosophy, which took the *Upanishads* as a starting point, but explored many directions of thought.

The arrival of Islam was not viewed with immediate hostility, as is now popularly believed. The Arabs and the Turks and Afghans were referred to as *mlechchha*, a term used from earlier times for those regarded as outside the social pale, therefore impure, and generally viewed as low in caste status. But other terms such as Yavana, Shaka and Turushka, familiar from pre-Islamic history, are also used suggesting that this "Other" was perceived as part of a historical continuity of peoples coming from western and central Asia. Curiously, they are not initially referred to by any religious designation.[7]

The Arabs were the first to use the term "Hindu" for all those living to the east of the Indus, *al-hind*. Gradually, the

---

7   Romila Thapar, 'Imagined Religious Communities? Ancient History and the Modern Search for a Hindu Identity' in *Interpreting Early India*, New Delhi, 1992, pp. 60-88.

term ceases to be geographical and acquires a religious connotation. It comes to mean all those who practice religions other than the ones familiar to the Arabs, namely Islam and Christianity. The use of this term is, therefore, not religion-specific but includes all the indigenous religions of India. Furthermore, it negates one of the essentials of the indigenous Brahmanical religions when it includes all castes – high and low, inside or outside the pale – equally, as Hindus. By this time, the central feature of the Hindu religion is said to be the worship of images.[8]

Iconoclasm and temple destruction become, therefore, an act of piety for the Muslim conqueror. But these are not merely acts of piety, for they were preceded by a few cases of the same in pre-Islamic times in India. Temples, when constructed by royalty or important personages of the court, were, in addition to their religious function and identity, statements of power and legitimation; they were also repositories of immense wealth. Raids on temples by Muslim rulers and generals, although greater in number than the preceding cases, nevertheless related to all these factors. They cannot be dismissed in every case as an expression solely of religious bigotry.

Islam was essentially a proselytising religion having successfully converted large parts of western and central Asia. But in India it met with not only a non-unitary religion, but also one that had little use for conversion. Given the centrality of caste to religion, one's religious identity drew substantially on caste, and therefore on birth. Conversions to Islam were either of individuals generally of high status, where conversion was an aspect of a social and political alliance; or, large scale conversions were frequently of the lower castes, where an entire caste in a locality would convert. This would be an aspiration

---

8　Sachau, op.cit., p. 112.

for benefits from a theoretically egalitarian religion, but were felt frequently as only aspiration.[9]

Despite the use of terms such as Hindu and Muslim, these did not denote monolithic social or religious entities. If the Hindus were fragmented by belief, caste and custom, so were the Muslims. Apart from the sharp Sunni-Shia differentiation, there was also a cleavage between those claiming foreign ancestry and the indigenous converts. Not only were the former, such as Shaikhs, Sayyads and Ashrafs, given high status in Muslim caste ranking, but even those among them whose ancestry was indigenous claimed foreign forefathers. In fact, however, only a few were of foreign origin, and even this was diluted over time through their having settled in India and intermarried locally, a classic case being that of Mughal royalty. For the large majority of Muslims their ancestry is as Indian as that of the Hindus.

Arab traders who made their homes along the west coast of India and married into local families, observed an Islam substantially indigenous as is evident from the cultural traditions of the large communities such as the Bohras, Khoja, Mappila and Navayat. Until recently there was only the vaguely learnt catechism that signaled an Islamic veneer in common between them and the Muslim peasant from Bengal or the Muslim herdsman from Kashmir. As in the case of the Hindus, the culture of the Muslim ruling class was also similar across the land. But the converted Muslim Rajput of high status had more in common with other Rajputs than with, for example, the Muslim Mappila of Malabar who had adopted local matrilineal customs.

---

9   S.I. Zaidi and S. Zaidi, 'Conversion to Islam and Formation of Castes in Rajasthan' in A.J. Qaiser and S.P Verma (eds.), *Art and Culture*, Delhi, 1992, pp. 27-42.

Given this fragmentation, relations between Hindus and Muslims were neither uniformly confrontational nor uniformly conciliatory. Relationships had to be negotiated and manipulated by each group separately, as had been done in earlier times as well, and they varied in accordance with social needs. Some of this occurred at the level of the court, where even though the new ruler was proclaimed in the mosque, his subjects remained Hindu in the main. A successful ruler had to bestow patronage on Hindu sects as well, as many did. Much more of this negotiation, however, was carried out, as it had been in earlier times, in the form of emergent social groups, with literatures, mythologies and practices that drew from varied sources. The dialogue between what we call Hindus and Muslims was sparse at the level of the priests and theologians, but animated between those who were breaking away from conventional religion and seeking a new area of discourse, as is evident from both the Bhakti and Sufi traditions.

The Bhakti sects inherited some of the earlier Bhagvata traditions, with inputs in some cases from the Sufi traditions as well. An ancestry for their ideas had also existed in the Shramanic traditions, some of which, such as Buddhism, had by now declined. Concentrating on the individual's search for release from rebirth, they placed an emphasis on leading the good life and devotion to deity. Many of the sects that have been included under this rubric preached a devotionalism that was also tempered by a concern for social ethics. This sometimes took the form of a universalistic ethic rather than being confined to the boundaries of one's own caste.

Attempts to arrange these multiple strands into a pattern recognisable to the European, commenced with Orientalist scholarship and the beginnings of colonialism in the late eighteenth century. A dialogue was sought with the brahmanas and the maulavis, who were seen as informants in the European study of Indian religions. This encouraged the notion that two monolithic religions, Hinduism and Islam, comprised the mainstream of religious experience in India. Relations between Christianity and Islam had their own history going back to the Crusades, and this history was written into Orientalist research.[10] Hinduism was a new experience and there was little awareness of the limited nature of a dialogue with the brahmanas, seen as its main exponents.

The priority given to orthopraxy over orthodoxy in the indigenous religions[11] escaped Orientalist attempts to understand them. Nor did the extensive British Indian ethnography of the nineteenth century and the detailed studies of religious practice from the Census Reports help to narrow the gap between the normative version of religion from the texts and the actual practice and belief on the ground. On the contrary, the distance widened in the nineteenth century with the emergence of the Indian middle class from the ranks of the upper castes through the process of colonialism. The middle class turned to textual sources for their definition of Hinduism, although ritual and social practice remained important to their religious identity.

Conversion to Christianity was far more limited than conversion to Islam, but the imprint of Christianity was much stronger in the various socio-religious reform movements among upper caste Hindus in the nineteenth century. This was also connected with the emergent middle class identity requiring a new ideology. These new sects were both reacting to and imitating the Christian model. The insistence on monotheism became the central feature of some, where, as in the Brahmo Samaj, there was a return to the *Upanishads*, in which the notion of Brahma was interpreted as a monotheistic idea.

---

10 E. Said, *Orientalism*, London, 1978.
11 F. Staal, *Exploring Mysticism*, Berkeley, 1975.

The worship of idols had been made into something of an embarrassment by the continual attacks from Islamic and Christian denouncers. Among some sects, such as the Arya Samaj, it was argued that idol worship was contrary to the *Vedas* and was the invention of the later and impure Puranic Hinduism. A fundamentalist current in the Arya Samaj argued that because the *Vedas* were divinely revealed they were the scriptural authority for all Hindus. This was an important issue since there was, at this time, a search for the single, sacred Book in imitation of the religions of the Book.

Within these various neo-Hindu movements, there was a recognised organisation based on office-bearers and functions and a schedule of meetings. This also encouraged congregational worship. The Arya Samaj established schools and colleges in imitation of the Christian missions. Going a step further, it initiated a method of reconversion back to Hinduism of those who had converted to Islam and Christianity. This was called *shuddhi* or "purification", a retrieval from the pollution of other religions, but contrary to the earlier norms of Hindu practice.

These socio-religious reform movements, as they are called, were largely of the upper and middle castes attempting to define an ideology for the middle class. They tended to ignore the religious articulation of the Bhakti tradition and others emanating from concerns as much of the lower castes as others. In western and southern India there emerged a series of anti-brahmana movements, which focused on caste and its inequities but were pointedly aimed at the brahmana interpretation of religion and society. Such groups created confrontations within the reconstructed Hinduism, by insisting on the centrality of caste. From this point on there was, among the Hindu sects, a confrontation between the notion of caste as the unit of religious identity and the notion of a religious community cutting across caste. This was not an altogether new idea since the Buddhists and the Jainas had already encouraged the notion of a community defined by religious loyalty, and not by caste. In some cases, groups identified by religious communities had, in effect, functioned like castes. The notion of a religious community now taking shape resulted in the evolving of the idea of a Hindu and a Muslim community. This evolution was historically different from what had existed before, since it was occurring in a colonial context.

Colonial authority in India projected Indian society and polity as dominated by two monolithic religious communities – the larger being the Hindu and the smaller being the Muslim, also referred to as the Hindu and the Muslim nations.[12] So strong was this conviction that even the initial periodisation of Indian history by James Mill was made along the lines of this division, where the Hindu, Muslim and British periods have come to be treated as axiomatic.[13] This periodisation as a perception of the past encouraged the notion of the separateness of Hindus and Muslims in India, and was also a contribution to constructing a Hindu collective memory replete with images of Muslim rule. Indian identity was projected solely in the form of religious communities. Thus when political aspirations and mobilisation are based on religious identities, the term "communalism" is used to describe this. References to Hindu and Muslim communalism increase in the twentieth century. Inevitably, when the demand for the representation of Indians in municipal councils and legislatures was put forward, it came to be conceded on the basis of religious com-

---

12 The word "nation" was used both by William Jones and James Mill, among others. They intended it in its earlier meaning referring to "peoples". But it reinforced its later use, when in the late nineteenth and early twentieth centuries, it gained currency in the contemporary sense of a "nation".

13 *The History of British India*, London, 1818-1823.

munity. The point of no return was the establishing of separate electorates by the colonial power. This vitiated the democratic process. Democracy was projected as the politics of numbers; therefore, majoritarianism was seen as necessary to democracy and numbers were counted by identity with a religious community. This also enhanced the idea of majority and minority communities. The culmination of these developments was the demand for and accommodation of a separate Muslim state and the eventual partition of India.

The genesis of religious conflicts in India highlights various features. The nationalism that spearheaded the struggle for independence was basically a secular movement, although it did use some religious symbols. Opposed to this category of nationalism were smaller groups that defined themselves through a religious identity. In these, nationalism consisted of a demand that a nation-state be created in which a particular religious community would be in a majority, and therefore have special status. There is a deliberate intertwining of nationalism with a religious identity. The success of Muslim communalism in creating Pakistan was not lost on Sikh communalists, who were more recently to demand a separate Sikh state of Khalistan. But its more dramatic impact has been to re-ignite what was once seen as the rather marginal expression of Hindu communalism, what is today referred to as the Hindutva movement.

Hindu communalism found expression at about the same time as Muslim communalism, in the 1920s. It provided an ideology for the Rashtriya Swayamsevak Sangh – RSS, a militant Hindu organisation, claiming to be cultural, and admiring of the Fascists in Italy and the Nazi movement in Germany of the 1930s. It was opposed to partitioning the country, but argued at the same time that the Indian nation was essentially a Hindu nation since all Muslims were foreigners, and in any case a minority. An Indian was defined as one for whom the geographical entity of India was both a *pitri-bhumi*/the land of one's ancestors, and a *punya-bhumi*/the land of one's religion.[14] By arguing that Muslims and Christians were of foreign descent, they were excluded on the first count, and since both Islam and Christianity were not indigenous to India, they were also excluded on the second count. Curiously, apart from Muslims and Christians, the Communists are also excluded on the grounds that their loyalties lie outside India, but in effect because they deny the centrality of religion in a democratic society. This definition of "roots" ran into difficulties with the Dalit movement of the untouchables. The Dalit leaders argued, in accordance with the theories of the time, that the earliest aliens were the Aryans who came from the north-west in the second millennium B.C., conquered India, subordinated the original inhabitants, introduced their alien religion, Vedic Brahmanism, and were those from whom the caste Hindus were descended. Since the Aryan identity of the *dvija*, twice born caste Hindu, is a fundamental component of the Hindutva ideology, it is now maintained by Hindutva ideologues that the Aryans were indigenous to India and spread from India westwards, civilising Asia and Europe.

In a certain sense Hindutva brings to fruition the challenge of Islam, in that it bases its organisation of Hinduism on the Semitic model. I have elsewhere referred to this type of Hinduism as Syndicated Hinduism.[15] There is an attempt to fashion a universalised Hinduism acceptable to all castes, for it is only a clearly-defined, monolithic Hinduism that can be galvanised towards the creation of a majority based on a unified, religious identity aspiring to political power. Such a fashioning

---

14 V.D. Savarkar, *Hindutva: Who Is a Hindu?* Bombay, 1928. The pamphlet was originally brought out by him in 1923.

15 *Seminar*, September 1985; also in expanded form in Romila Thapar, *Cultural Pasts*, OUP, Delhi, 2000, pp. 1025 ff.

inevitably borrows from upper caste belief and practice since the leadership and the more articulate following is from the middle classes and the rural rich. In recent years the Vishva Hindu Parishad (VHP), with views similar to those of the RSS, has attempted to focus activity on the worship of Rama at Ayodhya. (Rama was in origin the hero of an ancient epic, the *Ramayana*, and was later converted into an incarnation of Vishnu). The VHP and the BJP organised the demolition of the Babri mosque, built on a site, it was claimed, that was originally a temple commemorating the birth-place of Rama. Drama, ritual, processions, audio-visual and print media were all used to try and unify the Hindus. The political thrust of the movement was evident from the close association of the Bharatiya Janata Party (BJP), which used the movement to mobilise support and votes to bring it to power.

Equally important, an ecclesiastical authority was sought to be projected in the form of Shankaracharyas, the Dharmacharyas, the Sants and Sadhus, invited to *dharma-sansads* or meetings, where they proclaimed on Hindu belief and practice. These meetings were of an arbitrary collection of some heads of monastic-type institutions, some renouncers and some self-appointed 'holy men'. As renouncers the Shankaracharyas were and are respected, but they have not been seen as ecclesiastical functionaries. These institutions are, of course, quite different from the ecclesiastical structures of Christian churches. Yet, they are increasingly imbued with ecclesiastical authority even by the Government of India. Not surprisingly, Ayodhya has been described as the "Vatican of Hinduism" by the VHP, and for them it would seem the *dharma-sansad* is a higher authority than either the Indian Constitution as vested in Parliament, or the Supreme Court.

Hinduism does not have a historical founder, but there is now an attempt to give historicity to that which was once accepted as a-historical. By claiming that the birth-place of Rama is historically established and even archaeologically proven, irrespective of whether this is accepted generally by historians and archaeologists, Rama is brought on par with historical founders of other religions.

The need for numbers in majoritarian politics also makes it necessary that those with ambiguous religious identity, such as the Scheduled Castes or Untouchables, or Dalits – which is their preferred identity – and the Scheduled Tribes, also referred to as the tribal peoples, be identified as Hindus. Missionary activity, therefore, to "convert" them to Hinduism has been reactivated by the VHP and the RSS.

The rise of Hindu communalism is, in part, a continuing resentment against the creation of Pakistan, which it uses to question the loyalty of Muslims to India, and to target them as the enemy within Indian society. The Muslim reaction takes various forms, but more often is now reflected in an assertion of greater Muslim-ness through a process, which has come to be called Islamisation. This often brings about separatism in terms of localities, denominational schools, jobs, as also by an insistence on the continuance of a Muslim Personal Law, as distinct from an Indian Civil Code. This raises problems: some liberal Indians maintain that a society claiming to be secular expects all citizens to abide by a common system of education and a common Civil Code; others argue that given the pluralism of Indian society, if this pluralism is valued, then there are bound to be different schools and laws for different segments. The debate inevitably introduces the comparative question of how closely Muslim Personal Law conforms to Islamic texts in neighbouring Muslim societies.

To direct attention to the enemy within Indian society, hysteria is built up asserting that Muslims breed excessively and would soon outstrip the Hindus in numbers and become a majority. Violence is then organised to create fear among those marked as enemies. This is justified as a mechanism to assuage the fear that is created among the majority, of a possible return to power of the minority.

Violence is neither sporadic nor contained, as it was in the past. Gangs of rioters are available to political parties. Those who have to be gunned down, or homes and work-places that have to be burnt, are known in advance. Women are often the worst sufferers where, in political ideologies that subordinate women, the rape of the women of "the Other" is regarded as a legitimate form of aggression. Modern communications allow quick contact across the country and the linking of riots to events becomes easier. The media, always ready for sensations, frequently gives publicity to potential confrontations, ensuring future conflagrations.

Religion then becomes an avenue for political mobilisation. Conflicts are rarely over religion per se, but over political space, political control and access to power. Despite the rhetoric of political parties that "anti-social" elements should be debarred from politics, those who mastermind riots can more easily move into political office, using this ability as their qualification.

That Indian society is vulnerable to communal conflicts is due to various other factors as well. A society in transition is beset with fears and uncertainties, knowing what it is discarding but unaware of what it is transmuting into. Even the historical experience of the world over the last hundred years does not provide to such societies the clues to understanding an unknown future. The fears breed a sense of insecurity. Added to this is the competition inherent in a market economy accompanied by the enormous expansion that the Indian middle class has been undergoing, but resulting in an even more intense competition for appropriate employment and general insecurity.

Job opportunities are being further restricted among the middle class by the demand for "reservations". Castes that have been set aside in the past – the Backward Castes, the Scheduled Castes and the Scheduled Tribes – have been insisting in recent years on quotas of reserved seats in educational institutions and in government jobs. This acts as further pressure on the middle class. Hindu communalism has not come out frontally in opposition to the policy of reservations, since this would lose it the numbers, which it relies on for Hindu majoritarian politics. But, in effect, it has little space for the excluded castes, except to make token gestures.

The rise of Hindu communalism as a major ideology of the Hindu middle class has also led to the questioning of the validity of whether secularism is a viable policy for India. There is a debate on the meaning of the word, where in India, it has been understood to mean the co-existence of religions and not the separation of religion from state policies. Some argue that secularism as a concept can only be meaningful in a Christian context, and therefore is inapplicable to the Indian situation, or else that it is a western concept that is being forced on India.[16] There is, in the present, little support for those of us who maintain that secularism comes with the evolving of a democracy and with the institutions and infrastructure required of a functioning civil society. The strengthening of civil society is not just a return to an Enlightenment project: it is imperative for strengthening democracy and easing civil strife. It is to this emphasis on the centrality of civil society that we need to turn our attention.

---

16 T. N. Madan, 'Secularism in its Place', *Journal of Asian Studies*, 1987, Vol. 46, No. 4, pp. 747-59; also available in Rajeev Bhargava (ed.), *Secularism and its Critics*, OUP, Delhi, 1998.

Communal parties and organisations are aware of this but prefer to ignore it, as do those who support such organisations. The essentials of a civil society are brushed aside by the confrontations over capturing of political office, and appeals emphasise the separateness of the communities. This activity is not limited to India alone, for it also draws on the emotions and loyalties of erstwhile Indian citizens settled in other parts of the world. The support of such Indians to Hindu communalism or Sikh or Muslim communalism, also introduces the transnational dimensions of religious conflict, in which, what has now come to be called "the Indian diaspora" plays a significant role.

The Indian diaspora is in part the result of indentured labour being taken in the nineteenth century from India to work on plantations in other parts of the British Empire, such as the Caribbean or Fiji. Here the Indian population has now moved into middle class status and is anxious to both find and assert its own identity. In the present century, Indian migration was and is more substantially of professionals seeking better job opportunities to Britain and North America, as also West Asia. With the exception of Muslims in the Gulf, such migrants generally form a religious minority in the new land and are alienated from the majority in terms of religion and cultural articulation. The insecurity of the first generation of such migrants is carried over to the next and is increased by the hostility of other members of the host country. The search for identity goes back to the homeland, where the easiest link is the religious identity. This is intensified among those communities who see themselves as isolated in the host country. But these links also reproduce the tensions of the homeland among Indian communities.

Many of the professional immigrant groups are wealthy and make large donations to parties and organisations in the homeland, frequently to those using religion and culture as a front for other concerns. There is an intervention in the politics of the homeland for such funds to assist in financing candidates for elections to parliament, and on occasion to even provide the wherewithal for communal activities. The movement for Khalistan, the separate Sikh state, had its origin in the mismanagement of Punjab politics, but was heavily financed by the Sikhs of North America and Europe. Political parties and organisations supporting the Hindu cause receive even larger donations from Hindus outside India and the VHP has a very vocal presence in the United States. The Islamisation of Muslim society in India is frequently assisted with aid from Indian Muslims and other organisations in the Gulf. The communal problem in India, therefore, is no longer restricted to the borders of India, for it now has a trans-national dimension, which, if anything, will grow and not diminish.

In today's world of communities, perceived as separate but searching for collective identities, and of migrants and nationals, conflicts, ostensibly based on religion, cannot be cordoned off and treated as isolated phenomena. They impinge on all our societies in varying degrees. This implies an awareness of what the real causes of conflict might be and participation in seeking solutions. It is this that I have tried to put before you in writing of what is generally described as the religious conflict in contemporary India, but which is in actuality a conflict between the secular and the religious over the political future of this country.

Secularism and Secularisation

Indian Society and the Secular[1]

In speaking about Indian society and the secular, let me say at the outset, that secularism goes beyond just politics, although our political parties have attempted to reduce it to a political slogan: one party endorses it in theory, but hesitates to apply it properly in practice; the other makes fun of it since the party's foundational ideology is anti-secular. Supporting secularism or dismissing it, is not just a matter of a political slogan, it is deeply tied to the question of the kind of society we want. This is perhaps why it was widely discussed in the early years of independence, whereas now attempts are being made to scuttle it. Questioning the secular would mean seriously changing the direction that we have intended to give to Indian society: if secularism is removed from the constitution then democracy becomes a victim, with an unthinkable future.

If, however, we want a secular society, we would have to cease identifying ourselves primarily by religion, caste or lan-

---

1   The Asghar Ali Engineer Memorial Lecture, Jamia Millia Islamia, 19 August 2015.

guage, and start thinking of ourselves primarily as equal citizens of one nation, in theory and in practice. This involves mutual obligations between the state and the citizens and between citizens; and not just in theory, as of now, but also in actuality. The relationship of other identities such as religion, caste, language and region will inevitably become secondary: these latter would need to be adjusted so as to ensure that the rights of citizenship, together with what they entail, remain primary. Eventually the state will not be expected to support any religious organisation, even those it is currently supporting.

I would like to begin by trying to explain what I mean by the terms secular, secularism and secularising. Secular is that which relates to the world and is distinct from the religious; secularism involves questioning the control that religious organisations have over social institutions. This control is sought to be justified by arguing that it ensures morality. But the morality fundamental to secularism goes beyond any single religion and extends to the functioning of the entire society. Secularism does not deny the presence of religion in society; it demarcates the social institutions over which religion can or cannot exercise control. This distinction is fundamental. And finally, secularising is the process by which society changes and recognises the distinction.

When the term was first used in 1851, secular had only one basic meaning. It described laws relating to morals and social values as having been created by human society in order to ensure the well being and harmonious functioning of the society. These laws were neither the creation of divine authority, nor did they require the sanction of divine authority. Authority lay in working out, through reasoning and sensitivity, what was best for society in keeping with generally accepted values of tolerance and social responsibility, by those who constituted that society. Authority was exercised through laws. Social values, therefore, grew out of rational thinking, debate and discussion. This was needed to establish a moral code agreed to by the entire society and was not linked to any particular religion, caste or class.

What this means is that the laws and social values that govern the society should be observed as laws in themselves and not because they carry any divine sanctions: they have their own authority, distinct from religion or caste, or whatever. Religion involving belief and faith in a deity and in an afterlife continued to exist. However, the civil laws were sanctioned and upheld by secular authority, and did not require the sanction of any religion. Secularism, therefore, is not what it is sometimes said to be; it is not a denial of religion, it is a curtailment of the control that religious organisations have over social functioning. And I would underline this definition repeatedly.

This theory, after it came to be widely discussed, had various consequences; one being that it allowed people the freedom to think beyond what was told to them as being religiously correct. Again, this did not mean throwing religion overboard, but disentangling the codes of social behavior from religious control. And it did not make people immoral as some had feared at that time, as the threat of punishment for breaking laws could be enforced, and punishment came immediately and in this life. It was not postponed to the next life as in most religious codes. This made people think about the purpose of their laws, and such thinking is always extremely useful. The observance of the law is strengthened when people understand its purpose.

Having to reason things out meant that people had to learn to think independently. The thinking came from their education. Here too, the explanation of everything being part of a divine plan and requiring divine sanction was not always the answer to simple questions. Therefore education began to involve searching for explanations other than those based on faith and religion, or, possibly, even honing these explanations if there was evidence to do so. But preferably, social laws began to be drawn from rational enquiry into both the natural and the human world in which we live. Occasionally, there might even have been a small leap of imagination, ultimately to be explained by reason. Therefore, the explanations for the laws and a discussion of these became an essential part of education, and of thinking about the implications of being secularised.

Religion had originated as a personal emotional need, then extended to explanations of how one experienced life, and beyond that to how the universe functioned. This was all attributed to a supernatural power that was held in awe. Gradually, however, this personalised religion became a complex, organised religion, and took the form of institutions ambitious to control society and politics. With this change, religion also became powerful, both as the focus of belief and as an authority controlling social institutions through various religious organisations. In some places its power paralleled that of the governing authority – the state. It is this particular aspect of religion – the control that religious organisations have over social institutions – that the secular person wishes to see controlled and to be kept separate from the state. The distinction is important because we often overlook it, in saying that secularism denies religion altogether.

Secularism then took on an additional meaning. The state having authority over the making and observing of laws by human agencies should be distinct from religion, which has its sanction from faith and from deity. The authority of each was clearly different.

Social laws are the spine of a society. They should protect the right to live and they should ensure that there is no discrimination that affects life and work. This is crucial to protecting the points of change in the human lifecycle, for which laws are necessary: such as registering birth, marriage, or even divorce, processes of education by which a child is socialised into society, occupation and employment, and inheritance, generally of property. Actions linked to these come under the jurisdiction of civil law. To make this link effective, social laws have necessarily to provide the basic aspects of welfare in a modern state – the absolute minimum of which are equal access to education and to health care for all members of society, and to employment – and this is to be irrespective of religion and caste. If civil laws are to be universal and uniform, as they would be ultimately in a secular society, then we must guarantee this endorsement by the state. Discrimination on any count would be altogether unacceptable.

Religious authority, then, continues in a secular system, but is limited: it extends only to governing religious belief and practice. It has been argued that there should be no rigid barrier between religion and the state, but that there could be a negotiated, principled distance between them. This can allow for new alignments within the religion, or between the religions, or between religion and the state. The overall relationship would disallow the dominance of any single religion since each would have equal rights on the state, and the state on them, and equal status before the law. Nevertheless, there is a degree of stipulated separation in this arrangement, in as much as religious authority would no longer be controlling social laws.

This is not, of course, the same as what is sometimes described as the Indian definition of secularism, namely the coexistence of all religions. The mere coexistence is insufficient as religions can still be treated as unequal and some be marginalised, as they often are. The acceptance of coexistence, together with equal status before the law, can certainly be a first step. But we do have to ask how far does this go, and what should be the next step.

This definition based on the coexistence of religions is incomplete in many ways since the question of the jurisdiction of religious authority remains unanswered. The intention would, in any case, not be to put up barriers between state and religion; it would be to demarcate the activities that come under a civil jurisdiction and those that could continue to be controlled by the organisations representing religious authority. In a democratic system the equality would be essential, as essential as spelling out who controls which laws. In contemporary India the coexistence of religions exists, but their equality has yet to be established. The secular is less evident, and some might even say that it is virtually absent. Political and state patronage does not invariably distance itself from religious organisations; in fact, it is sometimes closely tied together, as we know.

Some oppose secularism by arguing that it is a western concept, not suited to India. Should the same be said about nationhood and democracy, both new to post independence India? And surely, our internalising of the new liberal market economy has a far stronger imprint of the west. To support the secularising of society does not mean subordinating ourselves to a western concept, but rather trying to understand a process of change in our contemporary history. Being a nation-state is a new experience of modern times, and is current now in every part of the world. We have chosen democracy as the most feasible system, despite its being new to us. I would argue that a secular society is essential to democratic functioning.

Let me turn now to the specifically Indian aspect of the subject, and comment on how I see religion and society in the past, in order to compare it with how it is viewed in our times. My argument is that colonialism introduced a major disjuncture in how we perceive ourselves and that we have accepted this without much question. Any deliberate social change with sizeable consequence becomes a little easier to handle if one can see the earlier historical forms of the society and its gradual mutation. The present, after all, does emerge out of the past. In the important area of the relationship between society and religion we have been nurtured on ideas about how religion functioned in India. These ideas came from colonial views of Indian religion that we have internalised without adequately questioning them. So a brief look at these might be useful.

Colonial perceptions were based on the European experience of religion in the context of European society. With reference to Europe, secularism is often described as the separation between Church and State. This is taken as a one-to-one relationship because generally the religion was a single monolithic religion. This was so strongly asserted that in past times those that questioned Catholic belief and practice in Europe were heavily punished as heretics. Some were burnt, some had to recant as did Galileo, and many faced the punitive actions of the Inquisition. Although Protestantism later was more flexible, the earlier experience was not forgotten.

This was the perspective of religion that was familiar to the colonisers. Their reading of Indian religion was through this perspective. Recent writing on Indian religion and society suggests that this was a defective view and therefore needs reinvestigation. The colonial image of Indian society projected two nations, the Hindu and the Muslim, defined by monolithic religious identities, and inherently hostile to each other. And because of their mutual hostility, a controlling authority from outside was required. This became one justification for colonial rule. As many historians have pointed out, this image was then imprinted on the history of India, especially on the medieval period, thus enforcing a distancing between the two religions.

The concept of majority and minority communities, identified by religion, was also introduced by colonial policy. This further consolidated the idea of monolithic religions, and these in turn fueled communal politics. Permanent majorities and minorities are, of course, contrary to the norms of democracy. A democratic majority is formed on each occasion when a large number of people come together in support of a particular opinion: the number has to be larger than of any other group, and those that join it are not restricted to membership of any previous affiliated organisation. Forming a majority, therefore, is not based on any pre-existing religious, caste or linguistic identities. The constituents of the majority change with each issue. There are no permanent majorities or minorities.

Anti-colonial nationalism tried to confront this image, as broad based nationalism needs to be inclusive, and to induct a range of opinion; it has also to draw on a shared history. The shared history is crucial. I would also like to quote Eric Hobsbawm who wrote that history plays the same role in nationalisms as does the poppy in the life of opium addicts: it is the source, it feeds ideas of identity. Anti-colonial nationalism did not question the monolithic nature of religious communities; it focused on denying their antagonism and projecting their coexistence. This became central to its idea of secularism, which did not fully succeed. One reason was that the colonial view of religion in India was, and still is, also foundational to the ideologies of what are now referred to as religious nationalisms, Hindu and Muslim, that went into the making of the communal landscape of India. In other words anti-colonial nationalism, and both the religious nationalisms, have built on the colonial construction of Indian religion; the first has borrowed much less so, the latter have made it foundational to their ideologies.

Before independence, the organisations propagating religious nationalisms were the Muslim League and the Hindu Mahasabha. These were not religious orthodoxies, but rather ideologies using religion for political mobilisation. Today, religious nationalisms include a range of Hindu, Muslim, Sikh and other religious organisations, politically ambitious and anxious to continue their control over community laws, to ensure a political constituency. History in religious nationalisms is not shared; it is divisive and becomes an arena of battle. The struggle over history textbooks is an attempt to ensure the projection of a history slanted towards one religion, and a denial of a shared history.

We may well ask, was this actually how religion functioned in relation to Indian society from early times? Have we looked analytically at our past? Have we examined the role of religious organisations from that past? What form did these organisations take, how did they exert authority, and which sections of society supported which particular organisations?

I would argue that the historical picture of religions in India was complex: it was not a simple binary of Hindu and Muslim, because religious groups took the form of an array of sects, and not of large monolithic communities. I see it in terms of two sets of relationships, each required for investigating the link between religion and society: the first was the interaction of sects with close social linkages through caste connections, present in every segment of Indian society; the second was the mediation with and through political authority, that then became a three-way process involving sect, caste and the state.

There was no church to bring together the sects into a single entity. In other words, I'm arguing for a much more decentralised way of looking at religion.

In the Indian past, the crucial relationship lay in the connection between multiple religious sects and many castes. The sect propagated belief; the caste often determined its social context. Status was measured through an interdependence of the two. Upper castes across religions, whether they observed caste restrictions strictly or not, tended to be more closely associated with the text-based formal manifestations of the religion, whereas the lower castes, perhaps being less text-based, were far more flexible. Caste determined the social code, maintained formally by those who claimed to be educated and knew the law. For most people, however, it was the hearsay of tradition. The authority of caste and sect over the social code needs now to be replaced by civil law applicable to all. This will require looking afresh at the civil law claimed by all religions to ensure its secularity and its endorsement of social justice. Both secularity and social justice are familiar as values but their application in social institutions is new.

Many valuable and meticulous studies have been made of religious texts that have enhanced our understanding of them. However, less attention has been given to examining the institutions created by various religions, both to propagate their beliefs and as agencies of social control. Rather than focusing on monolithic undifferentiated religious society in general, what may be more insightful is if we study the link between caste and sect in order to comprehend more precisely the interface between religion and society in our past. The link between caste and sect had a flexibility, even a fluidity, that monolithic religions lack. We could then ask whether the rigidity lay less in religion and more in caste discrimination? In that case the colonial construction of religion in India, so readily accepted by us, would need to be examined again. Perhaps we need to look more carefully at how caste in past times, and now class in its turn, has shaped and is shaping the relations between religion and society: which groups in society support which particular politico-religious organisations and why.

In pre-Islamic times there are no references to any monolithic type of Hinduism. Interestingly, what we today use as labels for religion, such as Hinduism and Buddhism, are not mentioned as such. Instead, there is reference to two broad categories of sects that propagated their distinctive ideas: these were the Brahmana and the Shramana. The basic differentiation was based on belief in, or denial of, divinity, and the theories of the afterlife. Brahmana referred to brahmanic beliefs and rituals; Shramana referred to the *shramanas* or Buddhist, Jaina, and other monks of so called heterodox orders, the *nastika*/non-believers, and their followers. The latter rejected the *Vedas*, divine sanctions and the concept of the soul. They were consequently associated with more rational explanations of both the universe and human life. Within each of the two, distinct sects with various beliefs were recognised.

Neither of these were monolithic groups. They were a collection of diverse sects. This duality of Brahmana and Shramana continues to be used in a variety of texts with reference to what we would today call religions, over a period of 1500 years from the edicts of Ashoka, to the accounts of Megasthenes, the Chinese Buddhist pilgrims, and Al-Biruni in the eleventh century AD. References are made in Brahmanical texts such as the *Vishnu Purana*, and in Buddhist texts, to occasional hostilities between the two. Interestingly, they use the same abusive terms for each other. The grammarian Patanjali of the late first millennium BC refers to the two, and adds that their relationship was comparable to that of the snake and the mongoose.

A third category, that is not mentioned, was of those discriminated against because of their caste or lack of it. Because of this, they had their own belief systems and forms of worship. This was a category intrinsic to caste: the equivalent of what we call the Dalit today is found in every religion under different names, such as *pasmanda, mazhabi* etc. The Dalit is present even among those religious sects that claim all men to be equal in the eyes of God. Technically all Dalits, irrespective of religion, should have the same rights, although this is not generally conceded.

Among the multiple sects that were emerging over time, some adhered to the orthodox, while others were supporters of the heterodox. The advantage of sects over monolithic religions was that sects shaded off from the very orthodox to those far less so: this allowed the less orthodox to assimilate new beliefs, and these were not treated as heresy. The heretics functioned in a stream of their own.

Our understanding of conversion would be much clearer if we could focus on sect and caste, wherever the evidence exists or can be traced back. This would provide a far better explanation than merely going on referring to Hindus becoming Muslims. How we look at historical interactions in the past, moulds, to a fair extent, our thinking about present-day interactions. It is, therefore, incumbent upon us to be far more analytical and precise in our historical exploration and explanation. We should not allow history to be reduced to, or dismissed, as political slogans of various kinds.

The creation of a sect was open and led to a plurality that became characteristic of every religion in India. This constitutes an important aspect in understanding the relationship between religion and society, and these relationships differ from society to society. We cannot assume, therefore, that the role of religion that emerged for Europe can be applied automatically to India – a mistake made by colonial scholarship. This does not imply that the meaning of secularism can change, but that the manner in which it is introduced into a society may vary.

Since Shramanism in the main was based on historical founders, it takes a fairly linear form, with segments referring back to a central teaching. The history of Brahmanism is far more complex. An early phase was Vedic Brahmanism focusing on the ritual of sacrifice, the *yajna*, invoking many deities, and specially Indra and Agni, and performed by upper castes. A variety of heterodox sects, pre-eminently the Buddhists, Jainas and Ajivikas, questioned these beliefs. Heterodox groups tended to provide rational explanations about social institutions and established a critical tradition of questioning orthodoxy, although eventually establishing their own orthodoxies.

By the early centuries AD, Brahmanical ritual became more individualised with a shift to the worship of Shiva and Vishnu. Sects of worshippers came together, differentiated by particular deities, as for example the Vaishnava Bhagavata and the Shaiva Pashupata. From the seventh century, religious belief and worship took the form of devotional sects, what we call the Bhakti sects. They arose at varying times in different parts of the sub-continent, the earlier recognisable ones being the Alvars and Nayannars in the south, to be followed by many in the north. Some, among the later ones, reflected striations of new religious ideas.

Some sects assigned to either Brahmanism or Shramanism received hefty patronage and became wealthy, powerful, established religions. This gave them status and enabled them to control social laws. Donations were made to sects and not to a monolithic religious entity, because this did not exist at that time. This continued to be the norm even in later periods.

Centres of the wealthy sects became the nuclei of education. This added to their authority and they could induct the elite. Frequently sects with large followings and authority began to function as castes in themselves, as for example the Lingayat in Karnataka, and many others in other parts of the country. They did not necessarily identify with the formal religions, and some actually opposed them. But in colonial records they were assigned to one of the formal religions.

With the arrival of Islam, and more so with the presence of the Sufis, the exploration of religious ideas – orthodox and heterodox – expanded; as did the number of sects. Some took orthodox positions, others held out mixed beliefs and worship. The latter were popular among the larger number of ordinary people.

The new presence was marked by the elaborate mosques and *khanqahs* built by royal patrons and the wealthy. The religious endowments became richer and richer, as is so in all well-patronised religions. As in the case of Buddhist monasteries and Hindu temples and *matha*s, these endowments tied to Islamic centres enabled their recipients to participate in the world of scholarship, and in politics. Detailed studies of the social institutions controlled by the various religious authorities that we refer to as Hindu, Muslim, Sikh etc., would be revealing as would their interactions.

As in earlier times, the sect remained the popular religious identity among the majority of people. This becomes more evident if we look at two processes involved in the coming of Islam – settlement and conversion. Today, its advent is projected at the popular level largely in terms of invasion and the subsequent political consequences. But there were many other avenues that took different forms, as in the settlements of traders, migrants, Sufis, and such like.

Muhammad bin Qasim's conquest of Sindh is known. But far more interesting were the settlements of Arab traders all down the west coast of India, from Sindh to Kerala. Some Arabs entered the service of the Rashtrakuta kings of the Deccan, dating to the eighth and ninth centuries. The more senior among them exercised their right to give grants of land to temples and brahmanas as had been the prevailing custom in the area. Arab traders inter-married locally and new communities evolved, with new infusions into existing religions. Inevitably, these became new sects, such as the Bohras, the Khojas, the Navayat, the Mappila and many others, among whom belief, ritual, and civil law did not hesitate to draw from existing practice. Therefore, no two were identical: Gujarati Bohras had little to do with Malayali Mappilas. Many such sects mushroomed all over, but have not been sufficiently studied as part of the history of society and religion.

This pattern continued into later centuries at the level of the wider society. This was despite the emergence of other patterns that arose from political power and administration. Such dichotomies run through history and only their constituents change. The newly emerging teachers of various persuasions attracted supportive followers. Until recently these remained the essentials of how a major part of Indians experienced religion, irrespective of having to declare conformity to formal religions in colonial times. This was prior to the ingress of Hindutva and Islamisation that have considerably hardened the boundaries and even altered practices. Many people today who identify themselves with the monolithic religion, whichever it may be, when pressed further, will mention the sect that they belong to, or the holy man whom they revere – the *baba*, *guru* or *sant* – who can be of any persuasion. This link is often more pertinent to the lives they actually live. And, interestingly, the sects that they identify with are generally those that were established in the last thousand years.

In the history of India, medieval history, which colonial historians called the Muslim period, is located in the last thousand years. This history has had a raw deal from religious extremists and politicians in being described as the age when, to quote the slogan, "We were slaves", the assumption being that Islamic rule tyrannised and oppressed the Hindu population. This is a continuation of the British interpretation of Indian history, eagerly taken up by religious nationalism. Viewed historically, the scene differs at many levels.

The interaction between what we call Hinduism and Islam had its moments of confrontations and conflicts in the face offs between competing politics and were manifested in various ways, and often through religious organisations. What was a largely political act at that time is often interpreted today as an entirely religious act, with the politics left out. Some confrontation was to be expected. Such confrontations were not new to the Indian scene if, in earlier times, the brahmanas and the shramanas had a relationship comparable to the snake and the mongoose; and this was probably a correct assessment, as we know that in some regions Buddhist monks were killed, and in others Jaina monks were impaled. In the subsequent millennium, in the last thousand years, the situation may not have changed strikingly. It was neither a culture given over to religious aggression as the colonial scholars maintained; but nor was it entirely free of such aggression. It was in fact a normal culture, similar to many others in the world at the time.

And, as in earlier times, this continued to be a period when striking creativity enriched facets of Indian culture, and we still live with these. The intellectual liveliness of the time, expressed in Sanskrit and Persian and in the regional languages, matched that of earlier times, although in different genres.

It was precisely this period that gave shape and form in various ways to much, although not all, that we now identify as Hindu in the landscape of present times.

Leaving aside for the moment the presence of interacting cultures practicing diverse religions, even some of the activities clustered around the Brahmanic tradition are most impressive. Throughout the second millennium AD, that is the last one thousand years, from Kashmir to Kerala and in between, there were scholarly commentaries being composed on Brahmanical texts and religious practice. Sayana's explanation of the *Rig Veda* is a fascinating glimpse into the mind of a learned scholar of the fourteenth century, with its mix of reality and fantasy. Social change draws out new commentaries on existing social codes. Kulluka's commentary on the *Manu Dharmashastra* incorporates a reaction to the social changes of the times, as in the debate over the status of temple priests viz-à-vis other categories of brahmanas, a matter of concern only when temples became powerful institutions, at a time simultaneous with the arrival of Islam in the sub-continent. The looting of some of the wealthy temples did not prevent the building of other equally wealthy ones with striking innovations in architecture.

There were many commentaries, digests, discussions on classical Sanskrit poetry and literary compositions. With the gradual switch to the regional languages, grammars required commentaries. New and prior philosophical theories are discussed in texts such as the *Sarva-darshana-sangraha* of Madhavacharya in the fourteenth century. Discussions on the Advaita Vedanta and Mimamsa schools of philosophy, to mention some, date to this period. There were explorations into theories in mathematics and astronomy, going from Ujjain to Baghdad and beyond, with Indian scholars at the cutting edge of knowledge. Classical Hindustani and Carnatic music was patronised by the courts of Maharajas and Mughals and in the homes of the wealthy.

In addition to Sanskrit and Persian, literary compositions of high quality began to be composed in regional languages that acquired a new standing in the royal courts and in places linked to religious sects. These compositions carried much of the thought and creativity of their own times, as is evident in the *Ramacharitamanas*, and the *Krittibas*, distinct from the Valmiki *Ramayana*, and much revered by Hindi and Bengali speakers. There were even alternate histories sung as legends by folk poets and bards, very different from the court chronicles that we quote. These were the voices of numbers of people, as also expressed in the *bhajans* of Meera and Surdas, and in the compositions of Thyagaraja. These were not the achievements of enslaved people. We today are unable to look beyond what we have been told by those who colonised us, and those who loyally continue to carry on with that legacy.

* * *

In this rather scattered attempt to look at some aspects of the past I have tried to underline the plurality in the articulation of religion in India, often in the form of sects and their interface with caste. To eventually disengage religious institutions from controlling the functions of civil society would help us in bringing about a more equitable society. The process of secularising society will have to address both religion and caste, and to that extent it requires a different kind of analysis from that of religions elsewhere. We have internalised the colonial version of the relationship between our religions and our society, and are experiencing its aftermath in the stridency of dominant religious organisations. We have also allowed some of these to become mechanisms for political mobilisation.

Secularisation, therefore, will have to be thought through with sensitivity, care and thoroughness. Although it cannot be a rapid change, nevertheless, a serious beginning has to be made to introduce secular values through establishing confidence in a secular society and explaining its necessary link to democracy. The resort to assassination to silence secularists can never succeed – it merely leads to the suffusion of terror that will one day rebound on those terrorising others. If there is one lesson that history teaches us, it is this.

A secular society and polity does not mean abandoning religion. It does mean that the religious identity of the Indian, whatever it may be, has to give way to the primary secular identity of an Indian citizen. And the state has to guarantee the rights that come with this identity, as the rights of citizenship. This demands that the state provide and protect human rights, a requirement that at present cannot be taken for granted. Such an identity, while adhering to human rights and social justice, would also be governed by a secular code of laws applicable to all.

A beginning could be made in two possible ways: one would be to ensure the secular in education; and the other, the secular in civil laws. Education means the availability of all branches of knowledge to all citizens without discrimination. Knowledge means updated information, and training young people to endorse the method of critical enquiry. I would like to add to this the need for young people to know what is meant by a shared history. Given that we are a democracy, we can perhaps work out how best this could be done.

Our civil laws were drawn up in colonial times, although we have made some changes after independence. In a turn to the secular we shall have to comb through the existing civil laws, to ensure that they conform to equal rights for all citizens with no exceptions. How differences between the civil laws and the laws of each religion and caste are to be resolved, will have to be discussed with the communities concerned, and not only with those currently controlling religious and caste codes. A uniform civil code does not mean merely doing away with the laws of one religious code: it means reconsidering, jointly, the social laws of all religious codes and working out a common secular civil code. In this process, injustice and discrimination against minorities and against the underprivileged, whether because of religion, gender or caste, will need to be annulled. Law does not remain law, if it can be manipulated to allow discrepancies. This is likely to be the most problematic factor in our turn towards secularising society. Is it not time, now, to start work on this?

The overwhelming projection of religiosity, not religion but the excessive display of religiosity, in the world that surrounds us, sometimes appears to be a surrogate for not coming to terms with real life problems; or, perhaps, it is due to our having become a competitive society with all its unexpected insecurities. Can we, instead, consider how we can make the reality of citizenship a guarantee of our social welfare, our well being, our understanding of the world, and our wish to bring quality into our lives? The secularising of society is not an overnight revolution: it is a historical process and will need time. But, hopefully, it will be assisted by the recognition that the state and society need to function in a new way. Implicit in democracy is the upholding of the ethic of human action: secularising society is an advancing of that very ethic.

Redefining the Secular Mode for India[1]

What would a secular society look like? Very briefly, it would be a society governed largely by humanistic principles, such as ensuring the social welfare of all its citizens. This would be done by providing a reasonable assurance of employment and income, health care, access to education, and a guarantee of human rights. Such a society is possible within the framework of any polity, but some are better equipped than others for this purpose. A secularising process is problematic since every society has multiple identities that have evolved through its history. A secular society is not anti-religious, but cannot permit religion to control its functioning.

First, I would like to emphasise that the prevalent Indian definition of secularism is not only inadequate but also tangential. Second, I would like to consider what is meant by secular-

---

1   Based on a lecture given at·the event organised by SAHMAT on 7 December 2011. A revised version was delivered at May Day Cafe on 1 September 2012.

ising society, as different from endorsing the secular. Third, I would like to argue that religious articulation and organisation has been historically different in India (and possibly also in China) from that of Europe, and our understanding of it needs rethinking. And fourth, I would like to argue that there has been in Indian thought, a strong potential for nurturing a secular society.

The definition currently popular in India either equates secularism with atheism which is incorrect; or else more commonly, it describes secularism as the harmonious co-existence of all religions, which is desirable but is not the same as being secular. To emphasise only the coexistence of religions gives no attention to the negative feature of this definition, that the religions were of unequal status. This is a potential source of conflict. Describing the religions as those of the majority and the minority communities has underlined the inequality. Furthermore, in understanding secularism as the co-existence of religions, religion remains the primary factor, in social functioning.

The ideology of secularism in Europe has a historical context. It was formulated primarily as a social and political ethic, which, at that point in eighteenth century Europe, was pertinent to many aspects of life and thought. As one aspect in the modernising of society, it opposed organised religious institutions that had a social and political control over society. For example, it contended with the control of the Church over education, as well as the exercise of religious identities in many areas of governance.

The need for a secular society coincided approximately with capitalism. Industrialisation and colonialism became dominant and gave rise to nationalisms of various kinds. Since nationalisms are now virtually universal and are present in the history of most societies of the world, the debates on secularisation and modernisation remain widely relevant in the contexts of nations everywhere. They have ceased to be pertinent to the history of Europe alone. But our historical experience has not been identical with that of Europe and we, therefore, need to work out the nature and function of secularisation in our own context. One obvious difference is the centrality of caste, different from class. Closely related to caste are sects, characteristic of the evolution of our religions. We have to know the nature of their function in our society, varying in space and time. Secularism in India is not a confrontation between Church and State since the institution of the Church was not a feature of Indian religion.

Ideological change goes together with historical change. The choice that is often posed today is between reinforcing religious modes, spoken of as "tradition" or "culture" from earlier times, or alternately, rethinking these. Such rethinking could introduce a secular mode into the functioning of our society. The first option does not work. Contemporary Indian forms of religious organisation are not the same as they were in pre-colonial times. History changes and so do the institutions linked to it. The experience of colonialism was a social and cultural disjuncture. When fundamentalist groups of all kinds speak about returning to pristine cultures and values, they ignore the fact that reconstructions of the past are, by their very nature, influenced by the needs of the present.

Religion has been made into the formidable counterpart of the secular, so let me define religion. At one level it is the personal belief of the individual, in terms of what she chooses to worship, how she chooses to worship, and the nature of the relationship between her and what she worships. This is the level that is rarely open to historical observation. The worshipper has a choice, as long as the worship does not conflict with the rights of co-citizens. At the other level of religion, and this is more important to the historian, is the way in which religious institutions function as social organisations as well. The study of these institutions and organisations illumines the nature of the society in which they are located.

There is always a tension between the two levels, between the informal and the formal. In the Hindu religions, for instance, this was illustrated by the *bhakti* form of worship in relation to temple worship; or in Islam, between the Sufi forms and praying in the mosque. This informality allowed more open definitions of each religion and permitted the presence of alternate forms. The formal religious organisations today – the varieties of the Samajs, the Jamaats, the Prabhandak Committees, and so on – are far from loosening their control on society; in fact, quite the reverse. They often play a political role, and are given publicity by the subservient media.

Religion involves belief in a deity or deities, which is/are believed to be the prime cause of creation. Deities can be in the image of the human or can be formless. Human society is said to function through a code of ethics and laws which are claimed as divinely sanctioned. There is a belief in an immortal soul and therefore in life after death either as rebirth or as Heaven/Hell, a belief tied into divine punishment if the social and sacred code is transgressed. The code governs the practise of religion, and is also the basis of the propagation of the religion and the organisation of its followers. Such organisations interpret these codes of behaviour and claim social authority.

This leads to the question of what is the secular. Secular ideas as potentially important to society have been a part of philosophical thinking, to a greater or a lesser degree, in virtually all societies although they may not always be recognised. Secularism in its broadest meaning, is a system of thinking that seeks to define the functioning of the universe and of human society without involving divine intervention.

This implies that it treats deity, divine sanction and the immortality of the soul as irrelevant to the functioning of society. It gives priorities to laws, social ethics and moral codes. It regards these as made by human societies and not by any God or gods. Laws, therefore, are not immutable and can be adjusted when required, without an appeal to divine sanction. When religious laws restrict social action, a secular policy could be a form of release from these. This means the primacy of civil laws governing the entire society. This, of course, also raises other questions, some of which could impinge on the role of programmes of affirmative action in relation to other identities.

Where religion focuses on the aspirations of the individual or a particular religious community, secular values by contrast, refer to and are ideally aimed at the well-being of the entire society. Policies relating to the entitlements of the citizen – social welfare, education, health, distributive and social justice and the rule of law can be, and should be, the constituents and primary concerns of a secular society. However, these have to be integrated as processes of governance, since they can also be abused by those in power. Ensuring the just practice of law becomes a necessity. These are aspects of the secularising of society.

The secular state is not expected to be the patron of any specific religious activity. Unlike post-Reformation Europe where the patronage of the king was generally confined to either Catholicism or Protestantism, Indian kings generally patronised more than one religion, and even some that were opposed to each other, such as Buddhism and Shaivism. Frequently patronage changed from reign to reign and they had a range of religions to choose from. The significant difference in the secular state is the negation of such patronage. A case in point is that when KM Munshi wanted the Government of India to finance the rebuilding of the Somanatha temple, Nehru did not allow it, arguing that the Indian government was secular and therefore the rebuilding of the temple should come from private funds.

Let us not forget that even private patronage to a religious institution is inevitably tied to the wishes of those that are wealthy enough to give grants and donations to these institutions. In earlier times it was kings and the aristocracy, today it is corporates and wealthy businessmen. Religious institutions are, therefore, not without a social agenda.

Moreover, all religions do not teach the same values. For example, attitudes to violence differ: Crusades, Inquisitions and Jihads are glorified in Christianity and Islam, the *Bhagavadgita* argues that if violence is required to meet the obligations of one's caste and fight against evil, it is legitimate. I have often thought of how different the message of the *Gita* would have been had the Buddha been the mentor of Arjuna on the battlefield at Kurukshetra, and not Krishna. But even with this history, there were people from all religions who preferred non-violence, as indeed not all Buddhists refrained from violence.

If secularism is not to be interpreted as merely the co-existence of all religions, then let me also firmly reiterate that it does not mean a turn to atheism, as is sometimes thought – even if atheism would solve some of these problems. The secularising of society is essentially the reconfiguration of entitlements to a decent life, to law and to ethics. It requires the relocating of religion to the extent that the institutions of religion do not have priority in the functioning of society. State financing should go to the institutions that are foundational to the welfare of society as a whole, and not to those with religious affiliations. It also requires that social ethics and human rights in themselves, unconnected with religion, should be the foundation of laws binding on all citizens.

It is often argued that secularism is alien to Indian civilisation and tradition. I would, therefore, like to consider the veracity of this statement. The constituents of secularism that make up the concept are not alien to Indian thought, although as a concept it was not given a label. Both history and philosophy provide evidence of a concern with these ideas in various forms. The most frequently evoked king in connection with religious tolerance is, of course, Ashoka Maurya. In his edicts, he calls for not only the co-existence of all religious sects but equal respect for those who represented them, irrespective of whether they were brahmanas or shramanas.

Akbar too, many centuries later, echoed these sentiments and called for respecting all religions, emphasising what he thought were their common features. Harshavardhana of Kanauj, like most Indian kings, patronised more than one religion – even those that were on occasion antagonistic to each other, such as the Buddhist and Shaiva. Similarly, Aurangzeb included brahmanas and *jogis* as recipients of his patronage. But this was not secularism, since the focus remained on the pre-eminence of religion. Royal patronage to more than one religion is different from secularism. Its purpose was often to invoke religious authority in order to serve political ends, to provide a kind of catchment area of support for the king as the patron.

However, what is closer to secularism but is seldom quoted these days, is Ashoka's definition of *dhamma/dharma*, which he defines as a social ethic rather than religion. Many of his edicts refer to what he thought of as the social responsibilities and relationships among various categories of people, and these were unconnected with any religion. This was an idea fostered by Buddhism, Jainism and other sects opposed to brahmanical orthodoxy. This hints at a step in the secular direction although it still cannot be called secularism, since secularism is tied to the concept of the nation and of modern society.

Viewed historically, religions are created by men and women in response to personal or social concerns. The organisations that grow from religious roots are mechanisms of propagating religious ideas, assisted often by access to resources and power. This encourages the creation of relationships ranging from co-existence to confrontations. These are situations of religious plurality, but are inevitably conditioned by a hierarchy of dominance and subordination. This remained characteristic of India over many centuries, although the status of sects could change over time. To some extent this was tied into the structure of caste society, where large caste clusters defined and adjusted their religion to accord with social needs. We today read their motivation as religious, but often the religious sect and its status represented the outcome of social and political assertion.

For the larger part of the Indian population religion has been neither monolithic nor uniform. For those calling themselves Hindus, there was no historical founder, no single sacred book that was viewed as the most authoritative by all, no ecclesiastical organisation culminating in a Church, no rites of conversion and no over-arching identity that drew in all related sects. Muslims and Christians had all these but they too until recently, were fragmented into sects. The practise of their religion responded to local needs, custom and caste, rather than an assumed monolithic unity. Thus the Mappila Muslims of Kerala and the Meo Muslims of Rajasthan had only a little in common in their practice of Islam, beyond praying in the mosque even if all of them did so. The social code or *shari'a* was considered essential to Islamic observance, yet the same *shari'a* did not hold for all Muslims. Sectarian confrontations have littered the history of Islam, not least being the continuing divide between Sunnis and Shias that accounts for so much bloodshed. As with Hindu society so with the Islamic, sectarian differences are frequently rooted in caste/*zat*, and region, especially in relation to customary law, and also in considering economic disparities. And caste applied across religions, especially in relation to Dalits. Every religion discriminated against them. The religious process, therefore, was different from that experienced in Europe, where Christianity was the sole religion, despite the split into Catholicism and Protestantism, and the Church was the singular institution.

It is only in recent years that there has been a process of what has been called Islamisation, where the intention is to wipe out divergence and have all Muslims observe a single official form of Islam. This is parallel to current attempts to reformulate Hinduism. The efforts of Hindutva, for example, are aimed at creating a Syndicated Hinduism, a religion that can be ordered and controlled – a Judeo-Christian type religion. The reason for this change is undoubtedly because such a version can be more easily manipulated and organised for political mobilisation, particularly as an opposition to the idea of secularising society.

In some ways a disjuncture in the understanding of religion in Indian society came with colonialism: colonial policy redefined the concept of religion in India. It cut across the pluralism, the blurred edges and the overlapping forms of the many religious identities, and instead created sharply demarcated community identities with a sense of religious uniformity within each community. Such identities had existed to a limited extent in pre-colonial times, largely restricted to the ruling class. But even the elite hardly saw themselves as members of a monolithic community, because upper caste practices differed from those of lesser castes, and had regional variations. The Muslim Sayyad, Momin and *bhishti,* did not see themselves as a single community; nor did the Sikh *khatri* mix with the Mazhabi Sikhs such as the Ramgarhias, let alone the brahmanas with the chandalas. The general population crossed the boundaries of formal religion and caste codes, and supported whichever deity or practice appealed to them, identifying themselves by sects that remained ever fluid.

In the late nineteenth century these identities were regrouped into separated monolithic units via the census. This denied them a shared history and replaced it with a history of monolithic religious communities, each occupying a separate compartment in society. Religious groups began to re-orient their relationships in the new context of the colonial polity. Such reorientations had also happened in the earlier past, but the earlier identities were more fluid, had greater continuity and plurality.

Moving away from supposedly divinely sanctioned laws is not impossible. In the last century we have experienced two major debates on religious law and society. The status of the *Shari'a* and its legal interpretation in a democratic society was discussed in terms of updating it in the period just prior to 1947, but the debate seems to have petered out with Partition. Subsequently, there was a debate on the Hindu Code Bill. Still later, changes in the status of the Dalits in India were a rejection of the *Dharmashastra* codes. Such steps can be extended further through secular laws.

To argue for a secular state in India today is not easy. Its implications are misinterpreted or misrepresented, often deliberately so. It is equated with westernisation and described as a western imposition on what is projected as the Indian tradition. Not surprisingly, the more materialist modes of westernisation, such as increasing personal wealth through neo-liberalism, with declining attention to the economic growth of the larger numbers of people, are not objected to. These are not seen as the imposition of westernisation through corporate capitalism, even though they are directly and overwhelmingly so. With the majority now endorsing an international market economy, any charge of westernisation through other forms is weak.

Adherence to this economy has introduced substantial change in Indian society: there is the insecurity of a competitive system, moving away from familiar moorings and creating new social mores. The resulting cultural alienation, not always recognised as such, brings many social problems. One among these is the visibility of middle class NRIs as role models, some of whom are attempting to recreate an imagined 'shining India' of the past, through deliberately misinterpreting history, and fostering religiosity as a palliative for alienation. This is attractive to middle-class India, because it means that no concessions need be made to a more equitable distribution of wealth or better living conditions for those below the poverty line. These latter changes would require the middle classes to be less concerned with chasing wealth alone.

As a result of these changes there is also a refusal to concede a kind of proto-secular thinking which has been present in Indian thought for many centuries. We need to remember that confrontations between philosophical ideologies, with some supporting religion and others opposing it, are not recent phenomena. They are a continuing feature of Indian history since earliest times. It is sometimes argued that philosophical materialism did not exist in Indian thought, as it did not produce a major text in the Indian tradition. Others claim that such texts did once exist, but were subsequently suppressed. However, the teaching was obviously known, was effective, and was powerful. It is referred to and reflected in lengthy passages in the texts of those trying to refute it. From the third century BC to the seventeenth century AD, there are references to debates on the questions raised by materialist philosophy with quotations from those supporting this perspective. Despite the erosion of texts, therefore, it remained a presence that had to be contended with.

A brief summary of philosophical views suggests that Indian philosophical schools and ideologies from earliest times were divided into two broad categories, and each of the two called the other *pashanda*/heretical or fraudulent. The two were the *astikas* and the *nastikas*. These can be loosely translated as the orthodox or conservative thinkers and the heterodox non-believers. The *astikas* accepted deity as the first cause, accepted rebirth and the conditions it brought as the result of actions in a previous life, and regarded the *Vedas* as divine revelation; and by contrast, the *nastikas* denied deity and theism, as well as rebirth and the immortality of the soul, and rejected the divine sanction of the *Vedas*. The *nastika* sects ranged from the Lokayata, later called Charvaka, to Buddhists and Jainas, all frequently in disagreement with each other, but nevertheless opposed to conservative views.

The heterodox were initially itinerant teachers, addressing the audiences that gathered in the parks on the edge of cities. The debates were sharp and contentious, the Buddha describing some participants as wriggling like eels around an argument, quibbling over the finer points. Logic was the lamp of learning. They held that the universe is self-created, and according to some its source is the combining of four elements – earth, air, fire and water. These elements also create the body with its tangible proof of life, which gets terminated at death. There is no immortality, no soul, and everything dies with death.

They argued further that evidence can come only from perception and from defining a cause, and not from inference – smoke can only be identified if a fire can be perceived.

Knowledge comes from the perceptions of bodily sense organs. One should rely on evidence, causation, and rationality, not on Fate or supposed divine sanction. Rituals are invented by brahmanas just to earn a livelihood. Caste is an artificial creation and is not divinely ordained. Laws are also man-made and can be changed. Whereas a few advocated a hedonistic life-style, many such as the Buddhists and Jainas propagated the establishing of social ethics as the mainspring of human behaviour, whereby the laws and values of society should relate to how one treats one's fellow human beings.

My intention in giving this rather inadequate summary is to point out that these ideas were constantly debated. They were clearly in opposition to Vedic Brahmanism, and to the later Puranic Hinduism. Not surprisingly, ritual texts of Hinduism, such as the *Puranas*, treat these ideas with sarcasm, but in the philosophical texts they are the source of serious discussion. Philosophical schools seeking to establish themselves had either to refute, or else, make some concession to heterodox thought. This is particularly so in the period from the eighth to the twelfth centuries AD, when, interestingly, the Hinduism of the *Puranas* was being widely established, especially among the elite. The references in these texts to the *nastikas* being the *mahamohas*, those that delude and create illusions, was to be expected, given the competition between the two.

The fourteenth century compendium of philosophical schools, the *Sarva-darshana-samgraha*, composed by the philosopher Madhvacharya, begins with a discussion of Charvaka views on rationality. Passages are quoted from Charvaka teaching and are refuted; nevertheless, even this refutation cannot hide the presence and significance of this teaching. Even though in Brahmanical texts, the heterodox are linked with peripatetic teachers, dropouts, and renouncers, all the same they could not be overlooked. Colonial scholars in the nineteenth century enquired about philosophical schools from their brahmana informants, who predictably gave precedence to the *astika* view, and the *nastika* was set aside. We today do the same.

Under the umbrella of what came to be called Hinduism in the colonial period, and parallel to the orthodox religion, were a variety of sects of many centuries before. These ranged from the Bhakti sects of the Vaishnavas, Shaivas and Shaktas, the Buddhist and Jaina sects, those of the Nathapanthis, and of the Sufis, among others. They were not necessarily atheist; in fact, few were so. But they reiterated the basic characteristic of religion in India, which primarily meant the freedom to choose or even to create one's religion. This happened when a group would come together with a teacher and be recognised as a sect; and the sect often became a caste. An example of this is the origin and history of the Lingayat sect and caste of medieval times. Its teaching was opposed to Vedic Brahmanism, and its caste base was mixed. But today it is both a distinct caste, with its own hierarchy of *jatis*, and a religious sect, playing a central role in the politics of Karnataka. In a sense this illustrates the point that the larger religion was a mosaic of sects, which possibly allowed smaller groups in society to co-exist with lesser confrontation. In the juxtaposition of secularism with religious organisations in such contexts, there are inevitably new questions seeking answers.

The history of religion in India is, therefore, different from that of Europe. If a secular response is to be sought it will have to be in the context of this difference. Hence the need for a new understanding of the role of religion in the history of Indian society, as well as a redefinition of secularism to mean more than just a co-existence of monolithic religions. In such a redefinition, the establishing of a social ethic from a secular position, far from being alien to Indian tradition, would be in the mainstream.

In what I have said so far, I am not arguing for the abolition of religion, or for replacing it with *nastika* philosophy. But I am arguing that we put religion where it belongs, namely, as one component of Indian society. It is by no means the principal feature that has subordinated all others, as some have argued. Furthermore, we should not allow religious identities to ride over the essentials of social functioning and governance. I have argued that the range of thinking from theism to atheism has been present in India almost throughout its history, and has been constantly under discussion. An awareness of this would be of help today before we rush to dismiss some ways of thinking, such as materialist philosophies, by calling them alien. That the social ethic and the laws that go to support it is not dependent on divine sanction, and that the existence of deities can be doubted, are ideas familiar to us since antiquity. In the past they were more openly debated but today this would be opposed for fear of the multiple claims to hurt religious sentiments. The real purpose of such claims is to deny freedom of discussion and to facilitate the political mobilisation of religious groups.

In Europe the Church hounded non-theistic thinking, and banned the texts and burnt the thinkers. In India, the *nastikas* occasionally met with a violent end, as when Buddhist monks were killed in Kashmir, and Jaina monks were impaled in Tamilnadu. But this did not prevent their ideas from being continuously discussed. We need to bring our heterodox traditions once more into the mainstream as an enviable heritage representing an impressive way of thought. This would legitimise critical enquiry and the rational basis of causation, so essential to knowledge and to social well-being. For obvious historical reasons, I am not suggesting that this tradition constitutes secularism. However, if secularism is treated as a philosophical concept, it could find some roots in earlier forms of Indian thought, should such roots be required.

The need to introduce the secular mode into governance in India is urgent for at least two reasons. One is that religions in India are being reformulated as monolithic structures with little flexibility. This disallows even the freedom of religious expression and reiterates religion as the central feature of social functioning. Belief is becoming hidebound. Social ethics have to conform to the supposedly immutable and divinely sanctioned laws. These are often inventions of our times to overcome the problems we face, and have little to do with earlier social codes. The ironic use of the term "honour killings" is a recent example of this. The intention is to disallow freedom to women and Dalits when they transgress the social code, by murdering them, and then justifying the murder as a way of upholding traditional caste codes.

Religious communities frequently claim that their sentiments have been hurt by something said in a particular book. This is an easy way to demand the banning of the book. Such books are those that suggest that we reconsider our identities and review our social codes. The source of such demands usually lies in a religious fundamentalist group, which claims to speak for an entire community, and gets away with it because the Indian intelligentsia takes it lying down. A demonstration of this inability to stand up to being browbeaten, was the recent decision of the Academic Council of Delhi University, to remove from the syllabus, a thought-provoking essay by AK Ramanujan, on the variant versions of the *Ramayana*. Is this because of apathy and unconcern, or the fear of yet more physical assaults by political gangs using the cover of religion; or, as in the cartoon controversy, not wishing to lose a political vote bank, even at the cost of destroying a basic function of education?

This is not altogether unconnected to the fears and insecurities introduced by various contemporary economic and social changes. The process of Hinduisation and of Islamisation, and such like, are seen as defense mechanisms, although they often aim at political provocation. The presence of religious fundamentalism is not always directly confrontational. More often it is subtle, and subtle in a variety of ways; in news reports on riots, in advertisements in the media, and in many programmes presented on TV. Subtlety has a lulling effect, and the idea of the secular finds decreasing resonance in Indian society.

The second reason takes me back to my earlier statement about the two levels of religious belief – the personal and the public. When religion becomes an organising agency and intervenes in controlling social relationships, it diminishes the possibility of a secular society. The secularising of society means that governance has to focus on what is essential: social welfare ensuring basic needs such as water, food, health care, access to quality education, income distribution and employment, and a guarantee of human rights; not just in law, but in practice. These are not to be treated as isolated items, as they often are, but as an integrated pattern of the polity. The ensuring of these essentials means pro-active governance willing to face confrontations from organisations geared to religion, and already controlling many of these activities, or where they are in effect a political lobby.

Negative discrimination continuing from the past cannot be annulled only by affirmative action in the present. There has to be a removal of the factors that encourage discrimination. It is only when a society does not have to make concessions to specific identities, and there is a universal availability of the constituents of social welfare, that such a society can be called free and democratic. We are a long way from that.

We today may perhaps still have the freedom to choose the values that should govern our society. Should we support a politics that allows religious communities to direct the form of our future and thereby continue to fracture it; or, should we demand a society that relocates religion through a process of ensuring the primacy of social ethics, laws and values as intrinsic in themselves and not requiring religious sanction? In short, the focus should shift from the co-existence of religions to the co-existence of citizens, with equal access to rights and a commitment to obligations, guarded by the vigilance of a free and just society.

Is Secularism Alien to Indian Civilisation?[*]

In choosing to write on this subject it is my intention to try and question the statement that secularism is alien to Indian civilisation and that it, therefore, follows that the secularisation of Indian society has no place in contemporary Indian values. This has become the slogan of supporters of Hindutva who project secularism as antithetical to Hinduism. My concern, here, is not with this kind of rhetoric of political mobilisation. I would like to address the proposition of secularism being alien to Indian civilisation as has been put forward by some scholars in a more thoughtful manner.[1] My concern is with two aspects

---

[*] First published in T. Srinivasan (ed.), *The Future of Secularism*, OUP, Delhi, 2007.

[1] T.N. Madan, 'Secularism in its Place', *Journal of Asian Studies*, 1987, pp. 46, 47-59; *Modern Myths and Locked Minds*, Delhi, 1997; and A. Nandy, 'The Politics of Secularism and the Recovery of Religious Toleration' in R. Bhargava (ed.), *Secularism and its Critics*, Delhi, 1998, pp. 297-344. The views of both have been debated, and this debate and much else on secularism in India is also reflected in R. Bhargava (ed.), *Secularism and its Critics*.

of this debate: one relates to the definition of secularism which also involves making a distinction between secularism and secularisation, namely the meaning of the concept and the process of social and political change that is involved; and the second with the fact that when secularism is posited as opposed to religion in India, the discussion is generally limited to only a segment of Hinduism, namely Vedic Brahmanism and some aspects of Puranic Hinduism, and the more extensive articulation of religion in India is not included.

I would like to focus, therefore, on these two aspects: the secularising processes implicit in the change to modernisation; and would also like to extend the meaning of Indian religion to include the religious identity of not just the few but of the larger population that would be involved in the secularising of Indian society. Furthermore, what needs to be examined, although this cannot be done within the limitations of this paper, is not merely what the religious texts say, but the manner in which religious institutions negotiate and establish their social functions. Secularism tends to be projected in India as an ideology that can be imposed, rather than as a process of establishing the rights of citizens, and introducing the changes required for this. There is, therefore, no specific historical moment at which secularism comes into a society with a clear blueprint for social change. It is better viewed as a process of gradual change affecting not just politics but the social and cultural life of society. The notion of the secularisation of society, therefore, is more appropriate than the limited notion of the ideology of secularism.[2]

The secularisation of society is linked to inclusive nationalism and the creation of a nation-state with an attempt to modernise society. It has been associated with modern economic patterns, such as those of capitalism and industrialisation, and

---

2   A. Vanaik, *The Furies of Indian Communalism*, London, 1997.

the enhanced use of certain technologies and sciences. It requires the establishing of democracy and the rights of citizens. It opposes a single state religion since it supports the freedom of all religions. Such changes are also tied to the privileging of individualism that distinguishes modernity from earlier times. Inevitably, in this pattern, religion is only one among other categories of identity. The secularising of society does not oppose religion but prefers that religious authorities should not control the institutions linked to social ethics, economic development and cultural change. Where there is an attempt at establishing religious nationalism, there the secularisation of society meets with confrontation from religious nationalism. However, secularism is not the antinomy of religion, and is quintessential to a modern society. A secularising society requires both the state and its citizens to determine social ethics as foundational to the nature and quality of the society that is being created.

The degree to which secularism is or is not alien does require some familiarity with both social philosophies and social practices from the past. But, unfortunately, discussions of secularism are frequently limited to seeing it superficially as antithetical to any and every traditional or contemporary religious articulation. Such discussions rarely pause to investigate even the critical assessment made of these orthodoxies by earlier ideological movements in past times, leave alone current views. Invoking religion also involves a reference to the wider range of established traditions, and not just to a selected few. In the case of India, the discussion focuses almost entirely on concepts from Vedic Brahmanism and Puranic Hinduism, to the exclusion of other religious expressions – both within and outside what is called the Hindu tradition – or else, on the ideas expressed by modern public figures, with little reference to the wider acceptance or rejection of such ideas. Defining religious traditions requires recognising differences in such traditions from higher to lower castes and from *dvijas*, the twice-born, to *mlechchhas*, those outside the social pale.

That secularism is alien is maintained through some statements that need to be clarified at the start.[3] The argument that secularism is inappropriate to south Asia because the majority of south Asians are adherents of a religious faith implies that a secular society is an atheist society, which of course is never the case. Religious faith does not debar secularism, since a secular society gives space to religion, but does not make it primary. It is also said that secularism is incapable of countering religious fundamentalism, but religious fundamentalism is primarily a political condition – especially in the contemporary world – and can be countered if the political inducement to fundamentalism is terminated. The secularisation of society protects it from religious fundamentalism. Where there is scant observance of human rights associated with a viable civil society, there, the turn to religiosity, if not to religious fundamentalism, is noticeable. Secularism and religion cannot be taken as equal ideologies, since they imply not only a different kind of thought process but also dissimilar social concerns. In the world of our century, it is not so much the attempt to marginalise religion through secularism that has strengthened religious fundamentalism, but the impact of globalisation and concessions to dictatorial political authority that has led to a parochial retreat into religion in many parts of the world.

The statement that secularism denies religion derives from the notion that the process of secularisation is embedded in the confrontation between the Church and the State, as has been projected in the history of medieval Europe emerging into modernity. Secularism is, therefore, seen as "a gift from Christianity". The argument generally made by those who support the notion of secularism being alien to India is that it is spe-

---

3　T.N. Madan, op. cit., 1987.

cific to European civilisation and to the nature of the particular contest between Church and State in Europe. It is inapplicable, therefore, to Indian civilisation (which is in any case commonly viewed as conforming to the religion and values of upper caste Hinduism). The modernising process in Europe loosened, modified, or even radically changed, European society from a system in which the Church (Catholic and Protestant) played a central political and social role, to a system where the Church is one among many other players concerned with the functioning of society. The contest in Europe was not between religion *per se* and the state, but between the dominance of the Church as an institution sanctioned by religion, over social functioning and the attempts of the state to intervene in this function.

That the articulation of secularist ideals is a post-renaissance feature in Europe indicates that some of its seminal ideas go back to pre-Christian traditions, as in the philosophies of Neo-Platonism that had views distinct from those of the Catholic Church. Together with this were European strands of thought and action that formed an alternative substratum to formal Christianity in Europe, as for instance, those of Giordano Bruno. These gave some weight to discussions on secularism but were not solely the outcome of an opposition to Christianity. Secularism is part of a modernising process and enters into the making of all societies that are undergoing this process. The question is whether such societies can draw on their own traditions to strengthen the process. Doing so would also mean being aware of the specificities of each society.

The interface of religion and society in Europe during the last millennium should not be applied indiscriminately to India, where the experience of such an interface has been fundamentally different. This difference is ignored in discussions on secularism and religion. Where there is no Church of a kind similar to the Christian Church – as in Buddhism, Hinduism and Islam – there the impact of religion on social institutions takes varied forms imprinted with local patterns of custom and behaviour. Thus, Hinduism did not regard belief as obligatory, but the performance of rituals – partially dependent on belief but more on social duty – was necessary, and one's caste and sect determined the rituals. Orthodoxy was subordinate to orthopraxy among the larger number of Hindus. Orthopraxy was an indicator of religious and of caste identity. In the case of Buddhism, social ethics encompassed religion. Adherence to orthodoxy was generally limited to the upper castes among all religions and these formed a small, although influential, percentage of society.

The departure in Hinduism came about through the recent political requirements of religious nationalisms. The need for mass political mobilisation required that religion be converted into something other than what it is. In many ways, the emergence of Hindutva, defined as 'Hinduness', is the reformulation of the Hindu religious system into one approximating Islam and Christianity – what I have elsewhere called 'Syndicated Hinduism'.[4] Hindutva requires that Hinduism, or at least a very visible part of it, has to change many of its premises, in order to be politically effective. By way of illustration, a few such changes are: the search for a founder of the religion and his historical location, so as to give historicity to the religion; the emphasis on a single sacred book, which becomes a tangible text for reference relating to social ethics and the moral code, and a focus of loyalty; and the attempt to build an ecclesiastical structure, such that it can be appealed to when there are conflicts involving religious institutions. A significant difference between Hinduism and Hindutva is that the latter disallows diversity,

---

4   R. Thapar, 'Syndicated Hinduism' in *Cultural Pasts*, Delhi, 2002, pp. 1025-1054.

and this makes the ethics of tolerance and, therefore, of non-violence and of equality, unacceptable to it.

To limit the discussion merely to secularism being that which is opposed to religion, is to confine it to the least important aspect; the major impact of the process of secularisation is on civil society – the issues of social welfare, the distribution of resources, and on human rights relating to citizenship and access to the law. This is essential to understanding that the secularising process in India will inevitably be different from that of Europe, although the difference does not annul secularism. Historical processes such as secularisation do not arise in a theoretical vacuum. It is appropriate, therefore, to investigate the wider Indian tradition for seminal ideas that may encourage the secularisation of Indian society.

There is also the question of differentiating between a personalised, virtually private religion and the social and political forms of organised religion that enables it to be used as a force for political mobilisation. This kind of distinction has parallels to what has been called religion-as-faith and religion-as-ideology.[55] The distinction is important to understanding the relationship between secularism and religion, since the first category does not necessarily present a confrontation whereas the second category can obstruct that aspect of civil law which a people may wish to change. The two are not, therefore, versions of the same religious articulation and there is a point when faith can sometimes be converted to ideology, and where this happens, the point in time has to be viewed historically. To diffuse the interference by religious institutions in social functioning requires a distancing of social ethics from religious control, as well as a transferring of power and authority from religious institutions to those associated with the state or civil society pertaining to the needs of the community. The latter get

---

5   A. Nandy, op. cit.

encapsulated in the norms of social ethics. Where social ethics are placed higher than the community's performance of religious ritual, there a potentially proto-secular presence can be detected. This also raises the question of whether the initial concern with social ethics preceded religion, as seems to be the case when viewed from a historical perspective. Religion seems to take over the defining and moulding of existing social ethics, transmuting the definition and giving it the label of the religion.

This, in turn, requires a definition of the word 'secular', recognising that it has undergone changes in time and place. The original usage of the word 'secular', from the Latin *saecularis* of Roman times, referred to celebrations that took place once in a long period of time; for example, the secular games in Rome. In Christian Latin it referred to those living outside the regulations of the Church, and by that definition not of the 'spirit' but 'of the world'. By extension it came to be used for that which was not religious and therefore acquired a negative connotation. But in the early nineteenth century, the meaning changed radically. Secularism was no longer used to differentiate the worldly from the religious, but was used to argue that social ethics and morality should be based exclusively on the regard for the well being of human society, without any sanctions from a belief in God. The connotation was no longer negative, and the focus shifted from religious sanctions to human society living in accordance with socially sanctioned laws pertaining to the common good. It is understood that laws emerge from the concerns of a society and need not carry the stamp of a religion. In its present meaning secularisation is associated with the modernising process, an activity carried out by human society without the authority of the supernatural. It is in this present-day sense that the argument about secularism could be made more insightful than it has been so far.

A search for equivalent words in Sanskrit or Arabic or Classical Chinese is, therefore, not very meaningful. Newly minted terms suggesting religious neutrality or negating religion (*dharma-nirapekshata/a-sampradayika/ghair-mazhabi*) do not define secularism, since they evoke a parochial and out-dated definition. On the relationship between religion and secularism there are two popularly held approaches in India: one argues that secularism confronts religion and this leads to a rupture; the other defines secularism as *sarva-dharma-samabhava* or equal respect for all religions. The latter, it is sometimes suggested, could mean that the state can interfere equally in all religions! This definition was coined when religious tension was vitiating nationalism, as it continues to do. The definition again draws on the medieval European meaning, which is irrelevant to India. It is inadequate since it focuses only on the approach to religion, whereas the more important aspect of secularism has to do with institutions referring to human rights and to civil society, and the relationship of the state to these.

A secular society, ideally, values the equal rights of all citizens, and freedom and equality among them. The function of the state is to ensure the access of these to all citizens, thus ensuring their well being. Implicit in this are notions of democracy, and, therefore, the right of citizens to support as independent individuals their own views on the issues before the state, and not have to be a part of a pre-determined majority; citizenship, which confers human rights, such as monitoring the state's upholding of law and order, maintaining codes of civil law, the general access to the law for redressing grievances, the right to education, health and social welfare; the right to state protection against community conflicts, even those that may take the form of religious conflicts; and the right to practice the religion of one's choice. The secularising process is more in the nature of changing the obligations of state and citizens, rather than focusing on relations between the state and religion.

The Church or its equivalent, where it exists in any religion, is a manifestation of the authority of particular religious groups. As such, it has to have a defined relationship with the state. The state is an alternative manifestation of the political, social and economic aspirations of the entire society in whose name it speaks, even if, in fact, it actually reflects the views of dominant groups in the society. Where there are religions without a Church, there sometimes a church-like organisation has been seen to emerge, in order to channel political aspirations associated with religious nationalisms. This again focuses on the authority of religious institutions, and is to that extent, a deviation from the focus of a secularising process.

The state can propagate economic and political policies, but it cannot propagate religious policies, since the genesis of religion impinges on the belief of each individual and is not primarily a social institution – although it can eventually become that, as it often does. There is a difference between religion as a personal belief and religion organised to become an institution with political, social and economic ramifications, and has then to be treated as an institution of society. Secularism assumes that all religions, to the extent that they are personal belief systems, are tolerant and treat their adherents as equal members of the religious community. The state may not intervene in this. But where religion is manifested in social institutions, as for example in educational institutions or the civil code, and in codes seeking sanction from religious authority to demarcate social groups, as in caste-based societies, there the question of the intervention of the state becomes relevant. Secularism is inherent to modernisation, and if the intention is to internalise modernity, then secularising society is inevitable. Nevertheless, inevitability does not imply a conflict, and there can be an interface between society and religion that adjusts more comfortably to the secularising process. It is this that I would like to explore here.

The process of modernising, and a shift towards the state being responsible for the welfare of its citizens, is associated with the nation-state. The recognition of the shift assists the process of secularisation. It, therefore, tries to decrease the anomie that can be created by the shift, and does this through bonding people by establishing human rights and equal status, as well as by the identity of citizenship. It is in the realm of social ethics that the shift is most visible. Human rights would imply that concerns earlier dealt with by the family and community or by the religious institutions, such as codes of marriage and inheritance, education, health, community living, access to the law, and so on, would now be the concern of the state, and at another remove, of civil society. Perhaps the most difficult aspect of this shift today is the attempt to annul privilege and hierarchy essential to the proper functioning of the nation-state, but not countenanced in earlier times.

In such a situation the religious control over social institutions decreases in importance since many of their functions should, ideally, be taken over by the state and by civil society. Where religious organisations resist the change, they tend to continue to incorporate features such as family, education and community living. The contest comes to be seen as between religion and the state, which is not representative of what is actually happening. The functioning of the ethics of community living becomes central to the secularising process. Therefore, a search for features in a religion that are conducive to secularism would focus on the question of social ethics.

In the nineteenth century, civilisations were defined by geography/territory, religion and language. Indian civilisation was located in the Indian sub-continent, the dominant religion was said to be Hinduism, and the language of the civilisation was, therefore, seen as Sanskrit. Such a definition has many historical fault lines, but since it is the accepted form even now, we may continue to use it, although pointing out the fault lines. Among the fault lines was the way Indian religion was projected. The reference was largely to the religion of the elite, and the tendency was to highlight the group of religions that were selected and placed within the rubric of 'Hinduism'. Others, as for example, Buddhism and Jainism, were marginalised.

What is actually included within the rubric of Hinduism are a vast number of sectarian identities – Vaishnava, Shaiva, Lingayat, Shakta, Natha, and so on. An over-arching label to include all these various religious sects was not used until recent centuries. But the religious identity and praxis that was more closely adhered to was frequently that of the caste. Given the link between caste and religion in India, there is multiple religious articulation across a spectrum of belief and social organisation. The secularisation of Indian society has, therefore, also to consider the nature of change in caste society. This substantially alters the picture from that of a single, clearly contoured religion. Protest against caste inequities was common in religious movements that stemmed from the non-orthodox, heterodox traditions. *Jatis* have their own mythologies and rituals, and the variations can sometimes be quite specific. A ritual specialist could in the past, through observing the ritual of a *jati,* have been able to identify approximately, its *varna* or ritual status, particularly where the code of the *dharmashastras* and *dharmasutras* was also being observed. Interestingly, until recently, *jati* identities continued to be evident even when a *jati,* or part of one, converted to Islam or Christianity, and many conversions were of this kind. What this means is that secularism in India cannot ignore *jati* identities that are differentiated social identities with some sectarian religious forms specific to the *jati*. Because the practice of religion is so closely tied to caste, the nature of religion is not similar to that of Europe, and in the Indian context the secularist dialogue has to include caste, which again makes it different from the European experience. This becomes all the more pertinent since both caste and secularism involve questions of social ethics, access to human rights and the availability of these to all social groups.

Indian civilisation has registered multiple religions as parallel strands, with some becoming more dominant in certain times and some emerging as independent religions. There have been degrees of continuity in some cases, and some fundamental differences in others. Religions with recognisable characteristics and influential in many parts of the sub-continent can be listed chronologically as Vedic Brahmanism, Buddhism, Jainism, Puranic Hinduism, Bhakti, Shakta, Islam, Sikhism, and what I would like to call the religion of the Guru-Pir tradition. To this may be added the input of Christianity and Zoroastrianism, going back to around the mid-first millennium AD, but with a more limited spread until recently. The evolution of religion in India is frequently seen only through textual sources, with a predisposition to privileging the brahmanical sources and socio-legal codes like the *dharmashastras*. But other religions and religious sects projected other ideas. Nevertheless there is a tendency to juxtapose all the sources and view them as manifestations of a single religion, barring the Semitic religions. However, when seen as independent religious articulations, their variations become apparent and point towards a complexity that is often overlooked.

There were, therefore, strong parallel traditions challenging orthodoxy in all the religions of India, and these tended to give greater weight to social ethics than to prescriptive texts regulating religious observances. The most powerful exposition of this comes from Buddhism. Although Buddhism later nurtured its own orthodoxy, the early emphasis on social ethics remained constant and was in turn to influence the form of many other popular religious sects through the centuries. I would, therefore, like to refer to the early teachings of the Buddha at greater length. The context to these teachings was the unease that many thinkers of the time had with the ideas of Vedic Brahmanism.

Vedic Brahmanism, in the first millennium BC, was the religion of the ritual of sacrifice and therefore the ritual specialist – the *brahmana* – was its key propagator. Its social beginnings are linked to the functioning of oligarchies and chiefdoms as pre-state societies and it drew its political authority from the patronage of clan chiefs requiring rituals of validation with claims of divine sanction. In the process of chiefdoms being transmuted into kingdoms and chiefs evolving into kings, the rituals of validation continued and became the rituals of kingship, and more so in the centuries AD when monarchies became the normal pattern. But Vedic Brahmanism had to compete with other religious sects and was gradually reduced to symbolic importance, except among its twice-born practitioners.

Buddhism and Jainism and a variety of heterodox sects were among those that questioned Vedic Brahmanism, and Buddhism was a recognised alternative. These sects reflect the historical changes that began in the mid-first millennium BC with the coming of the state and of urbanisation. Their influential patronage came from the non-monarchical clans of the middle Ganges valley and from some royal courts, but equally from the trading communities scattered all over the sub-continent. It is often forgotten that Buddhism had a widespread appeal as well as royal support for a millennium after it was first established, and in eastern India this continued for still longer, commanding the patronage of many communities in various regions. Buddhism and associated religions were collectively referred to as the Shramana religions. Buddhism cannot be dismissed as merely one of the many manifestations of Hinduism since it has been fundamentally different in belief and practice. The catalytic role of Buddhism can be seen not only in the emergence of later schools of philosophy – some confrontational and some supportive – but also in the evolution of aspects of Puranic Hinduism. Even as late as the eleventh century Al-Biruni, describing the religions of India, highlights the differences between the Brahmanas and the Shamaniyya (Shramanas).[6]

Yet it is largely the texts of Vedic Brahmanism and Puranic Hinduism that are quoted in discussions on the possible antecedents to secular concerns in pre-modern India. Because these texts either show no interest in what are today regarded as secular norms, or else are read to deny these norms, it is held that secularism is altogether alien to Indian culture. My contention is that if one is less selective in choosing the texts from early periods, then it is apparent that there were discussions among various groups on issues that do relate, sometimes directly and sometimes a little obliquely, to what we regard as significant themes in secular thinking.

The hallmark of Buddhism in the early period was the centrality of social ethics. Buddhism emphasised the relationship between the individual and society rather than ritual and belief in the supernatural. The Buddha was therefore treated in some brahmanical texts as a *nastika* and a *charvaka* – an atheist and a materialist. That the confrontation was recognised is evident from his rejection of the theist view.[7]

It is in the initial Buddhist ideas that one could search for seminal notions that might be conducive to a secularising of Indian society. There has been a debate as to whether what was taught by the Buddha can be called a religion since he does

---

6　E.C. Sachau (ed.), *Alberuni's India*, Delhi, 1964 (reprint), I, p. 21.

7　*Digha Nikaya*, I. 32,46 Brahmajala-sutta.

not postulate a belief in a deity. However, even though deities are incorporated a few centuries subsequent to his death, the centrality of social ethics remains a constant factor. It may be said that his contention was that a belief in human relations was more central than a belief in deity. The questioning of deity was not limited to the Buddha. Various groups of Lokayata and Charvaka teachers were even more vehement in regarding deities as unnecessary and religion as a foolish aberration. Such views persisted as parallel schools of thought to Brahmanic and Shramanic ideas well into the second millennium AD.[8] Ethics without religion was an established tradition among many strands of materialist and Shramanic sects and the ethical basis of laws was widely discussed. The Buddha suggested that the existence of deity was irrelevant, and rejected the traditional significance of Hindu deities. Eternity was embedded not in deity but in notions of *dharma/dhamma* (the teaching) and *nirvana/ nibbana* (the individual's liberation from rebirth).

The kernel of his teaching was in the *dhamma-cakkappa-vattana-sutta*, the teaching on the "turning of the wheel of law".[9] This encapsulates the four "noble truths", *ariya-sacca*, and the eightfold path of "the middle way", *majjhima pattipada*.[10] The basis of the four noble truths is the idea of dependent origination, *paticca samuppada*, a theory of cause and effect that becomes foundational to this ethics.[11] The argument is that suffering is caused by actions motivated by desire and the cessation of this leads to the extinction of suffering, and a condition of *nirvana*, liberates the person from rebirth and future suffering. Understanding the nature of causation is, therefore, of impor-

---

8   S. Radhakrishnan, *Indian Philosophy*, I, London, 1948, p. 277 ff.; D.P. Chattopadhyaya, *Lokayata*, Delhi, 1955.

9   *Samyutta Nikaya*, I. 191; *Vinaya*, Mahavagga 1.6.17-26.

10 *Majjhima Nikaya*, I. 167 ff.; Ariyapariyesana-sutta; III. 71-78 Mahacat-tarisaka-sutta; *Samyutta Nikaya*, 3. 94-99 Parileyya; II. 12.1 ff.

11 *Vinaya*, Mahavagga, I. 1. 1-7; *Digha Nikaya*, II. 30 ff.

tance to understanding the human condition, and the explanation is not to be found in divine revelation.[12] Liberation can be achieved by observing the middle way of moderation in actions and ambitions. Essential to this idea is the rationality of the argument linking critical thinking to causality.

His discussion of the middle way as the way of social and moral action is at the core of what can be called his social ethics. The centrality of the householder, *gahapati*, was the lynchpin in this.[13] The ethic, based on insight through knowledge, was encapsulated in conduct towards parents, friends, teachers and servants. The householder was not an enlightened being and had to be helped along by explanations of the moral code. Even the attaining of *nirvana* required such help and the Buddha used the analogy of the raft – those that had crossed to the other shore and been liberated by using the raft of enlightenment should leave the raft for the use of others.[14]

Dhamma was the universal ethic of family and community, propelled by *ahimsa* – non-violence, tolerance and respect for rights as embodied in codes of behaviour. As a code of behaviour it assumes the equality of all and the rules apply equally to all. The context to this is the story of the *mahasammata*, the great elected one, with whom the state began.[15] After a long, Utopian existence in the remote past, human society gradually began to develop conflicts and contradictions, eventually requiring the establishing of rules of family organisation and of private property. When even this failed to prevent conflict it was decided to elect one person to maintain order, to enforce the laws and to ensure the well being of all. The elected one was paid a wage that was a percentage of the produce. There is no divine intervention in this narrative as there was in the Vedic

---

12 *Majjhima Nikaya*, I. p. 160 ff., Ariyapariyesana-sutta.
13 *Digha Nikaya*, III. 180 ff., Sigalovada-sutta.
14 *Majjhima Nikaya*, I. 134-135, Alagaddupama-sutta.
15 *Digha Nikaya*, III. 84-96, Agganna-sutta.

myths of the origin of government, an intervention that continued to be referred to even as late as in the *Arthashastra*.[16] In the Buddhist texts the matter was settled by contract among equals in order to end the disruption of an earlier Utopian condition caused by subsequent social disharmony and intolerance. The state was neither a natural institution nor a divine imposition, but a necessity required when the actions of a society cause its disruption. Therefore, the state has obligations to prevent the disruption of society, which it can do by instituting social ethics. The social ethic is so central that the Buddha opposed caste hierarchy, because it creates inequality and this in turn encourages disruption.[17] The social ethic was to be taught in the *kutuhala-shalas*, the parks on the outskirts of cities, and through the preaching of monks.

By way of contrast, the *Mahabharata* also speaks of a social contract in an extract that dates to a period probably contemporary with the recording of the Buddhist texts. In the story of the first ruler Prithu and the establishing of a state there is recourse to a contract. But this is not among the people, probably because they were not regarded as being of equal status. It is a contract in which the brahmanas are involved, since they control social laws and the making of society and state, all of which derive from the gods.[18] It is intended to prevent the condition of anarchy – *matsyanyaya* – that follows in the absence of a state. The term encapsulates a condition of drought when the big fish in a pool eat the little fish. The mutual interdependence of temporal and spiritual power, represented by the king and the priest and central to the *Vedas*, is rejected by the Buddhist tradition. The *rajan* in the *gana-sanghas*/chiefdoms functioned for a long period without dependence on the brahmana.

---

16 *Arthashastra* 1.13.5-12.
17 *Digha Nikaya*, I. 92 ff., Ambattha-sutta; *Samyutta Nikaya*, 4. 398.
18 Shantiparvan, 59. 12-29; 94-119.

In the Buddhist texts, the upholding of *dhamma* was said to be the most important duty of the king.[19] An attempt was made towards the inculcation of these ideas during the reign of Ashoka Maurya. He developed on the Buddhist doctrine and made a point of calling upon the brahmanas and the shramanas (the Buddhist, Jainas and other Orders of monks) and members of religious sects generally, to be tolerant towards each other's teachings. All relationships should be based on mutual concern and consideration including those involving parents and children, employers and employees, and communities, professions and sects.[20] He called upon the gods to manifest themselves so as to persuade people of the righteousness of this teaching,[21] but he too did not attribute the teaching to deities. In the Buddhist tradition he became a pious Buddhist king, but his piety was expressed in a concern for social ethics and the welfare of people, and not in performing rituals directed at deities.

A significant difference between Brahmanical and Buddhist texts also lay in the concept of the *chakravartin*, the universal monarch. The Buddhist *chakkavatti* was the *dhammika-dhammaraja*, the king of righteousness or the righteous king, aware of the advantages of a society governed by *dhamma*. He was the turner of the wheel, where the wheel is that of the *dhamma*, the law,[22] unlike most *kshatriya* heroes in Brahmanical texts who were *chakravartins* because their campaigns brought them victories over their enemies. The latter were also expected to promote the law, but this was law pronounced by brahmanas, with the claim that it was sanctioned by deities: it was specific to caste and was conditioned by social hierarchy. The Buddhist understanding of law did not incorporate hierar-

---

19 *Digha Nikaya*, III. 59 ff. Cakkavatti-sihanada sutta; III. 72 ff., Parinibbana sutta.

20 Jules Bloch, *Les Inscriptions d'Asoka*, Paris, 1950, MRE III, pp. 96-97.

21 Op. cit. MRE IV, pp. 98-99; Minor RE, pp. 146-47.

22 *Digha Nikaya*, I. 59 ff., 88-89; *Majjhima Nikaya*, III. 172 ff.; III. 65.

chical differences and had universal application. The Buddhist concept of the *cakkavatti* does not detract from the recognition of power and sovereignty. Both of these require that the state ensure what we in modern parlance would call democratic functioning and concern for the welfare of its constituents. The highpoint of these functions were openness of thought and speech, observance of laws, insistence on frequent assembly to discuss matters of state, and the equality of all. The need for frequent assemblies was because the authority to rule was derived from those who constitute society, as is evident from the story of the *mahasammata*. What might have been a corollary to equality was the reference to wealth being acquired through labour, effort and righteous means.[23] Wealth should not be spent on useless rituals or on campaigns, but should go towards supporting livestock, agriculture, trade and administration.[24] It is repeatedly stated that the *chakkavatti* has to provide sustenance for the poor, apart from ensuring good administration and general prosperity.[25] Stealing and violence arise from poverty; therefore, in order to prevent poverty, the king must punish those who break the law.[26]

It is significant that Buddhism and Jainism were among the early religions to acknowledge the right of a woman to choose to become a renouncer and join an Order of nuns. This was not absolute freedom, but at least it permitted an alternate way of life to the conventional one. That this was much appreciated by women is evident from the sentiments expressed in the *Therigatha* compositions of Buddhist women. Religious sects influenced by Buddhism accorded the same freedom to women, who were also among their more respected practitioners.

---

23 *Anguttara Nikaya*, II, 69-70.
24 *Digha Nikaya*, II. 127 ff., Kutadanta-sutta.
25 *Digha Nikaya*, II, 139 ff.; III. 60 ff.
26 *Digha Nikaya*, III. 93 ff., Agganna-sutta.

By the mid-second millennium, Vedic Brahmanism was being superseded by Puranic Hinduism as the popular religion that competed with Buddhism and Jainism. There were attempts to appropriate the more attractive aspects of Buddhism, particularly when Buddhists themselves turned from treating deity as irrelevant to deifying a spectrum of beings. It is debatable whether the centrality of *karma* and *samsara,* with the individual being responsible for his/her liberation from rebirth, through his/her actions in this birth, was first popularised through Buddhism or through Puranic Hinduism.

The Bhakti tradition as part of Puranic Hinduism focused on particular deities, pre-eminently Vishnu and Shiva. Although some threads of Puranic Hinduism endorsed aspects of Vedic Brahmanism, the sheer diversity of the former led to differences from the latter in various significant ways: in the evolving of individual deities worshipped as icons; in forms of worship embodied in the rituals of *puja* as distinct from the *yajna;* in the emergence of temples as permanent places of worship; and in belief, especially in *samsara* and *karma* (actions and rebirth of the soul). Liberation from rebirth was the responsibility of the individual, but unlike Buddhism, Puranic Hinduism made liberation dependent on devotion to the deity. That the change from Vedic Brahmanism was substantial is indicated by the currency of new texts such as the *Puranas* and *Agamas,* written to explain the mythology, ritual and worship of emerging deities, and added to from time to time.[27]

Formal ritual was however by-passed by many teachers/ hymn singers/preachers/'holy' men and women, who emphasised a personalised worship. This coincided with a particular emphasis on social ethics although the deity dominated the ethic. Bhakti was a personalised devotion to a deity or the personi-

---

27 K. Chakravarti, *Religious Process, The Puranas and the Making of a Regional Tradition,* Delhi, 2001.

fication of the divine, and the worshipper could chose whom to worship, and how to worship. This flexibility allowed religious boundaries to be relatively fluid. The initial following was from among non-elite groups with an overlay of local forms of worship, but there was a gradual filtration upwards. Those who created the Bhakti movements in various parts of the sub-continent for over a millennium, belonged to castes ranging from the twice-born to untouchable/Dalit.[28]

Scholars have tended to sift the various strands of Bhakti according to deity, language, and emphasis on ecstatic devotion. But there is also the question of certain sects articulating a greater concern for social issues. This is apparent in their insisting on equality, not only in the eyes of the deity but also among worshippers, and setting aside or opposing caste norms in favour of a universal social ethic, as evident in the compositions of Dadu, Raidas, Kabir and Nanak, among others. The Virashaiva movement of the twelfth century is an example of a sect that opposed caste hierarchy and gender disabilities, and even questioned political sources of power. As such it was both a movement for religious reform as well as social protest. Similar to other such movements, it had a large enough following to enable it to evolve into a major caste by itself – the Lingayat. Opting out of caste inequality, even within the sect, strengthened the aspiration towards a universal ethic. They shared no common body of doctrine across sects, were frequently opposed to brahmanical doctrine, but were firm in their commitment to the ethics of social equality. That caste inequality continued should not be seen as the failure of these movements, since a major part of society conformed to their views. The filtration upwards tended to encourage new forms and objects of

---

28 D.N. Lorenzen (ed.), *Bhakti Religion in North India: Community, Identity and Political Action*, Albany, 1995; D.N. Lorenzen (ed.), *Religious Movements in South Asia*, Delhi, 2004.

worship, but the message of social protest was set aside by the dominant castes. The acquiescence of the lower castes in this mutation has yet to be examined.

The Bhakti religious articulation had regional manifestations and used the regional languages. There is a tendency to collapse all variations of Bhakti into one movement, but the manifestations differ to a greater or lesser degree even within regions, and this diversity should be recognised, apart from the two broad divisions of Nirguna and Saguna. There were mystics, but there were also those who protested against the inequities of social functioning.

After the arrival of Islam, the choice of teacher and deity widened, and ranged across Hindu and Muslim articulations of the divine. In this the Sufi teachers were a focus, merging with local society in some instances, and using the local idiom. The dialogue with some Bhakti sects, such as the Kabirpanthis, nurtured much innovative thought. Worshippers were seen as equal in the eyes of the deity and of the devotees, and to that extent there was a negation of social hierarchies. But the negation was not sufficiently universalised. The contribution of the Sufis in parenting, to some extent, the popular religions of the second millennium AD has been written about, but needs further exploration. The tension between formal Islam, as reflected in the *shari‘a*, and that as practiced and preached in the institutions of various communities encouraged by the more liberal Sufis and others, provides many insights into relations of power, formal and informal religion, and the life of communities.[29]

The Shakta religion overlapped with some of the Bhakti teachers, as also with the Sufi sects.[30] The latter gave religious

---

29 M. Alam, *The Languages of Political Islam in India*, Delhi, 2004, p. 81 ff.; R. Eaton, *The Sufis of Bijapur*, Princeton, 1978.

30 N.N. Bhattacharya, *History of Sakta Religion*, Delhi, 1996; *History of Tantric Religion*, Delhi, 1992.

sustenance to the *pirs* and *faqirs*, who held a similar status to that of the *gurus* and *sants*, and gradually the two mingled. *Gurus* and *pirs* included those who had been brought up as Hindus and Muslims, but had forsaken the formal boundaries of these religions to follow the more fluid teachings and practices of the Shaktas, the Bhakti *sants* and the Sufis, and sometimes to move beyond even these teachings. As late as the nineteenth century, the Meos of Rajasthan, for instance, were not clearly identified as either Hindus or Muslims, but followed the teachings and rituals of the *darvesh, jogi, jangam* and *samnayasi*. A century later, there were substantial attempts by the Arya Samaj and the Tablighi Jama't to convert them to a brahmanised Hinduism or to formal Islam.[31] Among the many striking expressions of worship among both Hindus and Muslims was the widespread following of Satya Pir in Bengal.[32] This pattern can be seen in many parts of the sub-continent. Recognisable characteristics are the absence of formal religious boundaries and the premise of social equality. In discussions on Indian secularism and religion, the impact of Islam is, with rare exceptions, either ignored, or else it is confined to the Islam of the royal courts and a few elite groups. Confrontations between the latter and the more popular sects are generally disregarded.

Those not in the upper levels of society expressed their religious needs through, what I would like to call, the Guru-Pir religion. This has been the religion with multiple sects – in all its varied manifestations – of the majority of Indians, for at least the last five centuries, or even earlier, with an inheritance in some of the earlier heterodox forms. It was a religion frequently propagated by renouncers. They spoke of personal devotion to any deity with a spirituality that underlined social ethics, expressed in a message not only of tolerance, but also of

---

31 S. Mayaram, 'Hindu and Islamic Transnational Religious Movements', *Economic and Political Weekly*, 3 January 2004, pp. 80-88.

32 Asim Roy, *The Islamic Syncretistic Tradition in Bengal*, Princeton, 1983.

social equality and a concern for the human condition. Equality was not limited to an underlying principle of the relationship among those who supported this kind of religion, but was extended to all men and women. The good society was central to their concerns, with a committed advocating of its principles, in however generalised a form. These were not incidental sects, but were the mainstream religion at the broadest level of functioning in most social communities, although they commanded little wealth and their teaching was often oral. Religious institutions claiming legitimacy from these ideas did exist, but their role was far more marginal than the institutions of the formal religions patronised by the elite.

The role of the renouncer in Indian society, as a figure of moral authority reaching beyond a single religious identity, also has a bearing on social ethics.[33] Some renouncers opted out of social obligations; others who were not identified with a particular religion, emerged as preceptors to communities, and preached an ethic of social responsibility. Mysticism apart, many more renouncers were concerned with the mainsprings of society, and how these could be directed towards the welfare of its constituents at all levels. It is as well to remember that this moral authority lay in not only challenging deity – as in the multiple myths of gods fearing the power accumulated by *rishis* through asceticism – but also in legitimating political and social protest. Gandhi's adoption of the symbols of asceticism was not an individual quirk or a Hindu identification, but was the continuation of a long tradition of linking moral authority, as distinct from religious authority, to protest.

The colonial state recognised only the formal religions of, what it called, Hinduism and Islam, and put everyone in either

---

33 R. Thapar, 'Renunciation: the Making of a Counter-Culture?' *Cultural Pasts*, pp. 876-913; 'The Householder and Renouncer in Brahmana and Buddhist Texts', Ibid., pp. 914-45.

one or the other slot. It is ironic that colonial ethnography is now among the sources of information on the Guru-Pir religious articulation during recent periods, as are the Gazetteers and Censuses; yet the distinctive religious identity of such groups was not recognised when these data were being compiled. This was despite the powerful oral tradition through which this articulation was, and is, preached and practiced. The followers of these teachings were the lesser of the lesser breeds without the law, and therefore almost socially invisible, except to evoke a certain curiosity. The rhetoric of the colonial interpretation of Indian society, as constituted of two monolithic communities, was all pervading. The socio-religious reform movements of the nineteenth century, where they were responding to these colonial interpretations, were circumscribed middle-class movements and tended to marginalise the religion/s of the majority of Indians. Nor did nationalism give recognition to these, despite Gandhiji's appeal to mass audiences, (as distinct from political parties), being couched in terms that echoed the Guru-Pir tradition. The religious nationalisms that are dominant today, have no place for religious articulations that cannot be firmly located in one of the two major religions, viewed as monolithic. The battle over places of worship, and the insistence on converting them from one religion to the other, is a case in point. This battle occurs in places where earlier adherents of all kinds of religious sects would have worshiped together.

Religious sects of the Guru-Pir tradition have often been described as the middle ground between Hinduism and Islam. My argument, however, is that this is not the middle ground, but the continuation of a religious tradition which modern scholars have relegated to a substratum status.[34] In going through the sources of pre-modern times, such religious

---

34 R. Thapar, 'The Tyranny of Labels', in *Cultural Pasts*, Delhi, 2002, pp. 990-1014.

articulations tended to be set aside in favour of the more accessible religious expression of elite groups with their easily available texts. Interestingly, the popular religious sects tended more easily to discard the norms of the *dharmashastras* and the *shari'a* and emphasised ameliorating the human condition with an ethic that went above and beyond established religion, and the applicability of which preferably was to be universal. Discussion of the interface between religion and secularism, or of the consciousness of ideas related to secularising Indian society, has to address itself to these articulations as well. This is all the more so since these religious articulations have been consistently and continually concerned about not just the centrality of social ethics, but also about actualising such an ethic. Such an actualising in the present day involves the relationship between caste, religions, the state and civil society. It is significant that at the level of *jati* there is also an acceptance of the idea of equality within the *jati*.

The close integration between religious and caste identity also raises the question of law and the state. *Dharma*, in the sense of law, was specified for each *varna* in the *dharmashastras*, and although these were not codes of law, they encapsulated ideal norms of social functioning. But what was not captured in the *dharmashastras* was that each *jati/varna* observed customary laws/*achara*, which did, on occasion, contradict the rules of the *dharmashastras*.[35] This was not peculiar to Hinduism, as there were the same discrepancies between the *shari'a* and the customary law observed by castes that had converted to Islam, as is evident from the differences in the customary law of, for example, the Meos of Rajasthan and the Mappilas of Kerala, both formally Muslim communities. Such customary

---

35 Such deviations from the norms are sometimes even mentioned in the texts, as for example, the practice of cross-cousin marriage. There is a debate on the acceptability of custom versus code. *Baudhayana Dharmasutra*, 1.2.3; *Gautama Dharmasutra*, 11.20.

law was often a continuation of the earlier *jati* practices, or resulted from intermarriage between immigrants and local communities. Distance from the norms, if not a refutation of these, may well have been more common than is supposed. Flexibility in law is also reflected in statements that where there was conflict, the king had the right to interpret the law, indicating perhaps a priority for custom over the code.[36]

Much has been written about the religious tolerance of Hinduism. The link between caste and religion could be one explanation for the relatively greater accommodation of alternate religions in South Asian history as compared to Europe. A religious sect, when it attained a critical mass, could be converted into a caste and accommodated with a variety of other dissenting groups. The sting of protest was removed by allowing them their own custom and ritual within the boundaries of their identity. The hierarchical placement of social statuses has some religious identities, but since the status has its own social boundaries, the religious identities could be more flexible. However, even where religious differences were relatively fluid, social hierarchies were less so. Protestors were not easily accommodated, and if possible were relegated to lower caste status. Where religious sanctions prevailed in the form, for instance, of the purity-pollution nexus, the status of the untouchable, being inherited, was immutable; and was at the receiving end of a fierce intolerance, in many ways worse than religious intolerance. The freedom to choose and practice a religion is not alien to south Asian tradition, but caste identity could curtail this freedom; therefore, religious sects seeking a wider following tended to oppose caste hierarchies.

Religions with established institutions such as monasteries, temples, *mathas, khanqahs,* mosques and churches sought the patronage of the local king and there was a competition for this

---

36 *Narada-smriti,* 1.10-14.

patronage. The larger amount of this patronage came from royalty, but Buddhist and Jaina institutions in particular also received extensive patronage from the communities of financiers, traders and artisan guilds, and from small-scale landowners.[37] Whereas communities were more selective in their patronage, in part perhaps because of more limited funds, royalty in India in all periods gave grants and donations to a range of religious sects. Such patronage was not neutral and the range of sects as recipients is striking. The basis for the selection was doubtless conditioned by the politics of these religious sects apart from the personal devotion or assessment of the patron. This is a contrast with European patrons confining patronage to a single sect. A medieval European king making a grant for the building of a mosque in Europe would be relatively unknown, yet this was done by non-Muslim rulers in western India. There were occasions when, for example, a Shaiva Solanki king annulled the grants to Jaina institutions made by his predecessor,[38] but generally Indian royalty seemed to have been aware of the political usefulness of patronising a number of different religious sects. This may again have had links with caste and regional interests. The Sultans and the Mughal rulers displayed the same catholicity and in most cases of patronage to non-Islamic sects the intentions would have been varied.

Incidents of religious intolerance often involved competition for patronage. The tensions were not only between the Buddhists and the Shaivas but also between the Shaivas and the Jainas, and to a lesser extent between the Vaishnavas and the Shaivas.[39] At one level, this has been taken as an expression of the co-existence of all religions or even of the neutrality of the

---

37 R. Thapar, 'Patronage and the Community' in B. Stoler Miller (ed.), *The Powers of Art*, Delhi, 1992, pp. 1–34.

38 Merutunga, *Prabandhacintamani*, 4.9.175.

39 R. Thapar, *Cultural Transaction and Early India*, in *History and Beyond*, Delhi, 2000, pp. 7-24.

state towards religion, but this would not invariably be a tenable argument. The reason for this patronage was not through any awareness of secularism, but because of the need to juxtapose patronage so as to satisfy religious groups in a context where the state was expected to be a patron of religion. Religious networks could also be viewed as potential catchment areas of support and loyalty. Quite apart from the personal religious predilections of a ruler, there was clearly an understanding of the function of religious institutions in a political and social context and the balancing of a number of such institutions. In some cases there may have been a policy of playing off one against the other, or in other cases the state indicating its power over the religious institutions. The pattern of patronage, because it was extended to groups that were thought to be politically and socially important or were intended to be made so, extended largely to the elite, whereas those representing larger but disorganised numbers, were generally ignored by the elite. These groups found their patronage among the lesser members of society whose support they claimed.

An interesting case of state patronage towards building a temple was raised immediately after Independence when in 1951 a Minister of the Central Government, KM Munshi, asserted that the Government of India was financing the rebuilding of the famous temple at Somanatha, raided by Mahmud of Ghazni in 1026, which by now had become an icon of Hindu-Muslim antagonism in the politics of religious nationalism.[40] Nehru categorically denied the assertion and stated that as a secular government, the Government of India would not finance the building of the temple. A private Trust was therefore established for the purpose. This was a departure from the earlier tradition and to that extent underlines a difference be-

---

40   R. Thapar, *Somanatha: the Many Voices of a History,* Delhi, 2004, pp. 197-201.

tween the policies of pre-modern states and those of a modern, secular state.

Secularism has to involve itself with contending the politics of religious institutions and religious organisations playing a political role. The dialogue is not about belief and faith, but about institutions and politics, and about the control of religious institutions and those that administer them, over aspects of civil society. Secularism adopts a code of social ethics that challenges the acceptance of inequalities, where these are proposed by religious ideologies. Rights have to be sought after and established through codes and practice, and they have to be backed by a philosophy that endorses these rights, and which does not require recourse to divine intervention or formal religious institutions. There is an element of what might be called proto-secularism available from earlier traditions, should contemporary Indians wish to draw on it. But this is at best an ambience and not an actuality for contemporary secularism, since the values associated with human rights and democratic functioning are of the contemporary world and not of the past. However, drawing from the past has the potential of assisting in the secularising of society without creating a complete disjuncture with what is regarded as tradition.

In referring to proto-secularism I am not suggesting that there was an attempt at establishing a secular society in India in c. 400 BC or even later. That this was not secularism is evident from the fact that whereas the appeal was to the individual to adopt a code of behaviour that was derived from values that we would today regard as conducive to secularising society, there was no requirement that the state should endorse this code or even establish and maintain institutions that would do so. In a secular society the onus is on the state and civil society to establish codes and institutions that would support secular values. The state recognises the existence of religion, but restricts the unquestioned activities of the latter to matters of personal belief. Politics should not function on the basis of religious communities, for the primary identity is the identity of citizens of a nation, and not members of a religious community. This space will be contested and has to be won by those in support of secularising society. But the contest does not concern religion alone, and has to extend to all those institutions and structures that are involved with the rights of the citizen.

Secularism as an ideology cannot be imposed, but when the structures that support the status quo are changed, then a secular society may begin to emerge. To that extent the ideology of secularism supports a particular kind of social change. This may be aided if there is a realisation that there are antecedents in the cultures of present-day communities that are sympathetic to secular values.

Religious nationalisms have a tendency to adopt forms of cultural nationalism. Discussions on cultural nationalism today need to define the cultures they incorporate. Existing definitions have veered towards the upper caste cultures and religions. The cultures and religious identities of others are set aside. Yet there are other traditions that might even have a larger popular appeal, such as those that I have referred to. It is important to the definition and the future of the secularising of South Asian societies that we explore the wider range of cultural traditions when we search for ancestral elements. Resort to a single religious identity is, in any case, self-defeating in a multi-religious society. Secularism is not just the confrontation between religion and the state. It requires new initiatives by the state and by the citizens in relation to the essentials of a secularised society. If citizenship is to be the primary identity it will have to place other identities of caste, class, religion, gender and language, in their appropriate places and will have to define the identities that go into the making of citizenship.

Historical Interpretations and the Secularising of Indian Society[1]

I have chosen as my theme a subject which is these days of much concern, namely, the secularising of Indian society. I shall be placing the discussion in a perspective which draws on history. This is not because I think that the Indian past was secular, but because the Indian past, if read with sensitivity, can be seen to be conducive to creating a secular society.

In the discussion on secularism in India, there is generally a reliance on the state taking a secular position as and when necessary. This leads to a certain dependence on state initiative and action. It seems to me that the secularising of Indian society is equally important. I see this as complementary to a secular state. The secularism of the state should preferably interface with the secularising of society.

I would like to discuss three aspects involved in the process of secularising Indian society. The first is the strengthening of civil society by insisting on defending the rights of citizens;

---

1   First published in *Counter Culture Perspectives: Selected Kappen Memorial Lectures*, Visthar, Bangalore, 2013.

the second concerns the state which has to activise these rights; and the third touches on the role of religion and religious institutions in civil society and the state. All three draw on the historical past, but some aspects of these are more embedded in the past.

Secularism in a modern society assumes the existence of religious pluralities, of their equal status and of the eventual emergence of a society in which the rights of the individual as citizens take precedence over religious identities. It sees a secular society as one in which social ethics is based on a current and continuing regard for the well being of fellow humans.

Secularisation is a cognate of a process of historical change and this process is closely tied to the modernisation of a society. The point that I would like to underline is that it is historically specific and relates to a particular historical situation. This historical situation is linked to the process of modernisation. To judge pre-modern societies as being secular or non-secular is somewhat anachronistic.

The modernisation of a society assumes the existence of a nation-state, of democracy, of industrialisation and investment, whether private or public, and of the emergence of a middle-class, professionally involved in this change. I am not endorsing this change as necessarily an ideal situation. I am assuming its historical existence in contemporary times, given our historical experience of colonialism and nationalism, and in the present day, the overpowering presence of globalisation. There are those who disapprove of the nation-state and of industrialisation, but have so far been unable to suggest workable alternatives. That we have arrived at these forms makes it necessary for us to build into them a just and ethical society. Such a society can only be built on a secular orientation. Modernisation is a package and secularism is a part of it. If we do not object to the emergence of a middle-class or to democracy, or to industrialisation, arguing that they are part of the modernising process, then we have little ground to object to the secularisation of society.

Secularism, therefore, does not assume a binary opposition between the state and religion. It is more a graduated but conscious movement towards changing society. This is of central significance to both, the concept and the working, of civil society. Secularising society would strengthen civil society and allow it to effectively monitor the state, ensuring that the state maintains the required impartiality towards religious groups. Basically these processes are intermeshed with democracy: if there is a snuffing out of secularism, there would be, to the same extent, a snuffing out of democracy.

The creation of a civil society is a relatively new experience for India, and the secularising of such a society is equally an innovation. It comes in a post-colonial period, which in some ways should make it easier for us to recognise its usefulness. But, equally, these are not alien ideas for modern Indians. The debate on these matters goes back to the writings of Ram Mohun Roy and others, and we have had, therefore, two centuries of discussion on them. It would be salutary for us if we could revive some of these earlier debates, which were often far more liberal than what we hear today.

Critics of secularism in India have raised various objections. One view states that because secularism is tied to modernity – and modernity is projected in this view as a kind of sickness – we should not want it, despite our having been part of a modernising process since the nineteenth century. However, these same critics do not object to the other changes brought by modernisation, such as the upholding of democracy in its contemporary forms, or economic liberalisation accompanied by industrialisation and invested in by multinationals. As weighty members of the middle-class, they accept the facilities of modernisation for themselves, but hesitate to extend them to those at or below the poverty line. But can modernisation be stemmed in a world of globalisation, which is what we have now opted to join? The changes are inter-linked and come in tandem.

Another objection relates to the historical past. Secularism is said to be essentially a response to Christianity in Europe and is, therefore, said to be alien to India. This, as I have tried to point out earlier, is an erroneous view of the history of the concept of secularism, which at one stage was concerned with confronting the Church, but which has since developed other dimensions linked with modernisation.

A further objection states that India has never been secular and never will be, because its essential identities were, and are, those of religious communities – each of which is uniform and monolithic. It is argued that community representation is now called for in the process of modernisation. Apart from being historically inaccurate, since secularism is not associated with pre-modern societies, this view strengthens the notion of majority and minority communities as the constituents of Indian society. It denies the historical fact that the identities of communities are not permanent. They evolve and transform with historical change. Therefore, monolithic religious communities have not been the constituents of Indian society over the centuries. This kind of communitarianism breeds its own problems, and more so for a society such as ours.

Tied to this is also the theory that the nation-state is not only irrelevant, but is the source of many ills. Therefore the state should give way to the community, defined by religion. History is ignored, there is a denial of nation, and no concern with the need for economic development, in whatever form. That there are some problems, particularly of economic development, which can only be handled through the intervention of the state, would also be unacceptable to this argument.

At the popular level, current views of secularism are broadly of two kinds. One is the view that secularism is opposed to religion, and the second, and more prevalent, is that of co-existence of different religions – encapsulated in the phrase, *sarva dharma samabhava*, arising essentially from the perspective of India as consisting of monolithic religious communities. This, of course, has not been the case since caste, region, language and sect were often more important than a presumed uniform, religious identity and religious identity lay in the identity of the sects.

Let me turn now to the relationship of secularism to the past. This is of considerable importance, not because the past was secular – it obviously was not if secularism is a part of the modernising process – but because in some societies, the historical links between the state, social organisation and religion were such that they are conducive in the present day to secularising these societies. In other words, it is easier for some societies to be secularised in view of what they nurtured in the past. I would like to argue that this is so for Indian society.

In speaking of secularism and history I shall be discussing three broad aspects. One is the multi-religious culture of the Indian past and what this implied for the viability of the concept of a religious community as we define it today, given that sometimes there was a convergence and sometimes a conflict among groups. Another is the perception that the Hindus and Muslims had of each other in the past. Associated with this is whether this perception changed with conversion to Islam. And finally, state patronage to religious groups needs to be considered since it is pivotal to the concept of secularism.

I would like to suggest that we need to investigate more fully the links between caste, clan, community, region, language and religious articulation. We have treated concepts such as community and religion in too limited and static a fashion. The word community is immediately linked to religion, and religion in turn is seen as an ecclesiastical structure dominating all activities. But communities in the past were identified by a range of factors that frequently and partially even overlapped. The present-day impregnable boundaries of communities would have been alien to the past. Similarly, religion was much more inter-twined with the social dimension than we allow for today. Since the present-day choice seems to be moving towards either the secularisation or the communalisation of society, we need to examine the links between religion and society, particularly from the period of the eighth century A.D. onwards, which saw established Christianity and the arrival of Islam in India. An awareness of the socio-religious landscape of even earlier times would also be helpful.

Religious articulation in the Indian past was much more nuanced than in Europe. This was in part because the pattern of religion was different. The history of religion in Europe and in west Asia is a linear history, starting with a historical founder and consequential sectarian movements, supporting orthodoxy or heterodoxy in relation to the initial religious teaching of the founder. In India, the initial religious articulation was a mosaic built on a multi-religious culture and it has continued to be that, although now the project of Hindutva is seeking to destroy the mosaic. Even in pre-Islamic times there were many indigenous religions and the concept of a single, linear religion was not prevalent. There was a network of castes and sects, some sharing boundaries and ideologies and some, discrete and diverse, creating a range of belief systems and practices. There was a consciousness of identification with varying religious forms among the differing social strata. This persisted into later periods. The relationship between religion and society that resulted from this was a different kind of experience from that of Europe. But in the eighteenth century, when Orientalists began to interpret the religions of India, the model was that of Europe, and we seem not to have questioned the resulting reconstruction, analytically.

The distinction between religious sects was generally categorised as what have been called Brahmanism and Shramanism, and these remained constant through a major part of Indian history. The religion espoused by the brahmanas was derived from the Vedic corpus; whereas that preached and practiced by the shramanas focused on Buddhism, Jainism and other similar sects. The practice of Vedic Brahmanism was largely confined to the upper castes as many rituals were forbidden to the *shudras.* The 'heterodox' sects – as the Buddhists, Jainas and others were labelled – were open to members of any caste.

The division into brahmana and shramana is reported by Megasthenes visiting India in the Mauryan period. The grammarian Patanjali, writes of the innate opposition between the two which is, perhaps, why the Mauryan king Ashoka, repeatedly calls for the need to respect both brahmanas and shramanas. There are Jaina texts, as for example the *Paumachariyam* of Vimalasuri, which speak of the brahmanas as heretics and liars. Some brahmana authors, such as Krishna Mishra, to whom the play *Prabodha-chandrodaya* is attributed, caricature Jaina monks as profligates and drunks. Al-Biruni, writing in the eleventh century, refers to many religious sects, and the Shamaniyya are mentioned separately.

This duality is easily visible at the elite levels and is evident from the literature. At the more intermediate levels there prevailed what we call today Puranic Hinduism, a category which covers even contradictory sects of various kinds, some supporting Vedic Brahmanism and others opposed to it. This was a truly creative expression in terms of the interface between religious articulation and social identity. The openness it supported was one of the reasons why sects with variant religious doctrines or differing social norms were all accommodated. It grew out of the need, often social and political, to assimilate and to incorporate, even if this meant new deities, rituals and beliefs. Or else existing deities were re-oriented as it were, with additional mythologies and rituals.

To build a uniform, monolithic religious community out of this kind of religious articulation is virtually impossible. Each segment was dominated by a relationship to either one caste or a cluster of castes. Where a sect cut across a range of castes, it usually ended up as an independent and separate caste. The social status of the various sects was dependent on who their patrons were, and it was not unusual for a relatively humble cult to be transmuted over a few generations into one of importance, especially if supported by royalty. The many aniconic deities that emerge as the focus of royal worship are part of this process, a case in point being the worship of Maniya-deo by the Chandella rulers of Bundelkhand. The social mobility of Tantrism and the Shakta cult makes a fascinating study in the interface between belief, ritual and a changing social identity. It moves from relatively confined fertility worship to a presence in some of the richest temples, as at Khajuraho. Obscure families acquiring the status of royal dynasties took their cults with them and amalgamated them with the worship of the more status-bestowing deities of Brahmanism. These social processes of family and caste mobility frequently gave direction to much that we recognise as 'Hindu sects'.

Further down the social scale, and initially more distant from these sects, were the belief systems and rituals of what we have called the tribal people, and those outside caste. These were the *atavikas* or forest-dwellers – the Nishada, Shabara, Bhilla, Pulinda – and the many hundreds of others, and at another extreme, of caste, were the Chandala, Dom and such-like. Theirs were frequently animistic religions with their own deities and rituals. Some contradicted Brahmanical ritual. Thus, despite the earlier Vedic sacrificial ritual involving slaughter of animals, in later times, animal sacrifice and the libations of alcohol, common to the animistic cults, were anathema to many brahmana sects. For upper caste Hindus these groups have been *mlechchha* or impure, and not part of their own religious identity for many centuries.

This variance may partially explain why the concept of *dharma* became central to an understanding of religion. It referred to the social obligations and ritual duties that had to be performed in accordance with one's *varna* and *jati* and the sect to which one belonged. The duties differed in accordance with caste status. Conforming to *dharma* demarcated the upper castes from the lower since it was expected to be more strictly observed among the former. The lower castes were presumed to be more lax. This raises problems for present-day attempts to project a universal and uniform Hinduism in the past and in maintaining that upper caste belief and practice define Hinduism, since the majority of Hindus were not of the upper castes.

We have to recognise that there was a distinction between the religion of the elites and of those low on the social scale. The hierarchy among sects often follows caste hierarchy. And most important of all, the religion of the actual majority of the population is rarely recorded in early historical sources. It usually has to be inferred from indirect evidence, for what has survived is largely the literature and visual evidence of the elite. We tend to extend this evidence to all social levels, which is historically an inaccurate procedure. But a faithful reconstruction of the religion of the majority would lead to some surprises. The beliefs and rituals of those at the lower end of the social scale are frequently part of what I have described elsewhere as perhaps constituting a kind of counter-culture. Religious boundaries are blurred, religious practices overlap, and mythologies are intertwined. This is not because the indigenous religions of India were necessarily tolerant, as we would like to believe, but because the religious articulation of the majority emerged from negotiating differences. Such negotiations can be potentially seminal to a secularising process.

I have stated earlier that the secularisation of Indian society would be easier than that of many other societies. Let me expand on this. Frequently, in the past, and even sometimes today, religious sectarian identity is subordinated to the identity of caste. The identity of caste takes into consideration marriage rules and personal law, inheritance laws, occupation, location and forms of worship. Therefore, that which goes into the making of what we today would call matters pertaining to civil society, remains central. Religious rituals among Hindus were according to caste, and caste determined who could enter which temple and where a person could offer worship.

The other side of this was that religious belief was often a personal matter. As long as caste regulations were observed, personal belief was of individual concern. Rituals presupposed certain belief patterns; nevertheless religious dogma was seldom over-arching across an immense social span. This encouraged a certain openness in these religions, different from the model familiar to us from the Semitic religions. This openness is now declining through the imposition of a uniform, monolithic view of religion, and by the communalisation of society. Many religious sects – as for example, those included in the Shramanic and Bhakti tradition, and others of a more esoteric kind – focused on the liberation of the individual soul, and worshippers could observe a variety of forms of worship. The projected relationship between worshipper and deity was not constricted by the requirements of ritual and belief. The argument that religious belief is a personal matter would not be altogether alien to the Indian tradition.

In this connection let me add that, for almost a thousand years, Buddhism was a major Indian religion and has left its imprint in various ways, even if the imprint is not immediately recognisable. The Buddha did not insist on a belief in deity, arguing that this was something that could not be proven. The Buddha also maintained that social ethics were man made. This element of rationality was not unusual in Indian thought. But we have tended to ignore it or even deny it. Alternate belief systems endorsed renouncers who could sometimes be dissenters, since they were bound neither by caste nor by ritual. Whether as *sannyasi* or *bhikshu* or *sufi* or whether as *pir, faqir, guru* or *sant,* they were widely respected, allowed their space and on occasion even supported as players in local politics.

Given the analogy of the mosaic, the question arises as to how conflicts and convergences were handled among sects. The convergences are evident in Puranic Hinduism, in the Bhakti sects and in many religious movements of an even more popular kind. Convergences led to break-away castes or the creation of new *jatis.* But there were also conflicts, as is to be expected from a complex society. Kalhana, in the *Rajatarangini,* mentions attacks on the Buddhists in Kashmir. Shashanka in eastern India is accused of the same according to Banabhatta, the author of the *Harshacharita.* The rivalry between the Jainas and the Shaivas resulted in each accusing the other of intent to harm. Scuffles of a violent kind over precedence at the Kumbha Mela between the Dashanamis and the Bairagis are depicted in miniature paintings.

These conflicts often had elements of the play of power, involving competition for royal patronage and tensions of an economic and professional kind. But the conflict was limited to specific areas and groups, and was not pan-Indian. There was no sense of a holy war – and *jehad* or a crusade. Religious intolerance was less severe when compared to Europe or west Asia, but acute intolerance took a social form, with untouchability constituting the worst form of degradation known to human society. Such groups were excluded from the religion and rituals of caste Hindus. We need, therefore, to investigate the reasons for either hostilities or assimilations, and to locate the social tensions involved. It does not help to either pretend that confrontations did not exist, or else to try and explain all hostilities as coming about only with the arrival of Islam in India. Both Christianity and Islam continued the caste hierarchies and discriminations of the existing social system and the articulation of these religions through a variety of sects became a familiar form.

A major issue in the observations on secularism in India is that of the relations in the past between, what are referred to in recent times, as the Hindu and Muslim communities. I would like to suggest that this is the wrong premise on which to start looking at the history of this relationship. There was a consciousness of different beliefs, of identities with different sects of Islam or Hinduism, but there was no consciousness of a uniform, monolithic Hindu community or a similar Muslim community until the last few centuries. Prior to that, alliances or confrontations were between smaller, localised groups, among whom the process of negotiation continued, albeit in some cases with new religious tones.

How then did these groups perceive each other? The use of "Hindu" as an identity by those whom we today call Hindus, does not gain currency until about the fifteenth century. Prior to that religious identity was based on sect and caste and an all-inclusive term was not thought necessary. 'Hindu' as is well known, was an invention of those who viewed the subcontinent from beyond the Indus and the name derives from the river – Sindhu. This goes back to ancient Iranian times. In the eighth century A.D. the Arabs referred to the area as al-Hind. It was initially a geographical term and Hindu was an ethnic identity. It was later used by extension to mean all those inhabitants of the sub-continent who practiced religions other than Islam and Christianity.

Equally interesting is the fact that the Hindus did not initially refer to those who arrived in India as followers of Islam, as Muslims. There were diverse forms of identity which have their own historical interest. The Arabs conquered Sind, but came more frequently as traders from west Asia. They were employed in high administrative positions in the territory of the Rashtrakuta rulers, and are frequently referred to as Tajikas. The Turks who came from central Asia and Afghanistan are described by the ethnic term, Turushka. Some were also referred to as Shakas and Yavanas, the former being the old name for the Scythians of central Asia, and the latter for the Greeks. The use of the term *mlechchha,* is a marker of social distance, used for those viewed as being outside caste society. Since a variety of people from tribals to local kings are variously called *mlechchha,* it cannot be assumed that it always carried a sense of contempt.

There is in the use of these terms a historical continuity since they mark the people as coming from west Asia and central Asia, with which areas there had earlier been centuries of coming and going. The labels used are similar to those of pre-Islamic times. There is also a suggestion of a certain familiarity, for, if people are given a name used earlier in history it does indicate that they are not perceived as entirely alien. What is also interesting is that even the Turks and the Arabs do not seem to see themselves as part of a single Islamic expedition. In the Turko-Persian chronicles, conquests in India and the establishing of Islamic rule through the Delhi Sultanate is taken back to Mahmud of Ghazni. The Arabs are generally ignored, even though their contacts and conquests preceded those of Mahmud.

Among Muslims in India, the majority were Indian converts to Islam. The process of conversion in the past requires an intensive study, as there are a number of popular misconceptions about conversion to Islam. The Turko-Persian chronicles seem to mention normative figures. They sometimes refer to fifty thousand infidels being either killed or converted, and an equal number of Muslim heretics being killed by zealous Sunni Muslim conquerors, such as Mahmud of Ghazni. The figure is evidently fantasy, to be used readily in any situation, and is unlikely to tell us much. What is interesting about the conversions to Islam is that they were of two main kinds: one was the individual who may have converted out of conviction or, if he was socially well-placed such as some Rajputs, he may have converted for reasons of political expediency; the other were conversions by caste, where an entire *jati* would convert, and these were by far the larger in number and more common.

Conversion by caste means that the stories of having to choose between conversion or death are, to say the least, exaggerated. In some cases there may well have been threats, but this was clearly not the norm. The question of why, in the same village or town, some *jatis* convert and others do not, is the more significant. Further, conversion by *jati* meant that many of the practices, especially those relating to marriage and kinship relations, inheritance and customary law of the *jati,* were not discontinued. This is clear from social practices maintaining the regulations of the *zat,* the equivalent of a *jati.* The Meos of Rajasthan, for example, even as Muslims, continue to observe particular social norms, prevalent among non-Muslims of their social status, but not observed by Muslim Rajputs of the same region. The upper caste convert would be more inclined to observe the *shariʿa*. In any case, his caste practices would be different from those of the lower status Meos. Such a situation finds endless repetition in other parts of the sub-continent.

Caste identities frequently determined both custom and religious practices. There are a number of communities along the west coast which trace themselves back to settlements of Arab traders, who over the centuries appear to have picked up wives and observances locally. The Khojas, Bohras, Navayats, Mappilas – to mention just a few – observed an Islam which may not have been recognisable to the Momin weavers in Uttar Pradesh. The Gazetteer of Bijapur, dating to 1881, describes the largest Muslim population as being those of the lower castes. They not only retained their original caste names, but also stated that they worshipped Hindu deities and celebrated Hindu festivals. Some prohibited the eating of beef and only rarely went to pray in the mosque. Have we prematurely rushed to identify these groups as either Hindu or Muslim, for they are better described as either Hinduised Muslims or Islamicised Hindus? They, and others like them, some now listed as either Muslim or Hindu, are in effect the actual majority whose religion was part of what can be termed counter-culture. They neither conformed to the orthodoxies of elite religions, nor constituted a uniform, monolithic community.[2]

What seems to become evident is that Indian social organisation takes precedence even over religious practices, which are claimed to be uniformly observed. But the actual practices conform more to caste rules than to the rules of the religion,

---

2   A parallel and useful study could be made with Indonesian and Malaysian history of the pre-modern period, which until recently also had multiple religions – some of Indic origin and some Islamic – in juxtaposition and in co-relation. Unfortunately, we always tend to compare Indian Islam with west Asian and Persian Islam. Yet the preconditions and the evolution of Islam in the south-east Asian region would probably provide closer and more significant parallels.

even among non-Hindus. This is, of course, changing in recent times. The fear of being a vulnerable minority is encouraging a move towards homogenising religious practices and politicising religious identities. That the fears are justified is being amply demonstrated in the wanton attacks, particularly in the recent past, on the persons and properties of those identified as non-Hindus.

The coming of Islam, therefore, did not create two monolithic communities – the Hindu and the Muslim – hostile to each other, as is the belief of those who support a communal interpretation of the Indian past. Readings of the history of the last thousand years are based largely on court chronicles, the authors of which had many axes to grind, not least the exaggeration of accounts of Islamic conquests and conversions. These are now ceasing to be taken at face value and are beginning to be examined more analytically – a process which historians have to adopt for every kind of evidence, whatever its religious or other identity. There are other data as well, such as varieties of texts of regional and local history, of compositions associated with popular religious sects, of the oral tradition of folk literature and even pictorial representations of worldviews. These are beginning to sensitise us to a different perspective of the societies of earlier times.

The picture that emerges is one of a constant process of cultural translation and social negotiation. This was a process which can be recognised for much earlier times and which continued, but the units of the transaction underwent change. Hostility or friendliness differed from situation to situation. Those that sought to be converted aspired to a different society or to different advantages, and these in turn required negotiating. The choice of the degree to which the new observances were to be followed varied from group to group, depending on its interests, and is reflected in the studies of regional communities and lower caste groups. It is these populations, marginalised in our studies of the past, which were and are the real majority if numbers are to be counted, not the brahmanised Hindu or the Muslim as defined by the theologian.

Turning to the third broad aspect, that of state patronage, this has been treated the world over largely as a matter of political expediency, although frequently efforts are made to disguise it as goodwill. The ruling dynasties of India have maintained a transparency about the need to privilege a variety of religious sects. The edicts of the Mauryan emperor Ashoka insist on both brahmanas and shramanas being shown respect, despite the king's own preference for Buddhism. The Ikshvaku dynasty seems to have decided on a gender division: the men patronised the Vedic sacrificial rituals and the women made donations to the Buddhist *sangha*. There is an ongoing controversy as to whether the seventh century king, Harsha of Kannauj, was a patron of the Buddhists or the Shaivas, so meticulously did he give to each. The Solankis encouraged the building of Jaina temples in Gujarat and also built a mosque for the Arabs with whom they traded. The Mughals, and this included Aurangzeb, made grants to Sufis and to brahmanas, and contributed towards the building of temples and mosques, and towards the maintenance of the *mathas* of the *jogis*. Akbar even invented a new religion, combining elements from the prevailing religions, which predictably did not survive.

When families of obscure origin rose to be rulers, as was often the case from the eighth century A.D. onwards, they elevated their traditional cults and merged them into the practice of the more established religions. The reverse process was also known. Royal families became the patrons of the cults of groups which were seemingly marginalised but whose loyalty was important to political stability. This provided a support of popular religious sects channelled through royal patronage.

Thus the Yadavas of Deogiri became patrons of the cult of Vit-thoba, which was in origin a cult of the pastoralists of the region. It has been argued that the cult of Jagannatha in Orissa has similar folk and tribal origins.

If many of these activities were assimilative, some were also exclusionist. The destruction of temples was among these. Temples were symbols of religious sectarian devotion, but they were also cultural idioms, they were financial treasuries, and they were political statements when they were built by royalty. Attacks on temples begin before the coming of Islam. Some are due to religious rivalries as between the Shaivas and the Jainas, some were raided by kings facing a fiscal crisis as in Kashmir, some were subjected to desecration as a sign of victory in a campaign as by the victorious Rashtrakutas against the Paramaras.

The temple was not just a place of worship. Like the church and the mosque it was also an institution. The destruction of temples therefore cannot be explained away simplistically as invariably an expression of religious bigotry. The other facets of this activity have also to be understood. This understanding has often to do with matters such as political and economic expediency, the demonstration of power and a punishment for disloyalty. Those Turkish conquerors who destroyed temples were doing so to cash in on iconoclasm, on the looting of wealth and on projecting this destruction as a symbol of triumph.

Characteristic of royal patronage in India was that it could change from ruler to ruler within the same dynasty. The choice of the recipient depended on the personal inclinations of the ruler as also on state policies. The tradition therefore was of multiple, although not impartial, patronage to various religious sects, irrespective of the religion of the ruler. But this policy of patronage to multiple religious sects is not secularism. It merely permits some religious sects to be comfortable. However, such a history of multiple patronage does make the secularising of society today more acceptable. By this I do not mean that the state should continue to follow a policy of multiple patronage. Such patronage to religious sects is a marker of a pre-modern society and is therefore not required now in a changed historical situation. But its historical legacy underlines the political acceptance of a multi-religious society and facilitates the transition from a multi-religious society to a secular society.

Let me conclude by returning to the issue with which I started, the secularising of Indian society. There has been some hostility to secularism, in part because it is projected as a denial of religion. I have tried to show that this is not the meaning of secularism. The more fierce hostility has arisen not from the fear of weakening religion but from the fear that if the politics of religious communities are replaced by the attempt to empower civil society, it will encourage a system that gives primacy to the rights and equality of all citizens, essential to the secularising of society. As long as some citizens are regarded as more Indian than others, and this differentiation draws from the notion of exclusive religious communities, concern with matters of social and economic change will be set aside and attention diverted to a pretense of safe-guarding religion and the nation.

The intensification of Hindutva has acted, as intended by its followers, to divert attention from the fact that almost half the population of India is at or below the poverty line and is denied even the most basic rights and amenities. Instead of working towards providing these rights and amenities to the tribals and the dalits, the focus has been shifted to the irrelevant question of the right to convert. The hype surrounding the issue as to which Indians are indigenous and which foreign, basing this identity on the false premise of whether they follow a religion which is indigenous to the sub-continent or is west Asian in origin, has led to the most inhuman and unethical behaviour on the part of groups claiming to defend Hinduism, and is directed towards those labeled as Muslims and Christians.

The insistence on identifying Indians by religious communities now determines which is the majority community and which the minorities. This kind of majoritarianism makes a mockery of democracy because it is a predetermined majority. Indian society, as defined by religious communities, is the product of a colonial perspective on Indian society. By insisting on this identity we are reinforcing the politics of colonialism rather than moving in an independent, democratic direction.

The secularising of Indian society is necessary to both improving the condition of those below the poverty line and those who are victims of majoritarian communalism. This requires the empowering of civil society which would have to be based on the centrality of social ethics – the creating and nurturing of values focusing on a concern and respect for fellow citizens. This is a necessary precondition for secularising society, and would in turn strengthen the secular policies of the state. Social ethics would involve legal order, political freedom, individual autonomy and material well being. And these, in effect, mean not only the equality of every citizen before the law, but more than that the access of every citizen to the law; democratic rights of representation assume unhindered adult franchise and would oppose ideologies which endorse social hierarchies; and material well being would involve a minimum economic security in the form of social welfare. Social welfare subsumes the right to elementary education and the availability of basic health facilities – the least that a modern state is expected to provide. Education is pivotal to this change. The right to a personal religious expression would be safeguarded in a consciousness of individual autonomy.

The failure so far to implement these requirements in any appreciable measure makes it evident that they cannot be left to the will of a government or to the whims of the state. It is now necessary for civil society to act towards the establishing of the kind of freedom implicit in these demands and conducive to endorsing social ethics. Let me remind you that almost two hundred years ago, in 1810, Rammohun Roy had stated that "The freedom of the political community is a prerequisite to the freedom of the individual". We have yet to achieve the fullness of this freedom.

Understanding Secularism[1]

It was only recently proclaimed that the end of history had arrived with the victory of global capitalism over socialism. Yet within the short span of these last few years we have witnessed and are continuing to witness the most dramatic resurgence of ideologies and aspirations which have a distinctly nineteenth century feel to them. These have brought back history, if ever it had indeed been ended, with a disquieting resonance. I am referring not only to the ethnic confrontations in former Yugoslavia, but more widely to actions motivated by theories of racism and of ethnicity, and of the permeation of religion into politics. Such actions are more than visible in the heart of global capitalism as they also are in the societies of our sub-continent.

The intellectually fashionable periodisation today speaks of history in terms of the pre-colonial, the colonial and the post-colonial. The latter two are familiar and subject to much discourse. Nevertheless generalisations are made about the

---

1   First published in *Nation and the World*, March 16, 1996

pre-modern tradition in India and these frequently derive from what is assumed to be the tradition, an assumption often based on the negation of that which is held to be characteristic of modernity. There is little hesitation in using colonial constructions of "tradition" or "community" or "culture" in speaking of an earlier historical heritage. A familiarity with the various pre-colonial associations of these concepts is regarded as unnecessary.

If, as some historians assert, cultural concepts are to be given priority in historical explanation, then surely these concepts have to be viewed from a historical perspective. It seems to me that this is all the more necessary in a society which even today carries so many "cultural survivals" from earlier times. Part of the reason for this unconcern with earlier history is the theory, disturbing for the historians, that all historical moments are isolated, fortuitous and contingent. The logic of this would justify even the rejection of history, and if the historical moment belongs to a post-colonial situation, its antecedents or mutations from a pre-colonial or a colonial time would be regarded as irrelevant. From a historian's perspective, this is unacceptable.

We are being encouraged today to take a fragmented view of ourselves and of our past where the fragmentation follows from the premises of nineteenth century interpretations of our past, and which had hopefully been replaced by a holistic view when we terminated colonial rule. In speaking of a holistic view I am not endorsing the claim of ruling groups to represent the whole, but am insisting that the relationships between various groups which constitute society be included, even where some of these are confrontational. Fragmentation has returned in many forms, the most prominent being religion-based nationalism, the kind of nationalism, which we had believed had been laid to rest at the time of independence. Added to this is caste and regional chauvinism. Some would view all these as products of the nation-state and argue that once the nation-state disappears so will these, but how this is to happen and what will replace the nation-state remains unclear. For the moment, the nation at least, is viable and apparent. It is more realistic for us to ensure its well being through actions that we regard as instrumental for the common good.

The return to a holistic view requires a reassessment of the relation of civil society to the nation-state. In this the secularising of our society, as part of the process of change envisioned in modernisation, becomes a central issue. I would like to argue that this is not a matter related only to religious identities and religious nationalism, but also has implications for other significant aspects of social change. Further, that although it differs from our pre-colonial past, such a secularising is not an attempt at alienating ourselves from our tradition, since the pre-colonial past has, in ample measure, ideas and institutions conducive to the secular.

Secularism in Europe has its own history. Its association with separating of religion from civic life, is only of recent times, accompanying the advent of the nation-state and the historical process of modernisation. The meaning of the word has changed in European intellectual history and therefore its exact translation cannot be sought in non-European languages, but as a concept it can be located in cultures where this historical process is taking place.

For the Romans "secular" meant a specific period of time, generally a hundred years, marked by holding games and worshipping the gods. Because of its association with the temporal, for a long duration it came to be used gradually as a description of the world that had existed for a long period. This was later contrasted with the Church, which had a briefer life.

Secular was initially taken in this sense as that which pertained to the world and not to the Church.

To speak of secularism as a western concept superimposed on India is historically incorrect, for it is not confined to the question of the relations between religion and the state, derived from the experience of the Christian Church. Within the Christian Church there was a substantial difference between the Protestant induction of some aspects of secularism and the Catholic confrontation with it. The Lutheran Scandinavian countries had a few problems with secularising these societies, not to mention the Catholic priests of Italy and Spain. Latin America is still battling with it. The crux of the confrontation is not around the religion of the individual or its negation, but over the question of the authority exercised by religious institutions or institutions inspired by religious identities, over civic life.

By the mid-nineteenth century the definition of secular focused on the question of ethics. It was stated that social morality, central to the secular, should have as its sole basis the well being of mankind to the exclusion of considerations stemming from a belief in God or in a future condition. The key elements of this morality were legal order, political freedom, individual autonomy and material well being. These are elements endorsed even by those who find modernisation antipathetic. The emphasis, therefore, is not on hostility to religion but on rational and moral principles governing society, principles which oppose the alienation of human beings, or the absence of social ethics. Yet there is persistence in arguing that the secular hinges solely on the conflict between Church and State. In the definition of secularism, the state has to adhere to and defend the values and ethics of a secularised society.

Where secularism is so interpreted, the evidence from pre-colonial India points to a relationship far more nuanced than it was in Europe and, in some ways, dissimilar. This was in part due to the multiplicity of religions from early times and in part to the nature of Indian social organisation, which was entirely different from that of Europe. There were certainly rituals to consecrate a raja and these were moments of intense religiosity. A new sultan was announced by having the *khutba* read in his name in the mosque. Interestingly, however, state patronage was bestowed in substantial amounts to a range of what may otherwise have been conflicting religious sects and institutions.

Cultural pluralism and its protection was accepted as the duty of the king. His protection of *dharma* was not religion in the modern sense for it enveloped the entire range of social obligations of which religious ritual was a part. This, however, is not what is meant by a secular society. Secularism is not expressed merely by the state protecting and ensuring the co-existence of religions. But, where there is evidence for this from the past, it increases the potential for locating those historical activities that would be conducive to the encouragement of the secular today.

The notion of a state religion in pre-colonial India also becomes somewhat meaningless when it is apparent that political power was relatively open throughout Indian history. Ruling families frequently came from groups ranked as socially low or from obscure families, where some made an effort to cover this up with fancy origin myths and claims to *kshatriya* status. But in the process of becoming politically established they tended to carry their religious cults with them and these had then to be recognised as part of the established religion. The entry of Shaktism into upper caste practice was in part due to this process. Where such kings could eventually claim to be the *avatara* of Vishnu, the centrality of a god as a focus of power, begins to pale.

Alternatively, an existing state sometimes had to extend its patronage not only to the established religious institutions, but even to a cult of the marginalised groups, in order to strengthen its authority. Although such cults are sometimes brought on par with upper caste religion, their local roots and specific meaning remain, and distinguish them from other such cults. Thus, the worship of the hero-stone among pastoralists in Maharashtra was mutated into the cult of Vitthoba, the Yadava dynasty encouraging its identity with Vishnu. This resulted in Yadava control over large tracts of the less fertile parts of Maharashtra. The same process has been sketched for many other areas especially at the turn of the first millennium AD.

If one takes a long view of the past, human societies have moved from the palaeolithic to the neolithic to the chalcolithic to urban civilisations and much more. Each change brought its own anxieties and bewilderments where power and authority were conceded by some and contested by others. As far back as 500 BC emerging kingdoms in the Ganga plain began to supersede the clans, and the beginnings of urbanisation brought further change. There was at this time a strong endorsement of social ethics. Buddhist thought maintained that ethical behaviour was socially determined and did not derive from deity, a clear separation of ethics from religion. The centrality of social ethics is a significant part of our cultural inheritance.

The history of religion has generally been viewed from the perspective of both the Hindu and the Muslim upper castes. Such religion was directed to a specific deity or deities and had institutions for channeling worship. Sacred space was demarcated by the temple and the mosque. Sometimes this was extended to the *matha* and the *khanqah*. Temples and *mathas* were closed to some lower castes and to untouchables; mosques and *khanqahs* were technically open, but nevertheless the clientele was discrete. There were orders of priests and monks, and there were *ulema*, there were texts held sacred, and there was a competition for wealthy patrons, particularly royalty. These were all characteristics of Christian Europe as well. But there, at the lower levels of society there was an enforcing of support for these institutions, whereas in India such support was garnered but did not prevent existence of alternative religious identities by the same people. The lower castes, viewed as servants of the temple, would have performed the requisite services but would not have been included among the worshippers. Their religious practice lay outside these institutions and was bounded by social codes of behaviour. Since these castes, which we now arbitrarily label Hindu and Muslim, formed the majority of the population, their religion has to be recognised as distinctive.

The religion of this majority was a mixing and merging of belief and ritual drawn from a variety of religious experiences, in which the formal differentiations of upper caste religions did not generally prevail. Frequently, the religious practices of these groups were unacceptable to those who defined Islam and Hinduism. Thus, brahmanas shrank from libations of alcohol and offerings of flesh, and the *ulema* could not prevent converts to Islam continuing to worship icons of the local religion. The recognition of these religions as central to the assessment of religion in India is a recent interest, having been substantially ignored in the Orientalist construction of Indian religion.

The claim that there was religious tolerance in Indian society is defended by recourse to texts. In fact, it was the juxtaposition of various kinds of religious practices and beliefs, tied closely to social organisation, which was the basis of both a relative religious tolerance and heightened intolerance based on social outcasting. Religious practices and beliefs could overlap among adjourning castes, but social distinctions were firmly demarcated. Religious tolerance was possible because of the enforcement of social boundaries, but when these were transgressed or seen as competitive, as for example, between the Shaivas and the Jainas in Karnataka, the tolerance disappeared and the conflict took a religious form. Violent forms of religious intolerance were local and did not develop into *jihads* and crusades. The co-existence of religions is again described as secularism, but this is not a sufficient description of secularism.

The religious reality in the past for the majority of Indians has been the recognition of a multiplicity of religions drawing marginally perhaps from the established ones, but far more rooted in the local cults, beliefs and rituals, and identified less by religion and more by *jati* or *zat*. This gave them a certain freedom to worship a stone, an icon, or a deity with which they alone had a dialogue. These were groups entwined by social regulations, but of a local kind. They maintained a distance from the brahmanas and the *ulema* for they were essentially unconcerned with the norms of the *shastras* or with *fatwas*, governed as they were by their own customary observances. This distance was not an idyllic or archaic freedom; it resulted from the segmentation or *jati* that kept them apart. The distancing in religious belief and practice, however, did not prevent an oppressive proximity in areas of civic concern, in the control exercised by those in authority over such groups.

Within the *jati/zat* there was a degree of egalitarianism. In the absence of democracy the ranking was held together by the coercion of those at the top and the acquiescing of those at the lower end. More often than not, within each broad category there was a certain consensus and some maneuverability. With the coming of democracy the coercive aspect should ideally fade away, but this will not happen easily and quickly, given the force of historical conditioning.

Caste as *jati* combined in itself kinship systems, occupation and access to resources, and rituals and beliefs. Further removed socially were the Dalits and the tribals whose religious practices were yet more different. There was, therefore, an immense diversity even in religions believed to be uniform, such as Islam and Christianity. Worship at temples and mosques was formal, but the perfect worshipper was the *bhakta* who chose his own deity, his *guru*, his own form of worship. Religious belief was bound by individual inclination, but religious practice conformed to that of the *jati*. The pressures to conform were pressures of society and did not emanate from a Church.

As in most pre-modern societies, hierarchy bound the segments into a whole, but it was not an immutable hierarchy. Osmosis between close castes did permit of some mobility, although this was dependent on the historical situation. Recruitment of upper castes in the case of brahmanas and kshatriyas took the form of incorporating new groups and assigning status. Inscriptions of the post-Gupta period from Bangladesh mention an increase of brahmana *gotra*s, which has been explained as resulting from the incorporation of people from local societies, a select few of whom were then given brahmana status. This became a feature in many areas where there was an expansion of the agrarian economy and state power. In the case of Ashrafs and Sayyads, who claimed foreign origins and therefore higher status, and frequently had high administrative positions, their ranks could also increase when after a few generations indigenous converts made the same claim. A change of status required a change in the way of life. Therefore, only those who could invest in the change were able to make it. Others sought to alter the ranking or express their dissent by initiating a new religious sect which, in negotiating with other religious groups, either negated or ignored caste ranking, but more often than not was transmuted into a caste. Both these features make a consistent pattern through the Indian past.

This does not make Indians more embedded in religion. But it requires that we investigate the relation between religion, politics and society in the pre-colonial period in terms different from the established ones. Monolithic, homogenous, religious communities, claiming to represent the majority or the minority, provide little explanation of the antecedents to the present functioning of society. They only foster the aspirations of some present-day political parties. But at the same time, the contemporary ideology of religious majoritarianism not only moulds religion into a new homogenous and militant form to enable it to function as an agency of political mobilisation, but it also makes a mockery of democracy by giving to the majority a predetermined identity. The fears of those labeled as minorities are also sought to be allayed by encouraging them to resort to uniformity and militancy.

This is not to suggest that there was an absence of communities in the past, but that the community identities were many and drew on caste, location, language, religious practice and belief, some of which intersected. These were not communities identified across the sub-continent by a single, recognised, religious mould. Communities are in any case constructed, which is why there can be intersecting identities, and these identities can disappear over time, or survive in variant forms. The current recognition of monolithic religious communities is also a construction, which grows out of the way Indian society was perceived in the colonial period. Social memory is also influenced by historical perceptions.

The induction of the secular into a society cannot be a partial experience, revolving around religion. It is a component of a bigger change involving primarily the introduction of democracy, but also of new technologies, and the emergence of a new social group, the middle class, which breaks away from earlier social identities. There is inevitably a search for new identities and in the Indian situation of recent times, encouragement has been given to religious identities, on the basis of a particular perception of what is regarded as the Indian tradition and Indian history. Secularism is no more a western concept than is the middle class or the nation-state even if all these are changes introduced to the world as a result of capitalism or colonialism.

The recognition of the secular relates to specific historical changes experienced by a variety of societies and may well in the next century result in varied manifestations. In Europe this change was associated with societies that had been confined to a single religion that evolved as a focus of power and therefore came into confrontation with the state. In India there has been a multiplicity of religions and the state did not need to confront them. This pre-colonial experience should make it easier for us to secularise our society provided we can cut our way through the impositions of the last two centuries. Religion in India, even if viewed in terms of Hindu and Muslim, has had a strong personal component and has not been dependent on a Church. It would, therefore, be regarded as natural that religion be a personal matter, a matter of faith, and neither the concern of the state nor of the self appointed theologians of any majority or minority community. To draw on a secular tradition from the Indian past would have less to do with religious identities and more to do with the questioning of social boundaries.

The problem of the monolithic religious communities, created and endorsed by colonial and, to some degree, national opinion, remains with us. If the nation-state has accepted these identities then the failure lies with civil society acquiescing in this acceptance. We are hesitant to recognise the elements of a different tradition, which I would argue is the historical heritage and which, although not secularism, would nevertheless, legitimise a secular social ethic. This in turn would empower civil society to strengthen democracy and prevent authoritarianism by the state. Secularisation creates new categories of cohesive social relationships that can monitor the activities of the state. The monitoring is not necessarily a self-conscious act for it is written into the legislation of human rights. These are opposed to any identity used for constructing monolithic, homogenous, religious communities, or for that matter even communities identified by race and ethnicity. Such identities are only too present in various parts of the world and are by no means absent in the sub-continent where they have become a source of opposition to the rights necessary to an enlightened society.

The secularisation of society is neither an easy nor a rapid change. The requirements of social justice and of social welfare, with precedence for subordinate groups and gender justice, have not been given priority in Indian development and are likely to be brushed aside by the demands of global capitalism. To try and hold back modernisation is now a fantasy. But we cannot be passive recipients of modernisation. In the absence of the practice of human rights and social justice, a modernised state can become merely another oppressive state, and where it appropriates the kind of nationalism that creates ghettos, it becomes a fascist state.

Ideologies of social welfare and social justice can be effectively put into practice by the state, but their continued existence, if not enhancement, should become the essential concern of civil society. This implies not just an expectation from the state, but more importantly, the ensuring of their presence in our institutions. It is only through empowering that which is secular in our society that we can hope to live with dignity.

HISTORICAL PERSPECTIVES

Contemporary Politics and the
Rewriting of History in India[1]

With the end of the Cold War there emerged two fashionable theories linked to history. These were encapsulated in the
phrases taken from the titles of two books. One was "the end
of history", and the other, "the clash of civilizations".[2] However, far from ending, history has been revived, literally with
a vengeance in some countries. In the Indian sub-continent
some are actively engaged in re-ordering the past and incorporating this into school textbooks. The governments in these
countries are least bothered that such a re-ordered history flies
in the face of current historical research: such a re-ordering
serves them in building the kind of national identities that will

---

1   Paper given at a seminar held at the Library of Congress, Washington
    DC in 2004. I would like to thank Peg Christoff at the Kluge Center of
    the Library of Congress for comments and questions that helped me
    clarify some of my ideas.
2   F. Fukuyama, *The End of History and the Last Man*, New York, 1992;
    S.P. Huntington, *The Clash of Civilisations and the Making of World
    Order*, New York, 1996.

support their political ideologies. Moreover, liberal democracy is not necessarily the goal of such ideologies.

This revival of history has, in turn, led to the reformulation of the concept of civilisation – a reformulation that is again supportive of the ideologies of world dominance. Civilisation no longer signifies the humanist concept of the eighteenth century. It has now incorporated the aggressive confidence of nineteenth century imperialism and continues to define territories by religious labels. Such a stance, combined with nationalism, often reiterates the ideologies of religious nationalisms.

Moreover, dividing the world into civilisations, whether eight or twenty-six, has little validity. It is now recognised that civilisations are not self-contained monoliths. They evolve from the intersection of cultures and societies, an intersection that questions the notion of segregated civilisations. The confrontation of civilisations, therefore, is used as a euphemism to justify the politics of contemporary conflicts. The concern with propagating a certain kind of history and the redefinition of civilisations, are not unconnected. They are mechanisms of political mobilisation, and the ideology that they endorse is eroding what were once regarded as essential values of a liberal, democratic, nation-state.

It has long been recognised that there is a link between theories of knowledge and the lens through which the theories are viewed. This has an application to scientific advances as well as the formulations of the social sciences. However, such links between knowledge and ideology do not justify treating political agendas as knowledge, as is being done, for example, in the official rewriting of history in the Indian subcontinent; and that too, a kind of history that does not draw on the discipline as current among historians. Far from advancing knowledge, this new history, on the contrary, is being used for forging an exclusive, narrow identity that can be exploited to support a chauvinist and sectarian political mobilisation in order to draw together religious groups identifying themselves as the majority community in the society. This is essentially an intellectual assault on the discipline, and the use to which it is being put is, at the same time, an undermining of history.

This method of creating an identity through doctoring history and intending it as part of nation-building, is familiar to us in the sub-continent from the treatment of history in India and Pakistan, and more recently, in Bangladesh and Sri Lanka, although the identities thus forged are in each case different. In India, the tragedy is that there has actually been a strong tradition of liberal and intellectually independent historical writing of an extremely high quality, which is now under attack. Furthermore, the defense of the discipline of history as an exploration of knowledge is also part of the defense of the idea of India as a democratic, secular society.

The independent nation-state of India created in 1947 had aimed to establish democracy, secularism and social justice. The debate on democracy was encapsulated in discussions not only on adult franchise and the holding of regular elections, but also on supporting civic institutions ensuring the rights of citizenship. Democracy is not just about elections, but also about how the social good can be made equitable and functional. A secular society implied that there would be no discrimination on the basis of religion and assumed that one could freely follow the religion of one's choice, as stated in the Indian constitution. Social justice requires that there be an equality of citizenship and a priority for human rights. Earlier governments endorsed these values, and although their practice was not necessarily adequate, at least the intention was clear. Negating these values was unheard of, even if they were problematic for some sections of society.

The undermining of democracy today lies in insisting that Indian society is constituted of communities identified by religion alone. Since in a democracy the wishes of the majority prevail, it is said that the Hindus being the majority community in terms of numbers, should determine public decisions. This, of course, makes a mockery of democracy, since a democratic majority is not a pre-determined majority. The decisions of a majority in the procedures of governance can and do cut across identities of religion and other identities. The focus of the decision is dependent on the issue in question. Reducing identity to a single, religious identity, is also a refusal to concede that actually Indian society in the past had, and has even today, multiple identities – of caste and social hierarchy, of occupation, of language, of religious sect, and of region. Religion was only one amongst these.

Pre-modern societies tend to regard social hierarchies as normal, and although there was some questioning of these, this was not an axiom of social organisation. Questioning hierarchies, in order to significantly change society, comes with modernisation. As in the case of most early societies, issues of human rights were not of significant concern, irrespective of whether they related to the availability of justice, employment, education, health, welfare or other minimum facilities. In the process of modernisation, and particularly after independence, these were seen as the necessary foundation to the development of the nation. But today, with the reversing of the values that Indian independence stood for, they are of little consequence. They are under attack from state policies, from the leaders of industry, and even more so from those support-ing a nationalism that gives priority to the Hindu citizens of India, rather than maintaining the equal rights of all citizens. This change is encapsulated in the notion of Hindutva, claimed to be the guid-ing force of current Indian religious nationalism. It is constantly referred to, and continually redefined, as and when it becomes necessary, both by the government and by the groups that make up the conglomerate of Hindu nationalist organisations, referred to jointly as the Sangh Parivar.[3]

Hindutva has become an item of 'double-speak'. It was coined as a concept referring to Hindu-ness, or as some argue, as a political slogan in the early twentieth century, and since then has been explained in various ways, depending on the occasion. It endorses the idea of Hindu Rashtra, that is a Hindu nation or state. It has also been equated with Hinduism, an equation unacceptable to those Hindus for whom Hinduism is not an aggressive politically oriented ideology, and for whom the Hindu religion does not require to be defended by organising the killing of Muslims and Christians. Hindutva as Hinduism is different from earlier Hinduism because despite its hostility to Islam and Christianity, it not surprisingly, carries the imprint of these religions in its structure and organisation. I have elsewhere referred to this new shape of Hindutva Hinduism as Syndicated Hinduism.[4]

---

3   The main constituents are the Bharatiya Janata Party (BJP) which is effectively the Party that dominates the central Indian government; the Rashtriya Swayamsevak Sangh (RSS) created in the 1920s and acting as the ideological core of Hindu nationalism, which superceded the Hindu Mahasabha; the Vishva Hindu Parishad (VHP) created in the mid-sixties and pushing for more aggressive policies in support of Hindu nationalism and with a considerable following in the Hindu diaspora; and Bajrang Dal, the youth wing of the VHP, associated more recently with situations involving violence; and the ABVP, the student wing. The well established Shiv Sena functions in Maharashtra and has a presence in support of Hindu nationalism, but is not generally seen as part of the Sangh Parivar.

The counterparts to such groups are not unknown among Muslim nationalists and Sikh nationalists. The latter were more active during the movement for Khalistan – projected as an independent Sikh state, a movement that has now become quieter.

4   See *Cultural Pasts,* Delhi, 2000, pp. 1025-1054.

Hindutva has also, rather perversely, been described as secularism. And now we are told that Hindutva is cultural nationalism. But we are not told whose culture is being made the national one, out of the many distinctive cultural communities that constitute India. Because cultural nationalism implies choosing a single culture and defining it as national, the choice is that of upper-caste Hindu culture. This would be something of a contradiction, because the Indian identity has historically evolved from multiple cultures across the social spectrum, as is normal to societies mutating within a changing history.

Despite its initial geographic and ethnic meanings, the term Hindu finally settled to being the name of a religion. It has been argued that the early religions of India were essentially religions of orthopraxy/ritual practice, rather than orthodoxy/conservative belief. There was no historical founder; no single, sacred text; no insistence on congregational worship; and no ecclesiastical structure controlling belief and organisation. Belief was open and ranged from animism to the most sophisticated philosophy. Religion was, therefore, a mosaic of juxtaposed cults and sects. Some of these had an inherent and close identity with particular social groups, recognised as castes, others deliberately cut across such groups. There was no single label by which they described themselves. They were identified as Vaishnava, Shaiva, Shakta, Lingayat, and so on. This permitted flexibility in belief, although not necessarily a flexibility across social identity. Intolerance was less of belief, and more of social practice. The Indian manifestations of Christianity and Islam, particularly at the popular and regional level, were also characterised by similar tendencies. Religion in India, therefore, had a specific articulation, different from what have been called the Semitic religions.

A new form is now being given to Hinduism through Hindutva. This is to enable it to act as an agency of political mobilisation. In order to do this it reformulates Hinduism, borrowing the structures of Islam and Christianity. It is concerned with the historicity of those now being projected as the founders of the religion; with giving centrality to particular texts in imitation of religions of the book; and in attempts to introduce a formal organisation of an ecclesiastical nature to pronounce on matters social and religious, and which cut across castes. This requires it to also endorse a particular view of Indian history and culture that has become part of the ideology of the religious nationalism of the majority. This is evident from the attempt to replace existing historical views that range over many historical explanations by a single view, supporting this ideology.

This change can be explained, partially, as an articulation of a new middle class. The middle class that has currently come to power is no longer the middle class created through colonial rule, drawn from the often wealthy, but frequently dominant, upper castes of India. The transition from dominant caste to middle class was relatively easier in the late nineteenth and early twentieth century – or so it would seem. The middle class of today is drawn from a wider social range, many more middle castes, as well as those erstwhile on the margins of the middle class. The component of dominant castes is less visible. It is, in some ways, an insecure middle class, seeking an identity that would require belonging to a well defined group, and anxious to monopolise resources, which it hopes to do through espousing a party based on religious nationalism. Hindutva provides a cause as well, since it asserts the primacy of the new middle class Hindu. The obsession with a single identity, as against the multiple identities of earlier times, is a modern phenomenon, in as much as it is focused on individual motivation and cuts across other identities. It is suspicious of those who are more than just superficially westernised, since it assumes that such groups endorse secularism -and this is ideologically opposed to religious nationalism. That the secularising of a society is necessary, ultimately, to the modernising process, is not an acceptable idea.

The increasing visibility of this new middle class also coincides with globalisation. As has been persuasively argued, globalisation does on occasion create choices, important for democratic functioning, particularly as regards the possibility of a multiplicity of choices in how it is to be implemented, if at all it is to be prevented from having an adverse affect on many societies.[5] On ground, globalisation has bifurcated those who can successfully ride the new economy from those who remain at the margins and are still aspiring to wealth. An attempt is being made by the latter to blur these distinctions, by creating a new all-India identity through the propagation of Hindutva. It is believed that all Hindus will automatically conform to it. Non-Hindus will be made to conform, if need be through violent means, as in Gujarat recently. Lower castes and Dalits will be attracted by the expectation of upward social mobility. And in any case, the cow is currently better protected than the Dalit.

From this perspective primacy goes to the Hindu in the definition of an Indian. This involves identifying the non-Hindu as the 'Other'. History, therefore, is viewed as the right of the Hindu to be the inheritor of the land, excluding the non-Hindu in this process. The group identified as the 'Other' is not actually a powerful group, whether it be Muslims in India or Hindus in Pakistan and Bangladesh. It is a weak minority but has to be projected as a threat. This enables the majority to give a political edge to its own identity. The identification of the 'Other', based on religion, is a reflection of how the majority perceives itself. The creating of the 'Other' requires the

---

5   J. E. Stiglitz, *Globalisation and its Discontents*, New York, 2003.

highlighting of difference, even if it is a clearly exaggerated difference, and difference gets mutated into deviance. Having created the 'Other', the defense of the 'Self' against the 'Other', leads to a persecuting hatred.

It could be asked whether the articulation of a national identity based on a single factor such as religion or race, would require there having to be an 'Other' at all? In the world of post-colonialism and globalisation there seem to be two kinds of 'Others'. One is the external 'Other', as among nations of the Developing World treating the First World as the 'Other': either to be envied or to be disliked. This kind of 'Other' may not have a marked physical presence but may be present in symbols, such as, the use of the English language, or wearing jeans, and more currently, the popularity of junk food and rock music, not to mention the perceived exploitation of economic resources. This kind of an 'Other' can be directly opposed, as is done in some Hindutva circles where various activities, ranging, as for example, from sending Valentine's Day cards or young women dressing in jeans to opening up the economy to multinational investment, are defined as western and therefore alien to Indian culture and interests. This 'Otherness' becomes complicated when Hindus subscribing to the ideology of Hindutva live in the First World and participate in its professional and economic activities, but believe that they are contesting its western culture by supporting the Hindutva agenda in India and by demanding that the rights of a Hindu minority community be recognised in countries of the First World.

Within the nation-state the more evident 'Other' is the enemy within, clearly demarcated, and in contradistinction to whom the identity of the dominant group is created.

The identities of both these 'Others' vary, of course, over long periods of time. They become more, or less, important as changes take place in history. The external 'Other' is perceived as either a rival (as in the Cold War), or as stronger than the dominant group of the nation-state. The identity of the internal 'Other' may also change, but it always remains a weak minority group, deliberately so chosen (and some would say deliberately so kept), because it is easier to construct a historical antagonism from the past with a group that is currently weak, and because it allows the dominant group to construct the 'Self' in whatever manner it wishes to.

The creation of an internal 'Other' is tied to a presumed collective memory. The 'memory', in turn, is created by kneading the past into new forms, claiming these as legitimate memory.[6] Such claims created to endorse the attitudes of the present are then used to restructure the past and justify the present. This is a circular process. The current hostility to the Muslims among many in the Indian middle class is frequently explained as due to a collective memory of the tyranny over the Hindus and their oppression, by Muslim rulers in the medieval past. That the articulation of this 'collective memory' can largely only be traced back to the colonial period is because such constructed memories keep changing with every major historical change. Since memory is part of a living society it is not permanent and can be formulated in any way.

The new attitude among those now in power is not unconnected with their trajectory of knowledge. I shall try and demonstrate this with reference to the way in which history is being projected. But before doing so, let me preface this by saying that the regular updating of knowledge through research, discussion and publication is essential to the advancement of knowledge. This involves the constant assessment and rewriting of studies that reflect this advance, as for example, even standard works in history. Indian history has been reinterpreted in the past two centuries. An initial colonial interpretation,

---

6   P. Nora (ed.), *Realms of Memory*, Vol. I, New York, 1996, pp. 1-23.

largely drawn from Orientalist research and the requirements of the colonial state, was followed by the questioning of this interpretation by historians sympathetic to the mainstream, inclusive, national movement. This, in turn, was questioned by historians of the last fifty years, teaching and writing in Indian universities and universities elsewhere, and who were intellectually wide-ranging Liberals, Marxists, non-Marxists, and such like, many grappling with the questions posed when history came to be treated as part of the social sciences. They covered a range of opinion. The most striking aspect of this kind of rewriting was that the changes of interpretation grew out of intense debates and discussions, as well as critical enquiries into the historical data and the generalisations derived from it – in short, through an advancement of knowledge.

The so-called 'new' history that is currently being propagated has been introduced in entirely different ways: through mangling existing school textbooks by insisting on deleting passages that were officially disapproved of; through surreptitiously changing the educational curriculum, without discussing the changes even with the government appointed Central Advisory Board of Education; through introducing new textbooks, without the normal pedagogical procedures of approval from a committee of educationists and historians; through trying to control the history syllabus of all Indian universities, by mandate of the fund-giving University Grants Commission; and through imposing the authority of the party in power, by arbitrary actions such as preventing the publications of the Indian Council of Historical Research which had been processed prior to the NDA-led government coming to power.

This change is not the result of investigating new theories of history; it is the imposition of an arbitrary history – virtually propaganda. It is a narrative intended to arouse emotions linked to a community, rather than reflect historical investigation. Such history is sometimes concerned with issues that are marginal to most historians, but which can be used to emphasise identity: for example, the statement that Hindus in the ancient past – and particularly Aryans – never ate beef, contradicts historical evidence, but has been useful to modern political mobilisation in demarcating Hindu from Muslim. There is a clear link between this negation of eating beef and the Cow Protection Movement of the nineteenth and twentieth centuries (now being revived) that acted as a deliberate wedge between the two communities. A belief in stories about the past, and inventing histories rather than investigating evidence, becomes a major enterprise.

The views that were at the source of what is now the Hindutva version of history are reflected in the writings and beliefs of the founding ideologues of Hindu nationalism. V.D. Sarvarkar's definition of an Indian required that he be a person whose *pitribhumi* (the land of his ancestors) and *punyabhumi* (the land of his religion) had to be within the territory of British India.[7] This for him disqualified the Muslims and Christians, and he added the Communists to the list as well. M.S. Golwalkar stated unambiguously that non-Hindus could not be citizens.[8] Further, that there had always been a single Hindu society and culture rooted in Vedic Hinduism. Islam intervened and tried to denigrate it, therefore Islam has to be opposed. No concession was made to the many religious movements in pre-Islamic India that questioned and challenged the Vedic religion, both in debate and in rituals. Among these were the Buddhists, Jainas, Shakta sects, the Nathas, Lingayats and many others, who expressed their religious commitments very differently from the Vedic. Hindutva also ignores the efflorescence of Hinduism through Bhakti – the devotional move-

---

7   *Hindutva. Who is a Hindu?* Bombay, 1923.
8   *We or Our Nationhood Defined,* Nagpur, 1945.

ments, which began in the pre-Islamic period in the peninsula but became widespread in the north in later times. These religious movements, which came to dominate the sub-continent and gave a new form and meaning to Hinduism and Islam, were often the result of the coming together of Hindu, Islamic and other religious strands. They are the source of much of the modern versions of Hindu practice and belief.

I would also like to argue that the theories being expounded in the Hindutva version of Indian history are a leap backwards to nineteenth century colonial history – the history that had been questioned by nationalist historians and discarded by more recent historians. Not only is it a borrowed history from colonial writing, but it also endorses the most simplistic aspects of certain kinds of Orientalism in defining origins and identities. Fundamentalist histories of various kinds in ex-colonies often draw on these initial colonial theories about their history. In this, the Hindutva version of history is no exception in forcing a return to nineteenth century colonial history. This is being dressed up as a new, original, authentically Indian version of history. It is none of this. It merely repeats much of what was said in colonial histories of India, about Indian society and culture. The presuppositions of the colonial authors are absent but the intentions are the same.

The colonial interpretation was carefully developed through the nineteenth century. By 1823, the *History of British India* written by James Mill was available and widely read. This was the hegemonic text in which Mill periodised Indian history into three periods -Hindu civilisation, Muslim civilisation and the British period. These were accepted by colonial and Indian historians, largely without question; and we have lived with this periodisation for almost two hundred years. Although it was challenged in the last fifty years by various historians writing on India, it is now being reasserted again. Mill argued that the Hindu civilisation was stagnant and backward, the Muslim only marginally better, and British colonial power was an agency of progress because it could legislate change for improvement in India. In the Hindutva version this periodisation remains, only the colours have changed. The Hindu period is the golden age, and the Muslim period the black, dark age of tyranny and oppression. However, the colonial period in the new history is a grey age, almost of marginal importance compared to the earlier two. The focus is on the Hindu and Muslim periods which, as we shall see, were part of the political ideology of the religious nationalisms of the early twentieth century.

Anti-colonial nationalist historians, often referred to as secular nationalist historians, had initiated a critique of the colonial period, but tended to accept the notion of a long, continuous Hindu 'golden age'. They did not distance themselves in order to assess the validity of such descriptions. Many were upper caste Hindus, familiar with the sources in Sanskrit and sympathetic to the idea of a glorious Hindu past. Insisting on such a past was, up to point, an attempt to compensate for the ignominy of being reduced to a colony in the present. Few argued that some aspects of the golden age might have been slightly tarnished – as for instance the existence of untouchability in social relations. Such arguments were not appreciated and were thought to be anti-national.

Similarly, the argument that the Muslim period was to be reconstructed from Persian and Arabic sources tended to attract upper caste Muslims to this study, and they too were sympathetic to what was stated in the sources, without questioning them too closely. The bifurcation of the sources was clear, and dominated by the religious literature of upper caste Hindus and Muslims. Even those who in the early twentieth century critiqued Mill's periodisation, merely changed the nomenclature from Hindu-Muslim-British to Ancient-Medieval-Modern, in imitation of the periodisation of European history. There was a debate over colonial interpretations, but the methods of analysis and the theories of explanation tended to remain the same as in the nineteenth century.

Mill's projection was that the Hindus and Muslims formed two uniform, monolithic communities permanently hostile to each other because of religious differences, with the Hindus battling against Muslim tyranny and oppression – a view accepted by most colonial writers on India. There was no recognition of the obvious segmentation within both communities, reflected in the varying histories of castes, social groups and religious sects. These formed the multiple identities negating the notion of monolithic communities. They also indicate that the history of these multiple communities, and even those defined by religion, was a complex history ranging over a variety of relationships, some of which were harmonious and some conflicting. These complexities have to be carefully investigated and explained from their varied perspectives. They cannot be dismissed with a simplistic mono-causal explanation.

The colonial view was further reinforced in the theory that the Muslims of India were foreign and alien. The subject was treated as if Muslims were – one and all – migrants, all claiming descent from the Arabs, Turks, Afghans, Mongols and what have you, who settled in India. This may have held true for a fraction of the elite, but as we know, the vast majority of Muslims in India were Hindus converted to Islam. The few claims to an origin beyond the frontiers of the sub-continent were more often claims to establishing a status rather than a statement of ethnic origins. The regional and linguistic variations among Muslims in India gave rise to many cultural and sectarian differences that militated against a uniform, monolithic religious community. Groups labelled as Hindu were also treated as if they were identical and conformed to a single, homogenous culture, although it is well known that the diversity among such communities was substantial.

Colonial historians read medieval Indian history as a record of religious antagonism between Hindus and Muslims. The basic sources were included as translations from Arabic and Persian texts in the multiple volumes of the *History of India as Told by its Own Historians,* translated and edited by Elliot and Dowson and published in the latter half of the nineteenth century. Chroniclers of the medieval courts were included, the assumption being that there was no writing of Indian history prior to the coming of Islam. The avowed intention of the editors, as stated in their 'Introduction' to the volumes, was to highlight religious antagonism, thus also demonstrating the superiority of British rule over Muslim rule in India. This reading was faithfully echoed by Indian supporters of either Muslim or Hindu nationalism. Aziz Ahmed, for instance, writing in 1963, characterised the sources of medieval history as consisting of two kinds, the Muslim epics of conquest in Persian and the Hindu epics of resistance in Hindi or related languages.[9] These are the concepts now being projected in the new textbooks. It cannot be denied that there was conquest, and there was, on occasion, resistance; but conquest and resistance were more frequently over territory, political power and status, and not necessarily even expressed in religious terms. Religion was not the dominating factor, as is clear from recent studies of these texts. Resistance involves a relationship of dominance and subordination, and such relationships existed in pre-Islamic times as well, and even after the arrival of Islam were seldom motivated solely by religious differences.

Further, not all the Muslim migrants were invaders since most came as pastoralists, traders, adventurers, and followers of socio-religious sects.

---

9 'Epic and Counter-epic in Medieval India', *Journal of the American Oriental Society,* 1963, 83, pp. 470-76.

The notion of majority and minority communities, identified by religion, was reinforced by the Census carried out regularly by British administrators since the nineteenth century. The primary division of society into Hindu and Muslim as politically viable communities throughout the sub-continent had not been used earlier. The category of Hindu incorporated Buddhist, Jaina, Sikh and various others, their previously held differences now being annulled. Different categories of Muslims, some of whom did not conform to orthodox social laws and had diverse religious practices, were also amalgamated into a single Muslim community. In the pre-colonial state, royal patronge had generally been separately extended to all these groups and their distinctive identities were recognised. The categories used in the Census data tended to restructure the constituents of Indian society as being essentially religious identities. These were then associated with numbers, and the Hindus became the majority community, and the Muslims were the largest minority community. This was reiterated in the setting up of Separate Electorates in the early twentieth century, also based on religious identities and their numbers. Terms such as majority and minority communities have gradually almost replaced the notion of Indian citizens.

This is not to suggest that colonialism invented contentious relations between groups of Hindus and Muslims. There were confrontations on various issues prior to the colonial period, but these tended to be localised confrontations on specific issues. Colonial readings of Indian history magnified religious confrontations and made them generic to inter-group activities; they also reiterated, more emphatically than was historically legitimate, the existence of two antagonistic communities throughout the second millennium AD. Inevitably, this historical reading, and the administrative measures that it encouraged, came to be articulated in political ideologies.

In the early twentieth century two new kinds of nationalism, other than the mainstream, inclusive, anti-colonial nationalism, acquired visibility. These were religion-based national groups for whom the identity of an independent nation-state was to derive from the religion of the majority community in the proposed state. Religion-based nationalism, essentially excluding the 'Other' – whether Hindu or Muslim – thus drew from the colonial interpretation of Indian history, and catered to the ambitions of a section of the Indian middle-class. It projected imagined uniform, monolithic, religious communities, and gave them a political reality. There was an entwining of communal historiography and religious nationalism. Muslim nationalism aspired to, and eventually succeeded in establishing Pakistan. Hindu nationalism is aspiring to make India into a Hindu Rashtra. The two-nation theory was essential to both the Muslim League and the Hindu Mahasabha in the early twentieth century. It continues to be essential to the communal movements of today. These nationalisms were not primarily anti-colonial, their opposition being to the other religious community. Thus V.D. Savarkar fully endorsed the two-nation theory, continually pledged his loyalty to the British government, and was accused of being among those who were in favour of the assassination of Mahatma Gandhi.

For Muslim nationalism, history became significant only with the conquest of India by various Muslim rulers, as is now reflected in the history textbooks of Pakistan and Bangladesh. Despite having a depository of sources in Sanskrit, particularly inscriptions, both countries lack the kind of scholarship that can integrate these sources into their view even of the medieval past. The parallel in Hindu nationalism was to see Hindu civilisation as the sole identity of India, all other cultures being foreign. The history of the second millennium AD is seen largely as that of Muslim conquest and therefore of foreign rule, despite the fact that the Muslim dynasties were settled in India and there were inter-marriages with Hindu royalty, including Rajputs. The study of Persian and Arabic sources is on the decline. Interest in this period has revived only with studies of regional histories. The nineteenth century colonial interpretation of Indian history is being projected once again, this time by Indians, in the new history textbooks for schools.

The proponents of Hindutva object to the history that has been written in the last fifty years. There is an insistence on calling it 'Leftist history', assuming that this will discredit it. In fact this history incorporates a range of opinions, drawing on a variety of theories of explanation and analyses, and is based on intensive research. The range enriches the understanding of the past. Its main concern was to ensure historical method and critical enquiry as the basis of this understanding. Many historians made extended analyses of some of the themes initiated by anti-colonial nationalism and questioned these, such as Mill's periodisation, the colonial concept of Oriental Despotism as the dominant political economy of India, and caste as a form of racial segregation. Other historians have explored facets of the social, economic and cultural history of India. A number of new and relevant questions have been raised, and sources used in fresh ways to answer these questions. These evolved from investigating the past through inter-disciplinary studies, and a familiarity with theories of explanation and of historiography from other parts of the world. The concerns of historians have widened out to include the study of changing forms of caste, gender studies, pre-modern and colonial economies, technologies, types of state-formation, the social context of religious sects, environment and ecology – in fact the normal components of what historians at the forefront of the discipline today regard as appropriate to historical investigation. Research of this kind established the legitimacy and recognition of the multiple voices and cultures that go into the making of the past and the plurality of religions in India for all periods.

This resulted in Mill's scheme being replaced by an alternate periodisation, based on wide-ranging historical change rather than the change in the religion of the rulers. The attempt has been to bring history into the purview of the social sciences, and this extends the scope of history as also the methods of analyses. The reading of texts as sources is not limited to a literal reading. There is a questioning of texts for new kinds of information that helps delineate the details in our understanding of the past. Historical research in recent times introduced new features that included more intensive testing of the reliability of the evidence rather than taking all sources at face value; encouraging a critical enquiry into the data; and seeking rational analyses on which to base historical generalisations. This is far removed from the politically motivated, mono-causal view of history that religious nationalism is propagating.

The Hindutva objection to this kind of history is in part on grounds that it is 'Eurocentric', although those who make this comment have read neither the work of the Indian historians whom they criticise nor the writing of western historians. 'Eurocentrism' is for them merely an abusive label, rather like 'Leftist'. What is more disturbing for them is that such history, irrespective of who has inspired it, challenges the claims to the culture that Hindutva has reconstructed of the past.

Another area of debate, crucial to the ideology of Hindutva, relates to the question of Indian origins and identities. Here the attempt is to reformulate these so as to prove the primacy of the Hindus, which primacy they could evoke in order to enable them to claim priority as the citizens of India. The beginnings of Indian history have to be rewritten to establish the genesis of Indian society as Hindu, and Hindu as understood in the Vedic corpus. The Indus civilisation as the earliest record of a sophisticated urban culture in the Indian sub-continent is now being read as having been authored by the early Aryans, those that composed the corpus of the *Vedas*. Calling it the Sarasvati civilisation rather than the Indus civilisation evokes Vedic connections. The contradictions in this argument are many. The *Rigveda* depicts a typically agro-pastoral culture and does not reflect an advanced urban civilisation of the Indus plain and western India. The date of the *Rigveda*, generally taken to be 1500 BC at the earliest, has in this view, to be taken back to 3000 BC or even earlier, which is untenable on the existing linguistic evidence. Since the archaeological and the linguistic evidence in this reconstruction are incompatible, the supporters of this new view give less attention to the linguistic evidence and interpret the archaeology according to their own ideas. Archaeological data is, nevertheless, described as 'scientific' and therefore irrefutable, arguing that the data speaks for itself. But, of course, pottery and beads do not speak. The reading of archaeological data is dependent on the person who is interpreting it.

There can be no visible remains of 'the Aryans' since Aryan is a language label and should be more correctly used as 'the Aryan-speaking people'. An archaeological culture can only be called Aryan – if at all – when there is evidence of the use of an Aryan language. The script of the Indus civilisation has not been deciphered so far. Nevertheless, the attempt is to equate the authors of Vedic Hinduism, labeled as 'the Aryans', with the most sophisticated of the archaeological cultures of the Indian past, the urban Indus civilisation. The obsession with Aryan origins came with the notion of the Aryan race in nineteenth century Europe and its application to the Indian past. That the term 'arya' was a term referring to cultural and social status in the past, is now ignored in favour of maintaining that all caste Hindus are 'aryas'.

The insistence on this interpretation is in order to claim that the Hindus have had an unbroken, lineal descent for five thousand years or possibly even more. In order to maintain that the Hindus are Aryans, and all others are non-Aryan and therefore foreigners, it has to be argued that the Aryans, and their language Indo-Aryan, are indigenous to India. This view is taken to such lengths that there was even a computer-based distortion of a Harappan seal attempting to pass off a single-horned animal as a horse. This was done in order to establish that the horse – associated with Aryans – was known to the Indus civilisation. Aryan presence, thus, has been made the key to Indian civilisation.

One is reminded of the parallels in the Nazi use of archaeology in the 1930s to prove the Aryan origins of Germans. The association becomes much closer now that it has been shown that the founders of Hindu nationalist ideology had connections with the fascists in Italy and Germany. Savarkar repeatedly expressed his admiration for fascism and ridiculed Nehru for opposing it. There was admiration for Hitler's solution to the Jewish population in Germany, and hints about the Semites in India, and elsewhere. B.S. Moonje, mentioned with respect in the RSS training schools, was greatly impressed by the organisation of the Italian fascists when he visited Italy in 1931, and it was said to be the model for the RSS training in India.

But even this theory of the Aryan identity and the *Vedas* as the bedrock of Indian civilisation, is a return to nineteenth century views. Among Indologists, both European and Indian, Aryanism in its racial dimension was the prevailing theory in explaining the origins and inter-relations of societies in Europe and parts of Asia. The centrality of Sanskrit and of the *Vedas* draws on the brahmanical tradition, but the definition of the Aryan repeats the views of European nineteenth century scholars who applied 'race-science' to explaining the past. However, these theories are turned inside out by arguing that the Aryans originated in India and were therefore indigenous to India, as also was their language; and by stating that it was from India that civilisation spread to other parts of the world.

Interestingly, even this insistence on the Aryans and their language being indigenous, and of India being the cradle of world civilisation, has an ancestry that goes back to the nineteenth century, to western, non-scholarly but influential sources. Madame Blavatsky who, together with Col. Henry Steel Olcott and others, founded the Theosophical Society in 1875, propounded similar views. They spoke of the Aryans from India civilising Egypt in pre-Vedic times. Olcott was closely connected with the brief merger of the Theosophical Society with the Arya Samaj of Dayanand Sarasvati, a merger that fell apart. Dayanand wrote of the migration of Aryans from Tibet into north India, and the Indian Aryan nation then civilising and ruling over the rest of the world. A much discussed question at that time was whether the British and the Indians could be related by blood, since they both belonged to the Aryan race!

Madame Blavatsky established many centres to propagate her ideas, especially in Europe, where theories of the occult in Hinduism and Buddhism were becoming increasingly popular. Such theories were said to have honoured Hinduism in the west. Few, however, followed up what was actually being said in the name of Hinduism; nor was there an interest in ascertaining the use that such ideas were being put to. In recent years there have been studies showing the links that these centres had with the germination of the Nazi ideology and what have come to be called the Ariosophists.[10] There was, therefore,

---

10 N. Goodrick-Clarke, *The Occult Roots of Nazism: Secret Aryan Cults and Their Influence on Nazi Ideology; the Ariosophists of Austria and*

a cross-current of Aryanism that linked a variety of European and Indian groups. The projection of Aryanism generated similar political ideologies.

At the time when Olcott was maintaining that the Aryans were indigenous, Jyotiba Phule, writing in Marathi, had a different take on the theory. Regarded by Dalits as a *mahatma* and a founding thinker, Phule supported the theory of an Aryan invasion, which he saw as an invasion of alien brahmanas speaking Sanskrit. As a result of this invasion the existing indigenous inhabitants were subjugated, oppressed and relegated to lower caste status. For him the lower castes were the rightful inheritors of the land but were denied this right by the in-coming brahmana Aryans. The conflict, therefore, was over the establishment of caste, which became the process by which the brahmanas appropriated the land of the indigenous peoples and rendered them without rights.[11]

This is different from the current Hindutva version, which follows the views of Col. Olcott and others, and where the crux of the theory is not the origin of caste conflicts, but the conflict of identities based on religion. The confrontation is between the reconstruction of an indigenous religion and religions that have their sources outside the territory of British India. The Hindu Arya is indigenous and, therefore, the inheritor of the land; and all other religious groups are foreigners.

That there was an invasion by 'the Aryans' was once held as the explanation for the arrival of the Indo-Aryan language in the northwest of the sub-continent. Few support this theory today. The focus has shifted to seeing the coming of the Indo-Aryan language through a series of migrations, prob-

<hr>

Germany 1890-1935, New York, 1992; *Hitler's Priestess: Savitri Devi, the Hindu-Aryan Myth and Neo-Nazism*, New York, 1998.

11 Romila Thapar, 'Some Appropriations of the Theory of Aryan Race Relating to the Beginnings of Indian History', in Daud Ali (ed.), *Invoking the Past: the Uses of History in South Asia*, Delhi, 1999.

ably small-scale ones at that. Such migrations would introduce new facets of culture that were interwoven, together with the languages, into the emergence of societies whose presence is recorded in the Vedic corpus. The interweaving of languages is evident from the presence of Dravidian linguistic forms in the *Rigveda,* which is the earliest compilation of hymns composed in Indo-Aryan. Furthermore, the earlier theory of Aryan race is no longer tenable as an explanation for social relations as described in this text. The theory is now seen as confusing sociological constructs and biological origins, and has been questioned.

The Hindutva version dismisses the arguments support-ing the Aryan speakers having come from the Indo-Iranian borderlands and insists that they were indigenous. The evi-dence of linguistic and cultural parallels between north India and Zoroastrian Avestan Iran are explained as the spread of Indian culture to Iran, even though the Iranian language of the Old *Avesta* is, according to recent scholarship, possibly a little more archaic than Indo-Aryan. That there are striking paral-lels and references to movements in the borderlands and the Indian plains. Furthermore, there is a refusal to accept that in-vasion and graduated migrations are two different processes, and particularly so, in the impact that they have on existing cultures and societies. Migration affects cultural change in different ways from invasion. The historians who argue for migrations are continually branded as supporters of the now defunct invasion theory, in an effort to discredit them.

Cultural change is a complex subject, requiring control over a variety of data, and some familiarity with explanations of cultural change. Migration has a gradual impact, where change is manifested in a slow transformation of language and aspects of ritual, and of social forms. Invasion is a serious dis-turbance, where change is relatively sudden and widespread.

These are not issues debated in Hindutva writings, since it is easier to merely insist on a theory than to discuss its implications. This is particularly so where the new theory is replacing existing history wherever it chooses to. Nor is there an understanding that history today is no longer just a narrative. It attempts to explain events. Explanation to be accepted has to pass the test of analysis. And analysis is completely absent in these theories.

We may well ask why are the proponents of Hindutva going back to colonial ideas of the nineteenth century, and claiming them as new and indigenous? Is it because of an intellectual barrenness and the intention of pursuing history as propaganda? It is assumed that Indian society and culture did not change in past times. This was also axiomatic of colonial views of Indian history. Indian society was said to have been so static that it did not register change. This in turn led to denying Indian civilisation a consciousness of history, since history assumes the recognition of change. In the current adaptation of this perspective, the Hindu period was one long, unchanging golden age. The notion of an Indian society unchanging over many centuries was questioned in the historical writing of the last century, and was discarded. But it is back again, in the new textbooks.

Those supportive of the Hindutva versions have not, over the years, produced any theoretical critiques of a seriously historical kind in refuting the mainstream historical interpretations of the last half century – perhaps because such critiques require wide reading and an intellectual understanding of historical problems. There has to be some familiarity with at least the minimalist historical method that is required from students of history – namely, a familiarity with the historical process of change, an awareness of the complications in handling source material, and of the theories of historical explanation.

The public abuse of a few selected historians, who are invariably referred to as 'Leftists' or even 'academic terrorists', does not constitute the refutation of historical explanation.

Going back to the views of the nineteenth century means that no attempt is made to understand the important historical questions of the interface of cultures and societies, and how these get transformed and evolve. There is the obvious fear that to concede such an interface would demolish the foundations of insisting on the single origin and identity of Indian culture. This has relevance to the study of society and culture as depicted in the Vedic corpus, the texts that are being quoted as the foundations of Indian civilisation, but which, it would seem, are not being analysed by those who claim to be using them in this manner. There is little interest in analysing the varying processes through which languages of the Aryan and non-Aryan speakers spread, since this raises questions relating to acculturation and the accommodation of differences – questions that have been raised and discussed by historians. Nor is there a concern, at a broader level, with commenting on how economies evolve, or customary law and castes change, or dominant groups emerge; or, how crucial these variations are, to understanding the nuances of change within cultures; or for that matter, cultural mutation through interaction with other societies. There is an apprehension that such analyses would challenge the simplistic, mono-causal explanation. The new history, therefore, is intended to close the mind to analytic capabilities.

History does not move through Either/Or generalisations, as there are many areas between the two that have to be investigated. There are many nuances and negotiations that are involved in how societies accommodate internal contradictions and external interventions. But the version of history and its teaching currently being introduced, is a kind of catechism –

one given question, one given answer and no discussion – as is evident from the history textbooks used, for example, in most schools in Gujarat. This will doubtless be the case soon in other BJP ruled states, judging by reports of recent changes in Rajasthan. This is a travesty of teaching methods. Textbooks are meant to encourage students to explore the how and the why of events. These sub-standard textbooks reduce the richness and complexity of Indian civilisation to making meaningless and banal comments about it.

The intention is that this version of history should become the only version, since other interpretations are being reviled and abused. Perhaps the most offensive action in the suppression of the earlier school textbooks in history, published by the NCERT (National Council of Educational Research and Training) and used until 2002, was the refusal to allow any discussion on the portions that were deleted from these books by the government.[12] These deleted portions significantly included seminal questions, such as the origins and history of caste. In a society where caste remains predominant, it makes little sense to not allow a discussion on the subject in schools.

Shifting the emphasis onto religion also detracts from the need to assess social hierarchies in Indian society. To continually project the Muslim and the Christian as the 'Other', diverts

---

12 Interestingly, this is again a practice that goes back to colonial policy in the nineteenth century. In schools in Gujarat, for example, one of the books used for teaching Gujarati was the *Narmadagya* by Narmad. The Department of Public Instruction, under orders from K.M. Chatfield, made major changes in the 1874 edition, and published the revised book in 1875 and made it the textbook, without getting a clearance from the author. Major changes concerned the relationship between the Bhakti poet Dayaram and the woman who was his disciple, Ratanbai. Chatfield insisted on a condemnation of the relationship on moral grounds, whereas Narmad had made no comment on it. S.Yashaschandra, 'Gujarati Literary Culture', in S. Pollock (ed.), *Literary Cultures in History*, Berkeley, 2003, pp. 600-601.

attention from the need to juxtapose ethical values such as tolerance with the notion of untouchability as a social reality. Apart from all else, the cultural empowerment of the weaker sections of society has no place in this curriculum. The demand for reservations in education and state employment, from and on behalf of the lower castes and the Dalits, makes the future insecure for a section of the middle class. The challenge from the under-privileged is opposed through supporting an ideology that effectively does not concede social equality. Civilisations of the past can be held up as models in the creating of ethical values, but it has to be conceded that they all had a poor track record of social egalitarianism.

In a society where other media, such as radio, films, television and newspapers, are significant to the creation of social attitudes, not always desirable, what is taught at school needs to endorse the positive attitudes and undermine that which is negative. In this context, the focus is more on the teacher than the textbook. Where alternative textbooks are available, there the teacher has a choice. But the Examination Board often curtails the choice, as do the examiners correcting the scripts at terminal exams. And, of course, the teacher is also susceptible to the influence of the media.

More than the media, the major source of information, not excluding prejudiced attitudes, now come from the Internet. The function of the teacher is, consequently, changing. It is less to provide information, more to equip the student to think about the parameters of the subject under study. The nature of the textbook, therefore, will also change. If information is subordinated to interpretations, then the contests over the latter will increase. This may result, hopefully, in the representation of knowledge in textbooks being taken far more seriously than has been the case so far.

History textbooks have advanced as the essential equipment of the nation-state, and are believed to be an aid in nation building. This function may have to be reviewed. The essentials of the discipline must begin to take priority over the more blatant political objectives of textbooks.

Let me conclude with the question of how the discipline of history and the future of education in India, so essential to the kind of society that we set out to build in 1947, can be defended. The state textbooks prescribed by the NCERT during the first NDA led government, and in many BJP ruled states during its second tenure – with their factual errors, apart from the revival of colonial prejudices – have been critiqued by historians. The difference between professionally acceptable history, and that which is being called history in the new textbooks, has to be made apparent. This requires an independent scrutiny of textbooks by historians. Such a scrutiny would include not only the textbooks published by the state, but also those used in schools run by a variety of organisations – the Shishu Mandirs of the RSS, the Madrasas of various Islamic organisations, the schools of the Gurudwara Committees, mission schools, private schools and state schools. Huge amounts of money are being channeled into these schools as donations and it has become essential that there be transparency about what is being taught. Identities are created through the process of schooling. It is necessary to ensure that schooling does not contribute to the enhancing of religious and social prejudices.

There is a need to revive and improve upon the earlier pedagogical procedures, and extend these further through consultation with specialists in education. There is a need for rationalisation in the approach to textbooks and teaching. The vetting of textbooks should ultimately be the work of practitioners in that discipline, and such books should not be subjected to the control of the representatives of various religious organisations. The educational process has to reflect advances in knowledge. This would also reduce the possibility of decisions about education being taken arbitrarily by powerful politicians. It would be an absurd situation if the educational curriculum had to be changed each time the government changes. Clearly there has to be a rationalisation of the curriculum. This would also require that membership of examination boards cease to be a matter of arbitrary social patronage and should better be aligned to pedagogical needs. It would also require the availability of a choice of textbooks from which the teacher can choose.

The current educational curriculum will encourage the next generation to be pliant, rather than questioning and exploring knowledge. Significantly, this echoes the agenda of colonial education and that of totalitarian states. However, this would ultimately affect the aspirations of the Indian middle class. Well-to-do sections of the middle-class can today send their children to private schools to prepare them for study and jobs abroad. The numbers of Indian students in the USA, for instance, exceeds those from other countries. Schools for other sections of society in India, therefore, tend to deteriorate. But with larger circles of rising expectations and competition, parents will have to start inquiring into the quality of what is being taught, and make demands for better education. Predictably, such concerns relate largely to subjects that are a prelude to high-income jobs, drawing on technical knowledge and expertise. Studies of societies, cultures and the creation of identities will tend to remain incidental and subject to political assaults, unless their centrality is understood.

It is not just a coincidence that the increased intermeshing of politics and religious nationalism, whether Hindu, Sikh or Muslim, was contemporary with the induction of India into the economies of globalisation. It is sometimes argued that a reaction to the transnationalism implicit in globalisation brings about a turning inwards, as it were, emphasising narrow ethnic and religious identities. The rising aspirations of the middle class are generated by the visions held out by globalisation and by the success of a small fraction of this class. But the downside is that for the majority of the middle-class these aspirations are not met, and there is a widening disparity between the suddenly affluent sections and the rest who remain on the margin. The latter are caught up in intense competition over employment and suffer from insecurities with the breaking down of earlier forms of broad-based community living. The propagation of hate as an expression of social relations diverts the inadequacies born of insecurities. The new communities created by globalisation, when threatened by the failure of what globalisation had promised, exploit religious identities as a cover for a cult of terror. And terror is increasingly becoming the language of communication, whether between groups or between states. Together with this and extending further down the social scale, there is a constant search for ways of upward social mobility, one of which is seen as recruitment into the well-financed, religio-political organisations of narrow nationalisms. The hatreds generated in the present are enhanced and legitimised by being projected onto the past. The rewriting of history becomes central to this new ideology. Organisations propagating the politics of religious nationalism are financed and supported not only by some local groups, but also by some sections of the diaspora – Hindu, Muslim, Sikh. The latter have no intention of returning to a less comfortable homeland, but nevertheless wish to intervene in Indian politics. The more ambitious and the wealthier among them intervene in the relations between the country of their domicile and their homeland and see themselves as a pressure group determining policies relating to the sub-continent. As in the case of the new middle-class in India, such groups in the diaspora are also grappling with the uncertainties of a new identity and status, in this case, in an alien country, and frequently coupled with a rather romantic projection of what is believed to have been the past of the homeland. The projection of their past in a new landscape becomes a volatile activity. Curiously, while such groups insist that the country of their domicile remain a pluralistic society with equal rights and protection for all citizens, they are not willing to concede the same for the country of their origin.

There are bigger and broader issues involved in these changes that go beyond history or the educational curriculum, for they are altering the principles of Indian society. Democracy, secularism and equal rights for all citizens as fundamental values are being threatened. Those citizens who are more equal than others, dictate the reading of the past, with a tunnel vision and mono-causal explanations. Liberal history runs counter to this, because it retrieves the multiple pasts and the pluralities of Indian society. This obstructs the use of history as propaganda. The exploration of this plurality becomes imperative, therefore, as does the secular voice in which it is articulated, if we are to prevent the closing of the Indian mind.

Communalism and the Historical Legacy: Some Facets[1]

The link between communalism and the interpretation of Indian history assumes significance because of the many occasions when communal organisations have sought the legitimacy of history in defense of their views. This is not however a one-sided process, for, such interpretations of Indian history, some of which are either no longer tenable or else are limited, are still adhered to by historians as well, especially those who are influenced by communal politics. I would like in this paper to touch on a few examples of the interlinking of communal ideologies and the interpretation of history.

The historian's relevance to the analysis of communalism begins with indicating the ways in which history is distorted by communal propaganda. Thus, when it is argued that certain events took place in the past, such as the destruction of Hindu temples by Muslim rulers, and it is required that these actions be avenged in the present, the point has to be made by histori-

---

1   First published in *Social Scientist*, Vol. 18, Nos. 6-7, June-July 1990.

ans that the politics of the past, whatever form they may have taken, should be confined to the past. The present cannot in any way redress the politics of the past, and those who would argue that this is possible are exploiting the past for purposes of the politics of the present.

When there is a distortion of history, as for example that the Taj Mahal was originally a Rajput palace, such distortions have to be corrected, for they percolate down to the popular perceptions of history and feed communal emotions. When a deliberate selection is made from the past of particular personalities who are then projected as heroes, such as Rana Pratap, Shivaji and Guru Govind Singh, all of whom belonged to the Hindu fold and are described primarily as being hostile to the Muslims, the intention is to propagate antagonism against the Muslims in the present day. There are other personalities, historically far more important, such as Ashoka and Akbar, whose message to Indian society was different, and they are therefore ignored in communal propaganda. These are all very obvious levels of the abuse of history, and this abuse has to be countered.

But there are many levels, more subtle, whereby legitimacy from history is sought by communal ideologies. Communal ideology perceives Indian society as constituted of a number of religious communities, politics is seen as the interaction of religious communities, and political allegiance relates to the religious identity. On this basis, political action is designed to further the interests of a particular religious community. The notion of the religious community claims a historical basis and takes the identity of the community as far back in time as possible, so as to add legitimacy to their politics. Such legitimacy is aimed at drawing in numbers of people.

This is also an attempt to maintain the status quo in society and not allow the kind of change that will accommodate the aspirations of those who are deprived of resources and status;

namely, the lower castes and the lower classes. Communal ideology is a diversion attempting to prevent radical movements. It ties in conveniently with a post-nationalist phase, where the middle-class does not wish to see the widening of the social base providing access to power and resources. Communal ideology is antithetical to liberal and radical thought and action, and where the communalists see themselves thwarted, they do not hesitate to recruit the urban underclass or the lumpens in an effort at criminalising activities, and thereby holding society to ransom.

The communalisation of Indian society has changed from the kind of communalism prevailing in the period prior to 1947, when communalism was essentially a mechanism of political mobilisation. In the period since 1947 it is not only a mechanism for political mobilisation, but has also come to pervade all aspects of life; particularly areas which are the most sensitive, such as education, the media, the forces of law and order, and even contemporary culture in all its facets.

Today the most evident communalism is that of what is called 'the majority community'. This does not preclude 'minority communalism', but because the numbers involved in the 'majority communalism' are so overwhelming, it is the most alarming. It is the communal ideology of the majority community that stakes maximum claim to Indian history, thereby legitimising communalism. However, historical analyses would question such a claim.

In looking at the past, there are two perspectives that are intertwined. Which are the theories of historical interpretation that have encouraged a communal view of Indian society? What is the evidence or the historical perspectives, which historians have ignored or neglected, and which might provide a different view, and which might in turn have discouraged the claim to the historical legitimisation of communalism? Within this context and given the dominance of Hindu communalism today, I would like to examine two connected concepts: the notion of the Hindu religion, and the notion of a Hindu community, going back to earliest times.

How was the notion of a religious community constituted from history; or, alternatively, what were the features drawn from the past, which went into the making of a religious community?

Among these an important component was the theory of the Aryan race. The theory gained popularity in mid-nineteenth century Europe, and was readily applied to India wherever the sources mentioned *aryas*. Its application had a definitive impact because it was argued that there was a racial segregation, which was seen as biological and therefore innate.[2]

The separateness was of two kinds: one between Aryan and non-Aryan, which has been widely used in analysing Indian history; and the other was the European concern to separate the Aryan from the Semitic. It was argued that there was an invasion by the Aryans who easily conquered the existing indigenous non-Aryans, frequently equated with Dravidians. Invasion became the explanation for the introduction of what was seen as an Aryan culture. The distancing of the Aryan from the non-Aryan led to the idea that the cultural history of India was the Aryanising of the non-Aryan, where there was little scope for seeing the reverse process. The separating of the Aryan from the Semitic may well have reinforced, even at the sub-conscious level, colonial historiography segregating the Hindu/Aryan from the Muslim/Semitic, even though the racial category would be inapplicable in either case. Even in terms of the theory, not all Hindus were Aryans; and certainly

---

2   As argued for example in H. Risley, *The People of India*, London, 1908.

the Iranian, Afghan and Turkish Muslims who constituted the majority of Muslims from outside India, were not Semites.

Another aspect of the theory of the Aryan race is, of course, the superiority of the upper castes, believed to be the pure or the relatively pure Aryans. They were the ones that observed the cultural forms essential to this identity and used an exclusive religion, Brahmanism, which was seen as the dominant religion. The religion of the upper castes became the framework for the construction of Hinduism in the nineteenth century.

The theory has been seriously questioned in recent years both by archaeologists[3] and by those working in linguistics.[4] This has raised a new set of questions as to how historians now view the evolution of a society and its culture – using indices such as ecology, demography, settlement patterns, language change among diverse groups and the interaction of belief systems.[5] Aryan is no longer seen as a term referring to biological race. The only identification is that of language, and, therefore, the correct form would be to refer to the Aryan-speaking people arriving in India, whether through migration or trade or as pastoral groups, and the evolution of a society and culture with elements taken from both the Aryan-speaking groups and others.

---

3   J. Jarrige, 'Excavations at Mehrgarh: their significance for understanding the background of the Harappan civilisation', in G. Possehl (ed.), *Harappan Civilisation*, New Delhi, 1982, p. 79 ft.; J.G. Shaffer, 'The Indo-Aryans: cultural myth and archaeological reality', in J.L. Lukacs (ed.), *The Peoples of South Asia*, New York, 1984, pp. 77-90. For a broader and more controversial perspective see C. Renfrew, *Archaeology and Language*, London, 1987.

4   T. Burrow, *The Sanskrit Language*, London, 1965, p. 379 ft.; M.M. Deshpande and P.E. Hook (eds.), *Aryan and Non-Aryan in India*, Michigan, 1979.

5   G. Erdosy, *Urbanisation in Early Historic India*, Oxford, 1988; T.N. Roy, *The Ganges Civilisation*, Delhi, 1983; Romila Thapar, *From Lineage to State*, Delhi, 1984.

The substantial use of a language dominated by Indo-Aryan was the major identity of north-western India at that time. Nevertheless, the theory of an Aryan race continues to dominate historical thinking and popular views of early Indian civilisation. Possibly one reason for this is that it was well suited to the middle-class, which in the nineteenth century was drawn from the upper castes, and saw itself, therefore, as distinct and superior. Its continuation lay in what was seen as the appreciation of Indian culture by Orientalist scholarship, and by the continuing belief in certain circles that such scholarship was not biased, inspite of demonstrations to the contrary.[6]

Orientalist interests in early Indian history were partly due to intellectual curiosity and partly to the idea that in India's present lay the past of Europe. The rediscovery of India's past, through a careful deciphering of the sources, established the bonafides of Orientalist scholarship among most Indian historians. The study of the past being essential to nationalist ideology, there was a tendency to rely on Orientalist scholarship for the reconstruction of the ancient period in particular. Orientalism had to grapple with a religion that was unfamiliar, and therefore had to be set up in familiar terms in order to be understood by European scholars.

Orientalism encouraged a brahmanical view of early Indian society, and even anthropologists, who more often work on the ground as it were, have tended to see Indian society and religion from the perspective of brahmanical texts.[7] Histories of Hinduism tend to be largely histories of the texts; and attempts to relate the text, the ritual and the belief to a historical context are far fewer.

---

6   See Edward Said, *Orientalism*, London, 1978, and the debate that this book has sparked off.

7   A case in point being Louis Dumont, *Homo Hierarchicus*, London, 1972.

The Orientalist attempt at integrating religious belief and practice into a coherent religion and a rational faith known as Hinduism,[8] was from the perspective of Semitic religions, since these were more familiar to such scholarship. These views had an influence to a greater or lesser extent on the socio-religious reform movements of the nineteenth and early twentieth centuries. Many of the projections of the Hindu religion today are also derived from treating it as parallel to some vaguely understood Semitic form. This is rather different from what the indigenous sources suggest.

The nature of Indian religions as indicated from early sources, indicates a different system from that of Islam or Christianity. There appear to be a series of parallel systems that go into the making of what has been called Hinduism,[9] but what may perhaps be more correctly called, Hindu religions. These parallel systems have a basic structure that is different from that of the Semitic religions. The major religious groups referred to in the early sources, are two: Brahmanism and Shramanism, and these are clearly differentiated.[10] Shramanism included the Buddhists, Jainas and other sects that were distinct from Vedic Brahmanism.

Shramanism, in most cases, was an institutionalised religion, which was not the case with Brahmanism. The two were organisationally separate, had a different set of beliefs and rituals, and had different social norms. Shramanic sects early on

---

8   D. Knopf, 'Hermeneutics versus History', *Journal of Asian Studies*, 1980, 39, 3, pp. 495-505.

9   Romila Thapar, 'Imagined Religious Communities? Ancient history and the modern search for a Hindu identity', *Modern Asian Studies*, 1989, 23, 2, pp. 209-231; G.D. Sontheimer, 'Hinduism: the five components and their interaction', in G.D. Sontheimer and H. Kulke, *Hinduism Reconsidered*, New Delhi, 1989, pp. 197-212.

10   As in the inscriptions of Ashoka Maurya, J. Bloch, *Les inscriptions d'Asoka*, Paris, 1950, pp. 97,99,112; also in Arrian, *Indica*, XI. 1-12; Strabo, XV.l, 39-41, 46-49.

established an order of monks, a *sangha*. Such orders came much later to Brahmanism, generally towards the end of the first millennium AD, and almost coinciding with the decline of Buddhist sects in many parts of India. Brahmanism assumed the precondition of a caste society, whereas this was not required of Buddhism or Jainism. Brahmanism emphasised the separate observances, rituals and practices of each caste, and made a sharp distinction between the *dvija*/twice-born and the rest. Shramanism tried to build a congregation of believers irrespective of caste.

Distinct from Brahmanism there also emerged at the turn of the Christian era, the Bhagavata sects and later the Shakta sects. These were manifestations of a variety of popular cults. Many evolved into a religious form, which has come to be called the Puranic religion. This became dominant in many parts of India in the first millennium AD.[11] It was significantly different from both Brahmanism and Shramanism, although it can be argued that it borrowed some deities from the former and some notions from the latter, especially the emphasis on individual salvation. The intensity of the idea of *bhakti* or devotion as a form of religious expression in some Puranic sects was a departure from the earlier religious manifestations, and particularly from the sacrificial ritual of Vedic Brahmanism.

In the multiplicity of sects that surfaced both in the first and second millennia AD, the identity of the sect was based not only on the particular deity, which was central to its worship, but also its location and the language which it used. There is a regional component that is extremely important, because much of the literature came to be expressed in the regional language and not only in Sanskrit. It would be worth investigating whether the use of Sanskrit or of a regional language did

---

11 R.G. Bhandarkar, *Vaishnavism, Saivism and Minor Religious Sects,* Strassburg, 1913.

not demarcate sub-sects within a particular tradition. Many of these sects gathered around them members of particular castes suggesting that perhaps their audience was constituted of a particular social class.[12]

What is interesting about the Puranic religion was its flexibility. It could therefore interact with tribal cults and forms of worship, and became an effective avenue of giving and receiving cultural forms. The worship of the icon, which became characteristic of many of these sects, and is therefore believed to be essential to Hinduism by outsiders, was unknown to Vedic Brahmanism.

In addition to this there is also the importance that is given to the private domain of belief, and which is in some ways characteristic of the indigenous religions and civilisation of south Asia. The requirement was that rituals and nodal practices be recognised, and these were often tied to caste identities. Beyond this, belief was a personal matter. The ultimate in the private domain of belief was the renouncer, who was respected at one level because of his insistence on his right to his personal belief, even if this insistence required him to quit society.[13]

These religious systems are not similar to the pattern of the Semitic religions since they do not constitute a single historically evolved religion. Hinduism cannot be described as a historically evolved religion with a founder, an ecclesiastical organisation, and with sects branching off and taking positions in relation to the teachings of the founder. The sects are often in origin independent cults, and are later associated with other sects. They come together in a kind of mosaic of distinct cults,

---

12 K. Schomer and W.H. McLeod, *The Sants*, Delhi, 1987. See the paper by D. Lorenzen, 'The Kabir-Panth and Social Protest', pp. 281-304.

13 Romila Thapar, 'Renunciation: the making of a counter-culture?', in *Ancient Indian Social History: Some Interpretations*, New Delhi, 1978, pp. 63-104.

deities and sects and the juxtaposing of these is often from social needs.

There is traditionally a lack of historicity regarding those who are being worshipped. Interestingly, the insistence on historicity that is emerging now as part of what is called New Hinduism (and which I have preferred to call Syndicated Hinduism[14] comes at a recent point in the history of Hinduism. Traditionally historicity was limited to each sect, for some had founders, were institutionalised and had sub-sects branching off. But whether all these sects can be placed under one label, Hindu, and can claim that they are historically evolved from a single origin, is a debatable question. These features are, however, characteristic of Buddhism and Jainism, which are to that extent different from Hinduism. These questions in turn relate to that of the existence of a single Hindu community, which identified itself as Hindu in opposition to the Muslims.

The term 'Hindu' has its own history and it is one that should not be forgotten. It derives from primarily geographical terms, Hindush, used in the Achaemenid inscriptions[15] of ancient Persia, and as al-Hind by the later Arab writers. The terms referred to the people living in the area of the Indus river and beyond, looked at from the perspective of west Asia.

The Arabs initially used the term as a geographic and ethnic term, and by extension, it came to be used for those who practised religions indigenous to India and therefore not recognisable as any of the Semitic religions familiar to the Muslims. This bunching together of all the indigenous sects and labelling them as Hindu, is alien to the earlier tradition where religious identity was by sect, and the term Hindu had not been used.

---

14 'Syndicated Moksha', *Seminar*, 1985, 313, pp. 14-22.

15 'The Persepolis and Naqsh-i-Rustam inscriptions of Darius', in D.C. Sircar, *Select Inscriptions*, I, Calcutta, 1965, p. 7.

The periodisation of Mill encouraged the reading of the Medieval/Muslim period of Indian history as more often the confrontation between, or less often the adjustment of, two major communities, the Hindus and the Muslims. There has been a tendency to project each as a monolith with clear-cut identities and demarcations. In this context, it is interesting to examine the perceptions each may have had of the other, since these would provide a better picture of the actuality than what the periodisation suggests.

An important question would be to ascertain the point at which people in India start calling themselves Hindus. It would seem that this came fairly late in the interaction between Islam and the existing religions of the Indian sub-continent. Similarly, the currency of the term Musalman also seems late. Kabir in the fifteenth century uses both terms.

Sources of the period of early contact tend to use the traditional terms, as used in the past for those coming from west Asia, or those regarded as outside caste society. Thus the term *yavana* used for Greeks, Hellenistic Greeks and others from west Asia and the eastern Mediterranean, continues to be used for the Muslims.[16] Alternatively, the term *mlechchha* is frequently used.[17] *Mlechchha* meaning impure, goes back to the Vedic texts and often referred to those who did not speak Sanskrit or observe the *varnashramadharma*, the caste ordering of society. *Mlechchhas* could be foreigners even of high rank, or could be those regarded as low in the social scale. Sometimes even the term Shaka is used[18] going back to the times of the Scythians. More specifically those coming in from the north-west, the Turks, were called by the ethnic term, *turushka*, but this in turn came to be used popularly to refer to Muslims.

---

16 *Epigraphia Indica*, 1952, XXIX, pp. 121-22.
17 As for example, D.R. Bhandarkar, Appendix to *Epigraphia Indica*, XIX-XXIII, No. 683.
18 Bhandarkar, loc. dt. No. 862.

These varying terms, each seeped in historical meaning, do not suggest a monolithic view, but rather, a diversity of perceptions, which need to be enquired into more fully.

The notion of confrontation requires some analyses of the nature of religious conflict not only in the period of Muslim presence in India but also in pre-Islamic times. Religious sectarian conflicts are known to earlier times. Thus both Hsuan Tsang in the *Si-yu-ki* and Kalhana in the *Rajatarangini*, refer to hostilities between the Shaivas and the Buddhists, where the former are described as killing Buddhist monks and destroying Buddhist monasteries.[19]

In Kashmir, the attack on religion was not restricted to inter-sectarian conflict, for in the eleventh century one of the kings, Harsha, anxious to replenish his treasury, ordered the confiscation of valuable idols and the looting of temples.[20] There are also many references to the antagonism between Shaivas and Jainas in Tamil Nadu, Karnataka and Andhra Pradesh, an antagonism which took violent turns with the destruction of Jaina temples or their forcible conversion to Shaivite shrines and the persecution of Jainas.[21] Hostilities between the Virashaivas and the Jainas seem to have been particularly acute.

More recently in history, there are references to fierce conflicts between the Sannyasi orders and the Vairagis in the latter part of the Mughal period. In each case, they are competitive sects and religious concerns are not the only reason for the conflict. These tend to be sects that are highly organised, and often literate. The competition is frequently for state patronage, or for control over commercial rights. In the case of the

---

19 S. Beal, *Si-yu-ki*, I, xdx; *Rajatarangini*, I. 307.
20 *Rajatarangini*, VII, 1091, 1100; VIII, 79, 113.
21 P.B. Desai, *Jainism in South India*, Sholapur 1957, pp. 23, 63, 82-83, 124, 397-402. *Epigraphia Indica*, V, pp. 142 ft., 255; XXIX, pp. 139-44. *Annual Report of South Indian Epigraphy*, 1923, p. 4 ft.

Sannyasis and the Vairagis, for example, they were also traders on a large scale. Pilgrimage centres, where the takings by way of offerings from pilgrims were lucrative and religious belief was bent to support commercialisation, became centres of contention between religious sects. There is, therefore, a play of power and an element of economic competition present in religious conflict, even if the conflict is sought to be presented as a matter of religious belief.

The same is true of the many conflicts between what have been called the Hindus and the Muslims. Such conflicts, first of all, should not be taken as conflicts involving two monolithic communities. They were not so in the earlier period either, where sectarian identity was more crucial than a monolithic religious identity. It was not the Hindus who attacked the Buddhists and Jainas, but particular sects of Shaivas.

The idea of a single Hindu community conditioned by a common religious belief, social norms and ritual practices, all extending across every region and including all castes, is not reflected in the early sources. There are references to communities, but these are communities based on location, on occupation, on caste and occasionally as a sect. These were not necessarily bound together by a common religious identity as in the case of the Buddhists, Jainas, Christians and Muslims. The *Dharmashastras* mention a variety of *dharmas*, as for instance *shreni-dharma* and *jati-dharma*, all pointing to the customary laws and practices of each. These identities could partially have overlapped. Significantly, there is no reference to Hindu *dharma*, which is a term of relatively recent origin.

Conflict is a social articulation, more so when it is conflict between groups representing the state or important institutions of civil society. The breaking of idols and the destroying of temples also brings in the question of temples and icons being symbols not only of religion, but also of the culture of politics. It is in this context that we have to examine the destruction of icons and temples by various Muslim invaders or rulers during the second millennium AD.

Attempts are being made today to build up hysteria on the issue of Hindu temples destroyed by Muslims. A mosque built on the site of a temple comes in very useful for arousing communal antagonism, since it provides a location for the confrontation, and therefore sharpens the focus. The demand that such mosques be destroyed or dismantled, and new temples be erected in their place, would play havoc with historical monuments. Today it is temples and mosques, tomorrow Buddhist icons and Jaina temples may also become the subject of such restorations. This process could continue to go back endlessly in time. If mosques are threatened today, there will be a demand that they be handed back to 'the Muslim community'. Recently, as a temporary measure, prayers were permitted in mosques normally classified as protected monuments under the control of the Archaeological Survey of India. Should this concession be made to all religious monuments from the past, there would be complete confusion regarding the protection and conservation of such monuments, in addition to its being yet another issue to fan communal hostility.

Every temple that lies in a state of disrepair is popularly believed to be so because of Muslim vandalism. But we know there are some temples which fell into disrepair because they lost royal patronage.[22] Given the ecology and climate of India, buildings require continual maintenance if they are to survive, and any shortfall in this creates havoc. This has happened not only to temples, but even to mosques built in the last three hundred years. It is necessary, therefore, to clarify which tem-

---

22 This happened, for example, in the nineteenth century to the Simhachalam temple in Vishakhapatanam district, and it was said that the temple was damaged by the Muslims. K. Sundaram, *The Simhachalam Temple*, Waltair, 1969.

ples had fallen into disuse and therefore decay, and which were wilfully damaged or destroyed.

In the case of temples known to have been damaged and then re-used for other religious purposes, as in the case of Jaina temples damaged by the Virashaivas, or the temple at Qila Rai Pithora in Delhi converted into the Quwat-ul-Islam mosque, another set of questions have to be asked. If the reasons were religious fanaticism, then surely the monument would have been totally dismantled and destroyed, rather than being converted to the use of another religion.

Is the vandalism, then, just pure vandalism motivated by a religious factor, or does it symbolise an act of conquest outside the battlefield, and the assertion of political power? Or, is it an act of incorporation, an attempt to somehow keep the earlier tradition alive in the newer tradition? Were grants made to temples revoked when they were converted into mosques, or was the control over cultivated land and other sources of revenue diverted into the hands of the caretakers of the mosque? If the grants continued, then there would be a rather mundane reason for converting a wealthy temple into a mosque.

When religious monuments such as temples and mosques are built through State patronage, or the patronage of those who are powerful and wealthy, then they are also part of the politics of their time, and there has to be a political reading of both the building and the destroying of such monuments. The politics of the past belong to the past, and to try and reverse their role today is to attempt the impossible. Nor does it solve present-day problems, and in fact only increases communal confrontation.

Religious fanaticism is also not always the full answer. Aurangzeb's destruction of the temple to Krishna at Mathura is often explained as fanaticism. Yet there is another aspect. The temple was built by Bir Singh Bundela, who was also organising political opposition to Aurangzeb. The temple was an act of defiance, a symbol of defiance: a situation where the religious and the political interlocked.[23] Both, the building and the destroying of the temple, are part of a political struggle involving the assertion of power.

There is a tendency to view the destruction of Hindu temples by Muslim rulers from the point of view of court chronicles, which underplay the political factor and emphasise the religious. It might be more salutary to enquire as to what the local people thought of the act. Did they see it as an act of sacrilege, or as an act of political conquest? As far as the court chronicle is concerned, the temple is a metaphor of power. Was it viewed similarly at different levels? Curiously, there is little reference in local sources to the raids of Mahmud of Ghazni against the major temples of north-western India, and virtually nothing in contemporary sources from further afield.

If the destruction of temples, or their conversion into mosques, was purely an act of religious fanaticism, then it is curious that those who built temples did not hesitate to become the builders of mosques as well. A text in Sanskrit, the *Rehamana-prasada*, is part of a treatise on the building of a large range of temples and palaces. Vishvakarma, the divine architect and also associated with artisans and builders, discusses in this text, a range of temple types pertaining to every sect. Among these is the mosque, the temple built for Muslims who build under the emotion of divine adoration or *sattvik-bhava*.[24] Clearly the guilds of craftsmen had a practical approach to constructing religious buildings, whether of the various Hindu or Muslim sects.

---

23 Personal communication from my colleague, Dr. Muzaffar Alam.

24 R. Nath, 'On the theory of Indo-Muslim Architecture', in *Sastric Traditions in Indian Arts*, Heidelberg, 1986, pp. 187-201; M.H. Dhaky, 'Notice on Indian Vastu text on the construction of a mosque', *Vishveshvarananda Indological Journal*, September 1977, XV, 2, pp. 1-7.

Professional groups, whether of Hindu sectarian persuasion or Muslim, would tend to have common interests. This also relates to the question of conversion, which is of central importance. The popular theory is that the local population was presented with the alternative of forcible conversion, or else death. The fact that political power lay in the hands of Muslim dynasties and yet the Muslims were always a minority in India, lends little credence to this theory. Nor does the totality of the Muslim population in India owe its origin to foreigners who settled in India. A small percentage came from outside. That many among them married and merged with the indigenous population precludes them from being called foreigners.

The majority of Muslims in Indian society were those who had converted from indigenous groups. The nature of this conversion has also to be analysed. Barring the few at the elite levels who were individual converts, the larger numbers tended to belong to castes that were converted.

At one level conversion from one religion to another is an intensely personal and private experience; it is an emotional experience where the converted person can take on a new personality and a new life-style. This process is reflected in the conversion of individuals. Where a caste, a *jati*, an occupational group is being converted, the earlier customs and memories of the group are not forgotten. This is not the case of a total change, but of what has been called a cultural translation where, for example, the prophet becomes the *avatara* or the *avatara* is seen in the light of the prophet.

Such cultural translations would be particularly noticeable in a society based on caste, where the earlier religious belief and observances also had a strong caste association. It is not surprising, therefore, that caste retained a hold on Muslim society, when it came to marriage and occupation, in spite of the egalitarianism of Islam in theory.

The Indian situation must also have puzzled Islamic theologians. This was the first society where there was an absence of a massive conversion of almost the entire population, and it was therefore different from Persia, Afghanistan and central Asia, of which they had had an earlier experience. What must have been even more bewildering was the fact that conversion is alien to the indigenous religions, where what was important to one's religious identity was the *jati* into which one was born, and from which one sought one's social and religious identity. Conversion is more specific to Semitic religions, where the identity is clearly demarcated. This was not so with the indigenous religions of India, where such identities could even be multiple or overlapping or ambiguous, depending on the social role of the identity. Thus, a king, Harshavardhana, is claimed by both the Shaivas and the Buddhists.[25]

The treatment of Hindu and Muslim society as monoliths by historians has tended to ignore the more important questions about these societies such as, how do various religious groups perceive each other? And do groups on conversion incorporate the myths and beliefs of earlier times into their newly acquired mythology? Texts in Sanskrit suggest that there was little dialogue with Islam, but the literature in regional languages provides a different picture. Popular religion, outside the circle of the Muslim courts and the concerns of the chroniclers of these courts, points to different perceptions. Ekanath, one of the most influential Marathi Bhaktas of the sixteenth century, composed a text on an imagined Hindu-Turka debate, in which there is to begin with, a heated confrontation on religious issues and polemics, with image worship as a key point

---

25 S. Beal, *Si-yu-ki*, Delhi, 1969 (reprint). D. Devahuti, *Harsha*, Oxford, 1970. S.R. Goyal, *Harsha and Buddhism*, Meerut, 1986.

of contention.[26] Ultimately, there is a consensus and accord between them.

However idealised such documents may be, they are invaluable for ascertaining the focal points in the perceptions of various groups. Some of the Marathi *bakhar* literature legitimises Maratha rule by first legitimising the preceding rulers, including the Mughals.[27] *The guru-shishya* relationship in the *bhakti* tradition of Maharashtra allowed brahmanas and Muslims to play the role of either guru or *shishya* in the same tradition, as is evident in the training of Sheikh Muhammad.[28] The eighteenth century Muslim saint, Shah Muni, wrote the *Siddhanta Bodha* during the period of the Peshwa brahmana rule, after Maharashtra had experienced the so-called Hindu revivalism under Shivaji. He uses a Puranic style myth to explain the origins of the Muslims.[29]

We are told that from Mahavishnu, the supreme ruler of the earth, sprang Paigambar-pir who descended to earth. From Paigambar, the Yavanas spread all over the world. A number of Paigambars established the *mlechchha-dharma*. Narayana created the four *shastras*, which the Yavanas call the Quran. The Yavanas call Narayana, Allah, and worship Mahavishnu with great devotion. It is interesting that even as late as the eighteenth century, the term Yavana is being used for the Muslims and *mlechchha-dharma* for Islam, although the term Musalman is also used sometimes.

These are not isolated examples. Some of the *mangalakabyas* of Bengal are other examples of such interlinks in the creation of what might be seen as a new mythology, where Puranic deities intermingled with the personalities of the

---

26 N.K. Wagle, 'Hindu-Muslim Interactions', in G.D. Sontheimer and H. Kulke (eds.), *Hinduism Reconsidered*, Delhi, 1989, pp. 51-66.

27 Ibid. p. 52 ff.

28 Ibid. p. 56 ff.

29 Ibid. p. 58 ff.

Quran.[30] What have been referred to as Bengali Muslim 'cultural mediators', were concerned that the local converts to Islam should not lose their earlier moorings, and were willing to create such a new mythology. This is equally evident in the folk literature of other regions with large Muslim populations. In Tamil Nadu for instance, the guardian figures in one of the cults of Draupadi are invariably Muslim.[31] This is not to suggest that the picture should be seen as an idealistic representation of harmony and peaceful co-existence. On the contrary, even these attempts at a new mythology suggest a certain kind of disjuncture. But the study of this literature is likely to move closer to the reality of how people perceived each other, rather than a focus on only the literature of elite groups. The monolithic nature of interpreting these relationships needs to be examined afresh.

The relation between religion and power is more evident at the level of court circles and elites, but it is not absent at other levels as well. When large state systems collapse into smaller ones, these links seem to become more apparent. Thus the eighteenth century provides many examples of connections between religious sects and power groups, and the use of the identity of a religious sect to wield power. The politics of the state of Orchha are a case in point.

Bir Singh Deo built a fort at Jhansi and garrisoned it with a military order of Sannyasis. The *mahant*, Indergir Gosain, was the governor and in 1735 he revolted, and in the subsequent decade set up a principality at Moth. He too built a fort and annexed villages from Datia and Orchha. In 1755, he was dislodged by the Marathas, but his disciple, Himmat Bahadur Gosain, regained the territory.

---

30 Ashim Roy, *The Islamic Syncretistic Tradition in Bengal*, Princeton, 1983.
31 A Heltebeitel, *The Cult of Draupadi*, Chicago, 1988.

Such a mix of religion and politics was not new to the Indian polity, for it can be noticed whenever religious sects become wealthy or come close to power. But the political role of such sects is more crucial in times and places of uncertain governance. The intervention of colonial authority in the late eighteenth and early nineteenth century has tended to blur our view of such activities. Some of the groups involved seem to be reasserting themselves in contemporary times with the resurgence of the Gosains, the Mahantas, and such others in contemporary politics.

Implicit in communal motivation is also the search for power by those who have lost power, and who now regard communal organisations as a mechanism for attaining power. Apart from the *mahants* and *sadhus*, who are in the forefront of organisations such as the Vishva Hindu Parishad, there is also a substantial Rajput lobby which feels that it should be the real inheritor of power, on the assumption that prior to the coming of Muslim rulers the Rajputs were in power. In many of the lesser states, during these centuries, dynasties claiming Rajput origins continued to rule. It is not altogether accidental that communal politics is at a premium in the ex-princely states of central and northern India.

The politics of religion invariably changes the nature of religion as well. Since a religion or a religious sect has a public following and a public face, its form has to be remoulded to enable it to play a political role. There is, therefore, a constant redefinition of these in history, an evolution that historians need to analyse.

In the case of the parallel Hindu traditions, the last two centuries have witnessed the emergence of the idea of a single Hindu religion, similar in some forms to the Semitic religions, which have been the model. Teachers or founders are sought in the absence of prophets. Certain religious texts, such as the

Bhagavadgita, have come to be regarded as sacred books in the Semitic sense, switching from the religion of ritual and practice to the religion of the book.[32]

Attempts are made to suggest the existence of ecclesiastical institutions commonly acceptable to all Hindus, and which can, therefore, proclaim on problems of religion. The building up of the institution of Shankaracharyas is now being used for defining, as it were, the identity of Hindus on a much larger scale than before.

The importance of missionary activities and conversions, as becomes noticeable on a visit to tribal areas in particular, is in direct imitation of Christian missions, and contrary to the practices and precepts of Hindu religious sects of earlier times. The need to have a single uniform Hindu community is born out of the politics of the last two centuries, as well as the changes in society under colonialism. The use of religious identities for purposes of political mobilisation grew from issues such as the notion of religious communities constituting the units of Indian society, from the question of separate electorates, and from the system of quotas, which focussed on the notion of representation.

The increasing involvement of religion in politics has resulted in the communalisation of Indian society. In this, the particular construction of the Indian reality of the past during the colonial period has been influential, and therefore, the significance of historical interpretations becomes central. It is perhaps possible now to see a typology of communalism. In the pre-colonial period, the recognition of a religious community was more limited, as language, ethnicity, caste and region

---

32 For example in courts of law, the oath is taken on the *Bhagavadgita* in imitation of the oath on the *Bible* or the *Quran*, even though the symbolism and the meaning of the former in the Hindu tradition is different from that of the latter in their religious tradition. There would be some Hindus who would not regard the *Bhagavadgita* as their single 'sacred book'.

were more apparent bonds. Religious perceptions and hostilities were more localised. It was difficult to use a religious identity for political mobilisation on a large scale.

The periodisation of Indian history in the colonial period encouraged the two-nation theory, in which the Hindus and the Muslims were presented as communities generally antagonistic to each other. Muslim communalism was encouraged and used by the colonial power, and its counterpart in Hindu communalism became more articulate in the period preceding 1947. The national movement drew on religious symbols to foster national unity, but these tended to remain distinctive symbols, a tendency which has been intensified in the post-1947 years.

The qualitative change between this situation and the communalism of today is not only the increase of communal ideology among all religious groups, but also the militancy and aggressiveness with which communal groups take public positions. In the past, where there were clashes between those who identified themselves as Hindus or Muslims, and the root of the confrontation lay in what was believed to be differences over religious practice, the initial attempt could be to sort it out through a dialogue to prevent violence. This was inherent in popular religious articulation, for it affected closely the people whose religious affiliations were at issue.

Today the question of dialogue does not arise. The Vishva Hindu Parishad has not called for a dialogue: it has only called for the destruction of mosques. Its cadres, and particularly its subsidiary, the Bajrang Dal, cannot be called a collection of devout worshippers, given that the prime function of the latter is to wield the stick whenever it chooses to do so. The Vishva Hindu Parishad has to be recognised for what it actually is; not a religious movement but a political organisation, using the front of religion.

Riding on the back of communalisation is also the criminalisation of society, which this militancy has encouraged. That this is as true of the overwhelmingly large 'majority community' as it is of the 'minority communities', creates a different kind of discourse on the question of communalism. Political fire-fighting is being directed towards communal issues, and other more basic concerns remain neglected.

Since communal ideologies draw on history, the past requires to be analysed in sufficient detail, and from a variety of perspectives, to counter the supposed legitimacy of that which is being sought to be propagated by communal ideology. The communal distortion of history, when it is widely propagated, percolates into the popular consciousness, and the dislodging of this distortion becomes a Herculean task. The analysis of popular perceptions of the past, therefore, also enters the historian's agenda.

Can Genetics Help Us to Understand Indian Social History?[1]

Viewing the human populations of India since early history, it is thought that genetic analyses can provide some evidence of their origins and of the social history. But the categories used in these analyses have emerged out of historical conditioning and consequently tend to bring the argument back to the historical. The classifications are almost entirely socially determined, barring the single exception of the biological difference of gender. The commonly used categories are race, caste, language, region and possible isolated habitats. Of these, race has been a dominant category in the last two centuries, and caste goes back to much earlier times. Language, region and habitat are of recent vintage.

The beginnings of Indian history have been beset with contradictory theories about the origins of the peoples that created the fundamental cultures in the making of India. These contradictions focus on the question of the origin of the Aryans and subsequently of the Dravidians. Were the Aryans a people from

---

1   First published in Aravinda Chakravarti (ed.), *Cold Spring Harbor Perspectives in Biology*, Cold Spring Harbor, New York, 2014.

central Asia with cultural similarities to those of West Eurasia, who migrated and settled in north-west India from where they spread across the sub-continent? Or were the Aryans indigenous to India, and according to some, spread their culture from out of India westwards? Attempts have been made to use genetic analyses to determine the identity of various population groups and attempt an answer to these questions. The problem, however, remains since no such groups have survived as a distinct entity from that period. Furthermore, the categories have been, and constantly are, redefined by historians and social scientists, and the redefinitions no longer allow of an unimpaired existence across the centuries.

Historical evidence about the populations of that period – the second millennium BC – is dependent on archaeology and history. Attempts have been made to co-relate archaeological cultures in Central Asia with textual references from the Old Iranian *Avesta* and the Indo-Aryan *Rigveda*. The closest is the Bactro-Margiana Archaeological Complex (BMAC) sometimes called the Oxus Civilisation, dating to 2300-1900 BC, but even this is problematic.[2] Skeletal material from archaeological sites cannot be identified as 'aryan' since this is not a biological concept.

The western Orientalist reconstruction of Indian history began with the Aryans as founders of Indian civilisation. This, of course, is not the narrative in the early Indian Puranic 'histories' which make no mention of any Aryans in this role. The invention of Aryan foundations, therefore, is a nineteenth century way of reading the beginnings of Indian history. The Vedic texts earlier were revered as texts of religious belief and practice, and not as recording the beginnings of Indian history.

The word *arya* has two social and cultural connotations widely used in history but separated by three thousand years.

---

2   F. Staal, *Discovering the Vedas*, Delhi, 2008.

The first is its meaning from Indian texts.[3] This undergoes change through the centuries. Initially it is a rather vague word used to describe those thought to be socially and culturally acceptable and worthy of respect; who used Indo-Aryan/Vedic Sanskrit as their language; and were relatively well to do. In the *Rigveda,* the Aryan is differentiated from the *dasa,* a word used to collectively describe the other component of the population. The *dasa* is associated with alien culture and speech, unfamiliar rituals and with evil and darkness. Some, however, were rich in cattle wealth and subjected to raids by the *aryas.* Presumably it was these rich *dasas* who occasionally were the patrons of brahmana rituals. Gradually, the use of the word was extended to mean a person to be respected and was therefore used for Buddhist monks and for royalty. By the turn of the Christian era, it came to be used for the *dvija*/twice-born upper castes, whereas the lower castes are described as non-*aryas.*[4]

This was read by nineteenth century western Orientalists as referring to two races: the Aryan, and the Dravidian – represented by the *dasas.* Both were language labels that came to be used interchangeably with race. The correct usage is Aryan-speaking and Dravidian-speaking peoples, but Aryan and Dravidian used as short cuts took on the meaning of race, ethnicity and culture. But the imprint of race was stronger. Similarities between Indo-Aryan and early European languages provided a basis for maintaining that there was an original Indo-European language spoken in Central Asia and that the speakers divided into two, with one branch going westwards and the other finally arriving in India. The language and culture of the latter became the foundation of Hindu culture. The Aryans inevitably were

---

3   Romila Thapar, 'The Rigveda: Encapsulating Social Change', in R. Thapar, *The Aryan: Recasting Constructs,* Delhi, 2008.

4   Manu, *Dharmashastra,* 10. 45, 57, 66-73, (Trans.) W. Doniger and B. Smith, Delhi, 1991.

the progenitors of the upper castes; and the *dasas,* said to have been subordinated by the Aryans, of the lower castes.[5]

The construction of the terms Aryan and Dravidian grew from the study of Sanskrit and Old Tamil. Sanskrit was recognised as having cognates with Persian and Greek, and a theory of linguistic monogenesis was put forward by Sir William Jones at the end of the eighteenth century. A few decades later Ellis and Caldwell argued for a parallel Dravidian group of languages. The Austro-Asiatic group, chiefly Munda, was regarded as dissimilar to both. The picture was one of multi-lingualism and each language was equated with a race. The equation was strengthened by the theories of what came to be called 'race science', which maintained that identification by race was based on scientific truth. Classification according to race was influenced by biological studies of the time and some degree of Social Darwinism. Colonialism appropriated the notion that the colonisers were superior and the colonised, inferior.

The nineteenth century study of philology in Europe, which advanced rapidly after the inclusion of Sanskrit as a comparative language, made a particular impression on German Romanticism.[6] Sanskrit was now spoken of as the ancestral language, a theory also advanced by those Theosophists who had made India their home. This led to a search for an Indo-European homeland in Central Asia, later to be regarded as the source for Proto-Indo-European speech. The Comte de Gobineau was now searching for the pure Aryan race.[7]

This in part triggered the change to look for the homeland in Europe and the notion that the original Aryan may have been a

---

5   Romila Thapar, *The Penguin History of Early India,* Delhi, 2002, pp. 98 ff.; T.R. Trautmann, *Aryans and British India,* Delhi, 1997.

6   R. Schwab, *The Oriental Renaissance: Europe's Discovery of India and the East, 1680-1880,* New York, 1984.

7   L. Poliakov, *The Aryan Myth: a History of Racist and Nationalist Ideas in Europe,* New York, 1974.

blonde Nordic. Measurements of the nasal and cephalic indices became crucial to proving racial purity. This turned into a major exercise in India, where there was a project to confirm the classification of races by these measurements.[8]

Max Müller's study of the *Vedas* in the latter part of the nineteenth century, and his reconstruction of the early Indian past, put the stamp of authority on the theory of an Aryan race. Although well aware of not confusing race and language, he nevertheless proceeded to do just that, as did other scholars of the time. He argued that the word *varna* used for caste in the Vedic texts meant colour, and referred to the fair-skinned Aryans and the dark-skinned *dasas*. Caste was much emphasised as the distinction between the upper caste Aryans and the lower caste Dravidians. One of the epithets used for *dasas* was *a-nas* which he read as without a nose, and this was at a time when the measuring of nasal indices was regarded as firm evidence, although the alternative reading is *an-as*, without a mouth, i.e. not speaking a comprehensible language. Situations of conflicts between the two are mentioned and this was taken as proving that the Aryans invaded north-western India and established themselves as conquerors. This idea has now been discarded and the preference is for a graduated migration and much mixing with existing inhabitants – except among those few who insist that the Aryans were indigenous. Differences in language and rituals were obvious. The structure of Dravidian languages was not the same as that of Indo-Aryan and therefore the racial distinction was also underlined.[9]

The Indian reaction to these theories was an acceptance of their main ideas, which suited the identities sought by the

---

8   H.H. Risley and E. Crooke, *The People of India*, London, 1915.
9   Sumati Ramaswamy, *Passion of Tongues*, Berkeley, 1997;
     T.R. Trautmann, *Languages and Nations: the Dravidian Proof in Colonial Madras*, Berkeley, 2006.

emerging middle-class. But these ideas were reformulated and eventually came to be used politically. The category of race was gradually replaced by caste. Since there was no word for race in Sanskrit, the term *jati*, which together with *varna* was used for caste, came to be used for race. The preference for *jati* was because its root came from *ja*, birth. This was partly responsible for the change.

Caste as a category of exclusion, or as a part of a social stratification, is a way of ordering society that is characteristic of the Indian sub-continent. The stratification is based on dividing society into privileged and non-privileged groups, the first constituted by the upper castes and the second by the lower castes. The normative condition was that social mobility was not to be allowed into the former, whereas control over the latter was not in effect possible. Three broad groups were outside the caste structure, and were often referred to as *mlechchha*: the untouchables/Dalits, regarded as ritually polluted, and who were physically segregated and formed a separate social system of their own; the tribal-societies of the forest habitats; and those that came from other lands and cultures. There was a belief that an immobile, frozen society could be created and could function without change through enforcing the code of caste functioning, especially rules of marriage.

Two systems of caste organisation were juxtaposed. One was *varna*, where caste society was divided into four hierarchical components: *brahmana, kshatriya, vaishya* and *shudra*. These are often spoken of by scholars as a form of ritual status where the normative texts, such as the *Dharmashastra* of Manu, determine identity and functions. The relationship of one to the other is crucial to the system and conformation, at least in theory, necessary. The other was *jati*, referring literally to birth, where there was again a hierarchical division. Here the rules of birth and marriage were derived from clan functioning with an emphasis on occupation, and codes were largely absent.

There was some attempt to find equivalences with the *varna* categories but this was problematic as *jati* hierarchies prevailed largely in the lower two *varnas*, and as such they were more flexible. Neither system was as rigid as was hoped for in the normative texts. The mixing of castes was regarded as social degradation; yet many castes, high and low, resulted from such mixing. The exclusivity of caste was maintained, but entry into an upper caste status could not be barred to other castes as is shown by the contradictions in the texts. However both, the Orientalists – brought up on a diet of normative texts – and the Indian middle-class drawing inspiration from the former, believed in the purity of descent of each *varna*.

Indian interpretations of the theory of Aryan race went from one extreme to another and shifted the identity of Aryan. Jyotiba Phule in Maharashtra turned the theory upside-down as it were.[10] He interpreted it as indicating that the original inhabitants were the lower castes who were made servile by an invasion of brahmana/Aryan aliens. The latter took away the land of the former through guile. He drew upon various myths as a support for his ideas. The cultures that existed prior to the coming of the Aryans were, therefore, the creation of the lower castes. This argument has been useful to the identity of lower castes, particularly after the discovery of the Indus civilisation in the early twentieth century. Phule's reading shifted the focus from race onto caste, with caste as the differentiating feature.

Upper caste authors ignored Phule. Bal Gangadhar Tilak argued that the Aryans trekked from the Artic where they originated, and one branch came to India. Later, when there was an insistence that the Aryans were indigenous to India, Tilak's

---

10 G.P. Deshpande (ed.), *Selected Works of Jyotirao Phule*, Delhi, 2002, pp. 23-100.

theory continued to be accepted by arguing that the North Pole was within British Indian territory![11]

The reverse of Phule's theory was propounded by Dayanand Saraswati, the founder of the Arya Samaj – the society of the Aryan race. Underlining the brahmana perspective, he stated that the Aryans were linguistically and racially pure, and migrated from Tibet into India.[12] They established the purest and finest culture in India, which should be revived. The upper castes were Aryan, and the untouchables/Dalits were excluded. The latter could be incorporated, once they had gone through a purification ritual. There were some common ideas between the Arya Samaj and the Theosophical Society, also active, particularly in South India during the later nineteenth century.

In the early twentieth century there was another shift in the identity of the Aryan.

V.D. Savarkar and M.S. Golwalkar changed the identification from caste to include religion. The Hindus were now defined not only as the primary citizens of India, but also as the Aryans in the Indian population. All others were aliens. The term Aryan was now given a religious connotation. India i.e., the territory of British India, had to be the land of one's ancestors, *pitribhumi*, and the land where one's religion originated, *punyabhumi*. Therefore, only the Hindus were eligible. This was to be a foundational argument to the more extreme Hindu nationalism of the later twentieth century, often labeled as Hindutva. The concept of the Aryan was now getting enmeshed in a variety of interpretations and definitions, very different from its earlier meaning.

The discovery of the Indus Civilisation/Harappan Culture in the 1920s, with a script, still unread, changed the picture.

---

11 A.C. Das, *Rigvedic India*, Delhi, 1920 (reprint 1987).
12 Dayanand Saraswati, *Satyarth Prakash*, (trans.) *Light of Truth*, Sarvdeshin Arya Pratinidhi Sabha, New Delhi, 1935.

The Aryans were no longer the bedrock of Indian history. The beginnings now went back to the Indus Civilisation. What was its identity? It dated to a period prior to that of the *Vedas*, its culture was urban; therefore, different from the agro-pastoral society of the Vedic texts. The nuclei were the cities, and these were unknown to the *Vedas*. Since the language has remained unread, claims have been made both by supporters of Indo-Aryan and Proto-Dravidian. One solution to the problem was to maintain that the Indus civilisation was identical with the Vedic and represented its archaeological counterpart. This was first suggested by L.A. Wadell in 1925, when not much was known about the cities.[13] The Hindutva ideologues in recent decades have been saying much the same, but encountering opposition from many archaeologists and historians who find it unacceptable in the absence of evidence.

The latter had generally distanced themselves from the variants of the theory. The initial argument had been that the Harappan cities declined due to the invasion of the Aryans. This was questioned for lack of evidence and the decline traced to environmental factors. Extensive archaeological work in the Indus plain and adjoining areas revealed a large number of settlements of varied archaeological cultures, contemporary with the Harappan cities, some of which continued into post-Harappan times. This has led to a revaluation of the process by which the Indo-Aryan language spread in northern India. It seems more likely that there were small-scale migrations into the north-west and settlements within the vicinity of earlier settlements, or even merging with these. The *Rigveda*, the earliest of the Vedic texts, is generally dated to between 1500-1000 BC. It shows linguistic elements and vocabulary from Dravidian and Munda languages, which indicates bi-lingualism, which in

---

13 L.A. Wadell, *The Indo-Sumerian Seals Deciphered*, London, 1925.

turn would suggest a fair degree of the mixing of populations.[14] This would come about through inter-marriage and the assimilation of each other's patterns of living.

Scholars have argued that even when cultures decline, there is always the possibility of some of their myths, rituals and belief systems, being continued through the oral tradition. This relates to the question of which of the two cultures was earlier. Archaeology generally provides reliable dates. Those for the Harappan cities point to a beginning in about 2700 BC for the cities in the north-west, and a slightly later start for those in western India. The decline comes a thousand years later, in about 1700 BC. Textual evidence is less easy to date. The date of the *Rigveda* is tied to evidence from elsewhere, such as the cognate words and concepts in the *Avesta* from Iran, and the names of deities in the Mitanni-Hittite treaty, of the fourteenth century BC. These sources have archaic forms of Indo-Aryan and are therefore probably a little older than the *Rigveda*. This would, in fact, date the *Rigveda* to a little later than 1500 BC. In any case, it cannot be contemporary with the Indus Civilisation. The question of chronology assumes centrality if the Harappans are to be described as Aryans, which is at best only an argument of contemporary political ideology.

Much of this argument is motivated by a concern to determine the indigenous and the foreign groups in the population. But we must remember that there were no cartographic boundaries in those days: the boundaries of British India, which are the ones used in these discussions, were the creation of British colonialism. Earlier, the effective boundaries were areas of common languages, practices, custom and political control, the last of which was blurred at the edges. These were often as-

---

14 P.B.J. Kuiper, *Aryans in the Rigveda*, Leiden Studies in Indo-European, I, Amsterdam, 1991; M.Witzel, 'Substrate Languages in Old Indo-Aryan (Rigvedic, Middle and Later Vedic)', *Electronic Journal of Vedic Studies*, 5.1, 1999, pp. 1-97.

sumed and not necessarily well defined. In the circumstances, groups can only be defined as conforming up to a degree to a particular culture, rather than being dubbed indigenous or foreign.

I have tried to trace the mutations of the term *arya,* and the notion of Aryan as an exclusive category. Its application has changed over the centuries, and new turns of meanings have been introduced even in the way it has been used by colonial and nationalist scholars. Clearly the connotation of race does not apply. To argue that they were an exclusive and self-perpetuating group is not meaningful. Historically, it makes greater sense to recognise that from the second millennium onwards there has been a mixing of the descendents of the Harappans living in various parts of the north and the west with other populations of the time; and subsequently with those that have migrated into the sub-continent at various times, starting with the Indo-Aryan speakers. The borderlands, in particular, had mixed populations. These peoples then moved eastwards into the Ganges plain, with further mixing with the local populations there. The same procedure was followed in the movement southwards into the peninsula. The degree of mixing cannot be ascertained, but linguistic traces of other languages in a given language can be used as a cautionary gauge.

There is now a turning to genetic data as one source for monitoring migrant and immigrant groups, and arguing for a clear-cut descent of some of these. The intention is also to apply the results to ascertaining the identity of the Aryans. But as I have tried to show, Aryan is a social construct, and therefore genetic information is unlikely to be useful, unless the parameters defining the groups for analysis undergo some rethinking. Genetic data and analyses, through the procedure of collecting and classifying samples, may have to consider alternative criteria. Since the data involve social history, there is a very long span of time to be considered; not only for mutation, but also for assimilation from elsewhere.

Genetic profiles often assume the claims of *varna*/caste categories as unchanging and exclusive to be correct. But being socially created, with no inherent natural rules, identities of *varna* undergo change. In the Vedic texts there is evidence of this. The most striking is the category called the *dasi-putrah brahmanas*. These are brahmanas identified as the sons of *dasis*. The word could mean either women of the *dasa* group, or else a slave-woman who would be of the lowest caste. In either case, the label is a contradiction in terms. We are told that they were at first reviled by the regular brahmanas, but when their superior ritual power was revealed they were eagerly assimilated into the orthodoxy. Their progeny would have been brahmanas, but with a mixed ancestry. Among the better known in this category was the much respected seer, Kakshivant.[15] A similar kind of recruitment to the brahmana *varna* takes place in later centuries, with the spread of Sanskritic courtly culture to outlying areas. Priests from local *jatis* who picked up a smattering of Sanskrit were recruited to perform the rituals. Their composition of Sanskrit inscriptions on occasion shows their scant knowledge. But over a few generations the family would become proficient and claim to be of the high status brahmana *varna*.

Another *varna*, thought to be concerned with purity of descent, is that of the *kshatriyas*. As the warrior aristocracy of epic times and the multitude of rulers that were scattered across the sub-continent from the late first millennium AD, they were also viewed as a caste that preserved coherence over long periods. But as it turns out they are among the most open groups, perhaps because political power was in itself open. References to *kshatriyas* occur in the later Vedic texts and in the *Puranas*.[16]

---

15   *Brihad-devata*, 4.11-15; *Aitareya Brahmana* 8.23.
16   *Vishnu Purana*, Book IV (ed.), H.H. Wilson, Calcutta, 1961 (reprint).

In both, there are long lists of succession and descent. Yet even the most respected *kshatriya* among them, Puru, the son of Yayati and ancestor to the protagonists of the *Mahabharata,* is said to have faulty speech, *mridhra-vac* (which would disqualify him as an *arya*), and descended from the demons, *asura raksha-sas* (a serious disqualification of high lineage).

In the late first millennium AD, adventurers of obscure origin or feudatories who rose to independent status, would, on setting up independent kingdoms, claim to be *kshatriyas.* Support came from brahmanas who prepared genealogies for them which occasionally were fabricated, and performed the necessary rituals for their legitimation as *kshatriyas,* in return for a fee which was often a grant of land. Such grants became the nucleus of those brahmana families who a few generations down claimed to be independent rulers of the lands granted, and these families constituted a new category *of brahma-kshatra,* mix of both.[17] Mention is made in the *Puranas* of kings creating a caste of new *kshatriyas.* A reference is made to a king of Magadha creating a new *kshatriya* caste. The groups from which he created this caste were lower castes and those outside the pale of caste society. Dynasties of the period from c. 500 BC to AD 400 are said to be of either the *shudra* or brahmana caste. Foreign rulers, such as the Indo-Greeks, are described as *vratya* or degenerate *kshatriya.* The category of *kshatriya* was open to various castes that might wish to claim it, as happened fre-quently from the latter part of the first millennium AD. Those claiming this status merely had to demonstrate their power in the open arena of politics.

The *shudra* caste, which was the lowest of the four, was also known to take on a variety of professions, from artisans to

---

17 Khoh Copper-plate inscription of Maharaja Hastin, *Corpus Inscriptio-num Indicarum,* Vol. Ill, (ed.), J.F. Fleet, Varanasi, 1970 (reprint), pp. 93 ff.

kingship. Those that ran the administration in many kingdoms were *kayasthas* who are said to be of mixed caste, sometimes linked to one *shudra* parent. Literacy was at a premium among these groups. *Kayasthas* in some instances are known to be authors of Sanskrit texts and as brilliant as their brahmana counterparts.

It would seem, therefore, that to take *varna* as a consistent and controlled genetic group can be contrary to historical data. Nor can the caste codes as outlined in normative texts – the *Dharmashastras* – be taken literally. These were the idealised norms, but obviously they were not widely observed, although the *varna* labels continued to be used. In fact, the *jati* structure of society is more reflective of social reality. But this network is perhaps too complex to allow for correct genetic analyses.

Categories of population groups are sometimes used as units of social analysis. But populations, of course, cannot be assumed to be static: they frequently migrate. This is more characteristic of pastoralists in search of pastures and water supply than of sedentary agriculturists. But the latter are also dependent on fertile soil and water and are known to have moved to many parts of the sub-continent in search of better conditions. The desiccation of the Indus plain led to migrations into the Ganges plain, and from there in time to western and eastern India. In both these areas, there were prior populations of agriculturalists with whom the newcomers would have inter-married and have adopted some of their cultural traits. Encroachments into forested areas, which increased from the late first millennium AD, would also have involved interaction with the forest dwellers. The frequency of *apsaras*, celestial maidens, entering the genealogies, is suggestive of marriage with women outside the caste. Activities linked to trade, by their very nature require travel and habitats in areas beyond the usual, with some degree of inter-marriage. All this creates a mixing of populations. The border areas of the sub-continent lave been home to a variety of peoples. The north-western borders received large groups of migrants from Central Asia, Iran and Afghanistan. The north-east became home to groups coming in from Tibet, China and Burma. The ritual specialists and the more learned members of the brahmana *varna* were particularly mobile from the mid-first millennium AD. So too were the low status *jatis* of architects and sculptors. Architectural styles in the royal temples of the Himalayan kingdoms reflect the hand of artisans from distant parts of the plains. This met the demand for specialists of various kinds in the new kingdoms. Brahmanas from Gauda (eastern India), Kanauj (central Ganges plain) and Kashmir were employed in courts distant from their homes. Some among these established new *gotras* and *pravaras* – subdivisions of the caste – have names which suggest recruitment from local *jatis*.

Another category suggested for identifying groups is language. If this is used, then precision can only be assumed for current language speakers. Languages also migrate and travel, and are used by speakers other than the original. Those associated with ritual and with social and political status, such as Sanskrit, are often the most sought after. The spread of Sanskrit to south India, a Tamil speaking area, indicates elite groups seeking status through adopting this language, quite apart from its use in ritual. This also raises the question of how a group is to be defined through language, since language also reflects social hierarchy. For example, how do we define speakers of English in India? Studies of language can, however, provide some clues. The migration of a language, or its intersection with other languages, can be traced to an approximate extent through comparative studies of syntax, morphology and phonetics – methods used in linguistics; but the methods have to be used with a careful control.

Social isolation and containment is not associated with castes, but with those that were excluded. It might be more useful to consider the DNA pattern among Scheduled Castes, who have been regarded as untouchables throughout history, and whose mixing with other groups was therefore limited. These groups, now referred to as Dalits, were isolated because they were thought to be polluting by brahmanas. They had their own social code, distinct from the rest. Other isolated groups were the Scheduled Tribes, whose habitat in forests encouraged their isolation. The best case of this would be the Jaravas of the Andamans. Others, such as Angami Nagas and Muria Gonds, may have ceased to be isolated some time ago. Comparative studies of such groups both among themselves and in relation to caste groups might be useful. The lower end of the social spectrum is likely to be more meaningful in studies of DNA from a historical perspective.

For the historian, and specifically the historian of ancient India, there are problems with using the results of what is termed ancient DNA. Samples collected from archaeological sites can be suspect for a variety of reasons. They can be contaminated through lying for a few thousand years in the soil, as in the case of burials, or in porous containers, such as urns or wooden coffins. There can be decomposition and the growth of bacteria, which would affect the result. Some maintain that the DNA breaks down after death. It would seem that ancient DNA might require new techniques in collecting samples and analysing them. Techniques are improving, but how reliable they are remains somewhat controversial.

Of the studies done so far, the results have been contradictory, and historians at least find it difficult to use them. For example, on the basis of some genetic studies, brahmanas are said to be a foreign group in the population. Others insist that there have been no foreign elements in the Indian population, which is difficult to accept given the historical evidence, and that the Aryans are therefore indigenous to India. This also touches current political ideologies on whether the upper castes or the lower castes should be regarded as the inheritors of the land. There is a tendency to pick up only those results that suit a particular theory. Genetic studies have largely been based on conventional views of the components of social history. The contradictions could be used to search for a different kind of analysis.

There is today a considerable focus on epigenetics – processes that are of concern to determinations and differentiations of cells. There is also an interest in epigenetic inheritance – developmental variations outside DNA. Not all information is specifically encoded in genes, and the information outside genes can be significant. Questions have been asked whether there can be genetic identity in two persons who have epigenetic differences; or, whether individuals can influence their heredity.

Mine is not an attempt to resist genetic studies of the population in India. I would, however, maintain that where identities based on exclusions or differentiations are used, it is important to recognise that these are not naturally given; they are socially constructed. The social constructions have also to be taken into account and, if need be, the units of analysis have to be re-adjusted. One must remember that there was a time when science was believed to have certitude and that 'race science' drew on this. Science has certitude within the parameters of known knowledge: but when the parameters change, the certitude also changes and has to be adjusted to the new parameters.

Rethinking the Concept of Civilisation as History[1]

I would like to begin by clarifying that in this lecture I am looking at the concept of civilisation as it has been used in reconstructing world histories. The term has had philosophical and other connotations that introduce dimensions different from the historical. I am, however, confining myself to the historical perspective.

The history of the world from pre-modern times has, in the last few centuries, been projected in the form of stages, some culminating in civilisations. However, in the light of recent studies of history, civilisation as earlier defined is becoming rather paradoxical. The concept is a construction that emerged at a particular point in European history in the eighteenth century. It was a way of organising the study of the past. Other theories of explaining the past now emerging in histori-

---

1   This is a marginally expanded version of the text of the Ambedkar Memorial Lecture of the Ambedkar University, Delhi, held on 14 April 2016. I would like to thank Romi Khosla, Kunal Chakrabarti and Kumkum Roy for their comments on an earlier draft.

cal analyses, may lead us to rethink the concept. Historians today try and peel events, viewing them as part of larger, and diverse contexts, as I hope to show.

A civilisation implies a kind of package with specific characteristics. Thus the territory of a civilisation has to be demarcated; its history is identified with a period of high intellectual and aesthetic achievement – what some might call "high culture" including an emphasis on humanism and ethics; associated with this is a premium on refined manners exemplified by the elite. In addition, civilisation is articulated in a particular parent language; it is symbolised by a single religion; it assumes that society is stratified and there is evidence of a state and governance; its elite is distinctive and dominates its surroundings; there is a marked presence of what are described as aspects of culture – art, monuments, literature, music, all of a sophisticated form; and above all, a civilisation records its knowledge of the world and attempts made to advance it. The definition therefore is expansive and covers many aspects of the life of a society.

I have two concerns in this lecture. One is that a civilisation draws on the identities of its creators and its participants, but the identities of both change in the course of history; and secondly, that concepts help us understand social reality, but they in turn have to be investigated, and more so where they claim to be foundational to understanding history.

The somewhat spare definition I have just given needs enlargement. The territory is expansive resulting from the ultimate success of the one from among a number of competing others. The dominant culture monopolises the constituents of civilisation to the near exclusion of the lesser cultures that then tend to be sidelined. What are taken as the constituents of a civilisation reflect the dominant culture whereas there is much more that goes into the making of a civilisation that has historically as yet remained in the wings.

Change is endemic to most societies, either from within or from contact with other societies. This can disturb the social equilibrium resulting in either increasing or decreasing the integration of its various units. A civilisation, therefore, cannot be static as its constituents inevitably change.

Let me begin with how and when the concept of civilisation first came to be constructed. Used in France in the eighteenth century, the concept assumed a departure from a prior condition. The Enlightenment understanding of history, together with social Darwinism in the subsequent period, placed human society in an advanced evolutionary stage. It underlined humanistic values as embedded in the literature, and the belief that rational beings could control the world around them.

German writers differentiated between civilisation and *kultur*/culture. Culture referred to what was thought of as intellectual and artistic in terms of value and ideals, and to morality. Cultures again were not compact, enclosed and static. Civilisation, however, had a broader spread and included more, as the definition suggests.

Why was it given a specific definition? Perhaps we need to keep in mind the ambience resulting from historical change at the time. Europe was moving from the imprint of an aristocratic, and what is often described as a feudal society, to being gradually remoulded by the start of industrialisation and the emergence of capitalism with new social categories. Entrepreneurs of various kinds were reformulating society, but at a slow pace since the mores of the previous society were still viewed as exemplary. The emerging vision required pointing up the glories of the European past in a more insistent way than had been done earlier with the Renaissance.

This change coincided, and not accidentally so, with the acquisition of colonies. When control over these colonies by European powers became more direct and fruitful, it had to be conceded that the colonies had their own cultures, but with the caveat that the European achievement in the past had been by far the highest and best. The colonies may well have even had civilisations, although these had been partially marred by the presence of the primitive in their midst. This subtracted somewhat from the achievement. Recognising this perspective on their past, the colonised also began to register their new ambitions among the evolving new groups of people, and were anxious to identify with a praiseworthy past to compensate for their subordination in the present.

In a sense the seed of the idea of civilisation may have existed in the differentiation that past societies made between the dominant society and those that used a different language and had a different way of life. One's own society was always superior. But the growth of the idea into a concept of civilisation was associated with historical change and the need for emergent social groups to claim new identities and a clearly defined heritage.

Civilisation assumed that what preceded it historically did not qualify and was labeled as barbarian. This dichotomy was present in the self-perception of ancient societies as well, but with a different connotation. Those regarded as 'the Other' were assumed to be uncivilised. For the Greeks it was the non-Greeks, for the Chinese the non-Han, and for the *aryas* it was the *mlechchhas*. If the Greeks called those that were its 'Other' as *barbaros*/barbarians, Sanskrit speakers referred to some as *barbara-karoti,* speaking in a confused way. The barbarians, irrespective of whether they lived as nomadic hordes threatening the civilised, or even in the midst of the civilised, were recognisable by their markers – difference of language and custom. The concept of civilisation assumed the existence of the barbarian as a kind of all-purpose counter-point to the civilised.

In the nineteenth century the dichotomy was further elaborated. Human society was said to go through three stages of change. Starting with savagery, it improved somewhat when it reached barbarism, and this was prior to civilisation. Only some societies evolved to the third stage. It was thought of essentially as a process of evolution, and used to point up the distinction between the stages.

The other more effective route was seen in the imposition of the civilised on the barbarian through conquest, an obvious attempt to justify contemporary colonialism. A classic example of this was that the Aztecs of Mexico were thought of as being less civilised, therefore performing human sacrifice, and the Spanish conquest thought of as civilised, brought this activity to an end.

The concept was now used in two ways. One was its role in colonial thinking. The other was the appropriation of social evolution by theories of explanation in anthropology, archaeology and history.

Colonial thinking was clear about the distinction between the civilised and its alternate – the primitive. The coloniser as the representative of a superior civilisation, introduced it to the colonised, the uncivilised primitive. In India, two divergent views – the Utilitarian and the Orientalist – emerged from colonial writers. James Mill and Utilitarian thinkers writing on the Indian past saw the territory of India as hosting two nations – the Hindu and the Muslim – each intensely hostile to the other. Its governance conformed to what was called Oriental Despotism, pointing to the absence of a civilised society. The colonised, therefore, required correcting in order to qualify as properly civilised.

The Orientalist view differed. It began with William Jones in the late eighteenth century enquiring of the learned brahmanas as to the texts he should study to understand India. He was directed to the *Vedas* and to Classical Sanskrit literature. Significantly, the Buddhist and Jaina texts were largely ignored. Jones' comparative studies of language and religion were a search for parallels to the Greco-Roman.

The Orientalists and Sanskritists in Europe disagreed with the Utilitarians. They argued that India did have a civilisation that needed to be recognised. Influential among them was Max Müller who focused on the *Vedas*, especially the *Rigveda*. Such studies led to the theory that the *Vedas* were the foundation of Indian civilisation. It was subsequently argued that it reached its crowning point in the golden age of the Guptas. Seeing India as a single unitary civilisation, specifically defined, made it easier for the colonisers to understand the colony, irrespective of how problematic these definitions were. We have inherited these colonial views about religion, language and history, with which we still grapple.

Dividing the world into civilisations provided portals to the study of global history. Association with a single language, and preferably a single religion, meant that each civilisation could be more easily monitored as compared to non-structured history.

Asia, it was said, could boast of three civilisations: the Islamic, with Arabic as its language; the Sanskritic Hindu; and the Chinese, associated with Confucianism. I have often asked myself as to why Buddhism was lost sight of in this typology? It was once the inter-connecting thread through most of Asia. It was made to disappear in India, it faded in Central Asia, and was on occasion actively persecuted in China; yet it emerged as a crucial Asian link in civilisational markers and ethical values. A deeper investigation of the critique posed by Buddhist thought to many existing Asian cultures, may help us redefine some aspects of Asian civilisations. Areas such as Central Asia and South-East Asia would be significant from the perspective of initial Buddhist cultures interacting with later cultural articulation.

However, the concept of civilisation when associated with anthropology and archaeology took a different turn. Patterns in the development of human societies drew from the theory of evolution, moving as a trajectory from simple to complex societies but with deviations that could allow or disallow further change.

It was held that human society began with the stage of savagery in the bands of hunter-gatherers. Subsequently, there were societies of agro-pastoralists. Many took shape as highly efficient herders of animals – especially cattle and horses – and in systems of cultivating crops. The institution of family and notions of property, that radically changed society, emerged slowly. This took them to the stage of barbarism that was extensive and diverse. They were identified by the typology of the material goods they produced, such as pottery and metalware.

Some remained at that stage, others moved to the third and highest stage, that of urbanism. As in the case of animal life, evolution did not move in a vertical line for all societies. For some, a horizontal movement became permanent. Those not recognised as civilisations were described as cultures. A culture was defined as a pattern of living. There could be many cultures encompassed in a civilisation, but its definition was based on the features selected and said to be its markers. The primary features of the civilisational stage were urban centres, literacy, and the existence of a state, therefore high culture alone did not suffice.

This archaeological-anthropological trajectory formulated in the early twentieth century, has lately been extensively debated. The critique has suggested alternate ideas but has not annulled the theory. It has, however, been problematic in a few instances where earlier definitions of civilisation were already in use, as for example, in India. According to the archaeological definition of the twentieth century, the Harappan cities are the foundation of India's civilisation. These predate the generally accepted date of Vedic culture by quite a few centuries. For some of the Orientalists of the nineteenth century it was Vedic culture that was foundational to Indian civilisation, the Harappan cities not being known at that point. But this culture lacked some of the fundamental components of the civilisational stage, as for instance, urbanisation and literacy.

Harappan cities were not only elaborate urban systems, but were carefully planned by people who understood the working of urban centres. The location of public functioning was concentrated in one area – in some cases on an artificially constructed mound – and was distinct from an expansive residential area. Other features are familiar to us from our school text-books – a sensible lay-out with planned roads, a remarkable drainage system, warehouses and granaries, and complicated defenses at the city gates. Among the other aspects of an advanced urban culture was the central role of a system of writing.

We now have a somewhat contrary situation where archaeology informs us that the foundations of Indian civilisation lie in the pre-Vedic cities of the Indus Civilisation, but the Orientalists of half a century earlier had projected the *Vedas* as the foundation, and this continues to be preferred in some circles today. There is a significant difference between the two. Whereas lengthy texts are absent in the Harappa Culture even though a writing system is in use, the *Vedas* are oral compositions of a high order, but with no evidence of a contemporary writing system. It is difficult to identify the urbanism of the

Harappan cities in the descriptions of settlements in the *Rigve-da*, the earliest of the *Vedas*. Inevitably there are controversies today about the origins of Indian civilisation.

The concept of civilisation popular among nineteenth century historians was, of course, not the archaeological one, since that was excavated later in the early twentieth century. Yet it is the nineteenth century definition that is more often the one thought of by many people when they refer to Indian civilisation. I would, therefore, like to discuss the definition of Indian civilisation that has prevailed in the popular imagination since the nineteenth century.

The territory chosen was that of British India. The confidence of colonialism made it seem that it would be permanent and stable. Earlier names for parts of the sub–continent such as Jambudvipa, Aryavarta, Bharatavarsha, or even al-Hind, had shifting boundaries. But even British India broke up into three nations in the twentieth century. This was not unusual as every century has seen changing alignments in the borders of the many states and kingdoms comprising the sub-continent. There are no permanent boundaries in history.

In pre-cartographic times, defining boundaries with any precision was problematic given the absence of maps. The more common usage was that of frontier zones marked by geomorphological features, such as mountains, rivers, forests and such like. For instance, Manu describes Aryavarta as the land between the Himalaya and the Vindhya and the eastern and western seas. A study of frontier zones suggests that sometimes much the more interesting historical inter-actions took place in such zones. Frontier zones have the advantage of looking both inwards and outwards, and they even have the choice of deciding, which was which.

For a variety of reasons the geographical focus of high cultures shifted. The Harappans occupied the Indus plain and its extension but their artifacts are found as far west as the Gulf, and contacts with Mesopotamia have been discussed. The authors of the Vedic texts initially locate themselves in the Panjab and the north-western borderlands, and then moved eastwards to the Ganga plain. The second urbanisation had its epicentre in the middle Ganga plain. In general histories of India, the peninsula and the south are sometimes off the radar in this period, probably because the archaeology of their impressive Megalithic cultures differed from the cultures of northern India, as also did the Dravidian language associated with that area.

Speaking of frontiers and from the sub-continental perspective, the Kushanas were half in and half out. Their fulcrum was the Oxus valley. We may well treat them as integrated into north Indian history, but it would be worth asking whether they in effect, may have looked upon north-western India as a frontier zone of their own Central Asian kingdom? And if so, how did they see it? Did Kushana polity focus more on Central Asia and China? Indian texts have less to say about the Kushanas but they are a presence in the Chinese annals of the time, the *Hou Han Shu*. Indian writing of early times lacks curiosity about frontier zones and beyond, as compared for instance with Chinese inquisitiveness on the subject.

In controlling territory within India, the Guptas and the Cholas were approximately mirror images, one having a northern perspective and the other a southern one, separated by a few centuries. The Turks, Afghans and Mughals, irrespective of their origins were firmly ensconced in northern India. Interestingly, the Mauryan and the Mughal states incorporated the northwest borderlands but not the southern part of the peninsula. Territorially, neither made it to being a fully sub-continental empire. Identifying people with territory has now become complicated with the frequent inputs of those working on DNA analyses to determine migrations and the mixing of populations.

So in terms of the territorial base of the civilisation we are not speaking of a compact sub-continental area but of parts of it, that hosted a variety of cultures. The variations are pertinent to the notion of constructing a civilisation. But these are frequently ignored when selections are made of what goes into civilisation as a package. This applies not only to India but to other civilisations as well. In Asia, it would be as true of West Asia and China. What this suggests is that we should be sensitive to changes in the frontier areas, both overland and maritime. We should be open to how they may have contributed to the creation of what we call civilisation, since this would be pertinent to the evolving of cultures in various parts of the sub-continent. The view from the other side cannot be overlooked.

It is interesting that there was such a substantial interest in Buddhism among Chinese scholars but comparatively much less in Brahmanism, if, as we like to believe that the latter was central to Indian civilisation throughout history? At the same time cultures within themselves also evolve over time. This makes it necessary to see civilisation not as a permanent entity but as a continuous process also registering historical change.

Language is often a good barometer of historical change. We know that all languages mutate. Given the array of Indian languages the change was impressive, both through mutation and through contact with other languages. This poses a couple of questions for the historian.

One is that we don't as yet know what language the Harappans spoke. Attempts to read the Harappan symbols as Indo-Aryan or Dravidian have so far not succeeded. The Vedic corpus refers to the *mlechchhas* and the *dasas* as different from the *aryas*. They either spoke the Aryan language incorrectly, or not at all. They worshipped other gods and observed unfamiliar customs. There is also the puzzling group referred to as the *dasi-putrah brahmanas,* something of an oxymoron. Can the sons of *dasis* be brahmanas? But there they are, and respected by the brahmanas. It seems that more than one language was being spoken and more than one cultural group involved.

But let's leave aside the yet inexplicable and turn to certainties. For almost a millennium the language most widely used was not Sanskrit, but various Prakrits, though they all co-existed. The Jaina texts were initially composed in Prakrit, the Buddhist in Pali, another form of Prakrit. The Prakrits are related to Sanskrit, but their use was differentiated. Discussions on causality in thought, *dharma* and *ahimsa,* rationality, the existence or not of deity, and such ideas were discussed, not by all but by a number of people, in Prakrit. The evidence of inscriptions points to Prakrit being the initial common language used by both the royalty and the populace, with Tamil used in the south. The earliest inscription in correct Sanskrit dates to AD 150 with a lengthy statement issued by Rudradaman, a ruler of central Asian origin. Prakrit travelled to Central Asia, South-East Asia, and together with Tamil to the trading centres of the Red Sea. It was initially the main language associated with those who came from India.

Learned brahmanas continued to use Sanskrit. But its use on a larger scale, or the emergence of what has recently been called 'the Sanskrit cosmopolis', dates to the later period from the Guptas onwards. This was when it came to have a monopoly as the language of learning, creative literature, administration, and was the language of those aspiring to status. It expanded further with courtly culture, in newly established kingdoms. This required its use by local court poets, but also in official documents, where occasionally the scribe could even make mistakes. However, in Sanskrit drama women and lower castes continued to speak Prakrit, presumably as befitting their inferior social status.

Newly established kingdoms from the late first millennium AD onwards, when hard pressed would use the emerging regional languages, especially when new castes of local origin became upwardly mobile. However, Sanskrit was pre-eminent for over a millennium in virtually every branch of learning, and more so in courtly literature and administration and in religious scholarship, composed more frequently by upper caste authors.

The history of this prior patronage explains in part its high status at the Mughal court where brahmana and Jaina authors interacted with scholars of Persian, also patronised by the Mughals. Translations of the *Mahabharata* and the *Bhagavadgita* and other Sanskrit texts from Sanskrit into Persian, done jointly by brahmana pandits and Persian scholars, are well known. Such activity was not limited to an interest in religion but was more effectively a form of translating cultures. Patronage to Sanskrit in medieval times, as one of the languages of learning and formal religion, is borne out by the numbers of literary texts, commentaries and digests, that were composed in the last thousand years under multiple patrons.

This continued into modern times, with patronage from the colonial state conscious of the upper caste connections of Sanskrit. The literatures in other languages received less attention as carriers of civilisation. It might be worth doing a survey of what was composed in these languages throughout history, to gauge the lineages of thought and articulation. This in itself would be insightful in evaluating the role of the single language as a civilisational idiom.

Any text of any kind and in whatever language, assumes an audience. All composition is in essence a dialogue. If a text is written by the elite and uses the language of the elite, it reflects the elite culture, and can at best only indirectly reflect the participation of other cultures. To that extent it curtails our understanding of the civilisation.

Much the same can be said about choosing a particular religion as the single one to represent a civilisation. The colonial readings of religions in India described them as monolithic. But were they so? Many colonial scholars tended to see Indian religions through their knowledge of the medieval European past, with its single monolithic religion of Catholicism and later Protestantism. It is debatable whether religions in India were monolithic and unitary. Virtually every religion was articulated and propagated through a range of sects, each having the choice of being either autonomous or associated with another.

These religious sects have a long history. Their survival is also in part conditioned by their closeness to particular castes or caste clusters, nor is it unconnected with the patronage of royalty and the wealthy. This highlights the inter-face between religion and society, an aspect seldom given enough space in the concept of civilisation. By bringing together virtually every religious articulation other than the Muslim and Christian, under the label of Hinduism, the extensive divergence as characteristic of religion in India, with its unique qualities, was denied.

That Indian civilisation was characterised by a singular and monolithic religion, is unlikely. *Dharma*, which we today take to mean religion, was viewed as consisting of two streams. One was Vedic Brahmanism. This required a belief in Vedic and other deities. It insisted on the sanctity of the *Vedas* authored by the gods, and held that each mortal had an immortal soul. Strongly opposed to these beliefs were various groups jointly referred to as Shramanas, who doubted or rejected deity and the immortal soul, and treated the *Vedas* as authored by humans. Across the centuries *dharma* was defined as the two streams of the Brahmana and the Shramana, or the *astika/*believers, and the *nastika*/non-believers, which we today regard as the orthodox and the heterodox. The *nastika* consisted of Buddhists, Jainas, Ajivikas and those of such persuasion, including the Charvaka, with their philosophy of materialism. Interestingly the initial social context of the Shramanic rejection of Vedic Brahmanism, was urban.

This dual division was referred to in the edicts of Ashoka Maurya (*bahmanam-samanam*), in the account of Megasthenes, (Brachmanes and Sarmanes), as well as in that of Xuanzang, and continued up to the time of Al-Biruni – a period of fifteen hundred years. Patanjali, at the turn of the millennium AD, mentions it in his famous grammar, and adds that the relationship between the two is comparable to that of the snake and the mongoose! The Shramanas in some *Puranas* are called the great deceivers – *mahamoha* – who deliberately mislead people with the wrong doctrines. They are, therefore, *pashandas* – frauds. Sometimes the Buddhists refer to the brahmanas with the same epithet.

We are told that on some occasions the relationship between the two became violent. A deeper investigation of our history of religion may show us as being less tolerant and non-violent than we claim to be. We can certainly take pride in the absence, so far at least, of something like the Catholic Inquisition that forced people to make statements dictated by the Church or to recant. Nevertheless, the degrees of intolerance and violence that prevailed in the past and were linked to social and religious issues, need to be enquired into.

Intermeshed with religion and society was social oppression and the exclusion of those declared to be without caste or of the lowest status and polluting. Caste discrimination against the large numbers of lower castes was linked to ritual pollution and perpetuated by economic subordination. This was the Indian equivalent of the observance of other forms of discrimination in other civilisations. The practice of treating demarcated members of society as polluting, negates the idea of a tolerant society signifying as it does extreme intolerance, and a low rating in social ethics.

In practice, this was observed by every religion in India and by most communities. Surprisingly, it is rarely mentioned in discussions on ethical values and humanism in Indian civilisation, neither in the texts of the high culture nor in later discussions of Indian civilisation. Our current concern with this aspect we owe to the debates on defining the nation that began a century ago.

Yet, at a quite different level there was a dialogue and much discussion between brahmanas and shramanas on philosophical questions, such as, on the definition and use of logic. By the mid-first millennium AD the Shramanas were also using Sanskrit in philosophical discourse. But eventually Buddhism was to be swept away in most parts of India, leaving the Jainas in the main to defend and continue the traditions of the Shramanas.

The last thousand years have been quite striking in terms of the changes that were introduced at various levels in what we would regard as aspects of civilisation. The landscape changed. Temples and mosques replaced Buddhist monasteries and *stupas*. Some of the most magnificent Hindu temples dedicated to divergent sectarian deities, and also Jaina temples, were constructed in this period. These were endowed with land and their committees of control were into substantial commercial enterprises, as had been so with some of the Buddhist monasteries in earlier times. Economic enterprise was open to all religious institutions and places of worship, nor have these held back, since many have had and still have, substantial wealth to invest.

The religion that we today refer to as Hinduism also had roots in the teachings of the medieval Bhakti sects. These encouraged new forms of worship, some reflecting ideas from the presence of other religions, and they taught in the regional languages. In the transition from the Vedic to the Puranic religions there was a distancing of the later from the earlier, acknowledged among some, not all. For the majority of people Vedic belief and ritual as such, although patronised by royalty, became peripheral. Much of the teaching, attracting substantial numbers, was oral since the larger numbers were not literate. The result was a multiplicity of sects of every kind either drawing from or opposing the more formal religions. This receives less space in the classic descriptions of religion in Indian civilisation.

What I am suggesting is that the conventional description of what constitutes Indian civilisation, is partial. It barely touches and generally ignores the contribution of those below the elites and the upper castes. The concept of civilisation needs to draw from a far wider spectrum if it is to represent more than just the dominant cultures. This critique applies equally to descriptions of other civilisations. One could argue that the concept itself is therefore limited. Let me try and explain this.

The compactness of civilisation is in part because of its land-based and demarcated territory and the social origins of the cultures it encapsulates. But many of the achievements resulted from the commingling of groups, elites and non-elites, both within this territory and those on its frontiers, and sometimes beyond. The commissioning of a monument or a cultural object may lie in the hands of a wealthy patron but its creator is often a lower caste professional. Styles can therefore be a reflection of localities and popular trends, not limited to the elite and drawing in others.

Icons of the Buddha illustrate this. The Gandhara image from the north-west is Indo-Greco-Bactrian in features and style, whereas the one from Mathura has little of the Gandhara style and is strikingly different, as is the one from Amaravati in the south. It changes again in Borobudur and Angkor in Indonesia and Cambodia, as also in Dunhuang and Lung Men in Central Asia and China. The images do not conform to a single aesthetic, but do suggest the richness of the dialogues that must have taken place, unfortunately unrecorded, among those sculpting them. Surely some *shilpin*s and *sthapati*s – as artisans and craftsmen – also travelled with the traders, brahmanas and Buddhist monks to South-East Asia and Central Asia in the early periods, to assist with constructional problems, or the precision, if not also the aesthetics, of iconography?

How are forms transmitted to distant cultures? The idiom in a new context should surely be read in that context as well? The diversity points to the inspiration not being limited to a single elite source, yet the creators of the icons find little place in discussions of civilisation. How were the complexities of the Sanskrit manuals converted into visual forms by artisans not educated in Sanskrit? This is the interface that civilisation is all about, not the separation of the two.

Texts requiring scholarship travelled with brahmanas, Buddhist monks and traders. Many ventured beyond the frontiers, creating innovative mixed cultures that challenge the existing civilisational models. This would be more marked in the formation of new states, especially in distant lands. Some Indian texts were rendered into local languages and adjusted to local perspectives in an effort to imprint their own culture and influence patronage. The variations speak volumes. In the controversial additions to the *Hikayat Seri Rama* of Malaysia – one of the many versions of the story of Rama – the patriarch Adam carries messages from Ravana to Allah. Other variations are similar to those known in India, but what these say remains outside the delineation of the single civilisation.

Adaptations provide another perspective. It is being argued that the original Javanese version of the story of Rama, drew, not on the Valmiki text, but on the narration of the story in the much later grammatical work, the *Bhattikavya?* The question is why? The choice of one from a diversity of sources needs explanation, especially now when some insist on cultural singularity. Even if it is a transaction between high cultures, the cultural presence of the 'Other', is crucial to explanation.

Central Asia provides parallels. The carriers of the cultures were the same as those that went to South-East Asia, but the Buddhists drew greater attention. Buddhist monasteries marked the staging points of the trade routes that went from China through Central Asia and Northern India to the Mediterranean. This was the Old Silk Route. A healthy patronage encouraged each monastery to host murals of the highest quality illustrating narratives from the Buddhist texts, in the context of local history. Their versions become in a sense, a commentary on the Indian texts, an attempt to see a part of India from the other side of the border. Do their perceptions confirm our current view of Indian civilisation?

The involvement of Indians in this trade continued until the last century, although latterly in segments because of historical changes. For over a millennium it had cut across what were identified as the separate civilisations of Asia, civilisations whose distinctiveness we have thought of as being crucial to their identity. But in each case the achievements, be they in philosophy, religion or the arts, drew on the interaction of these cultures rather then originating in isolation. The traders took the initiative and the rest followed.

Indians and Chinese in the past came to South-East Asia through a maritime exploration. This linked up ports and hinterlands and required traversing the Arabian Sea, the Bay of Bengal and the South China Seas – an Indian Ocean route, linking the segments of the chain from North Africa to South China. This is not a compact land mass but the contacts it nurtured impacted civilisations. Like the Silk Route it virtually created it own cultures. Can we call it a maritime civilisation? It boasted of multiple cultures – high and low, literatures in various languages, architecture and art that competed in quality with that of what we call established civilisations. Above all it demonstrated that ultimately knowledge advances when there is an exchange between those in the know, irrespective of where they come from.

This is superbly demonstrated in the study of astronomy and mathematics across Asia, dependent on this exchange for many centuries. This was not just a casual mixing of ideas. It involved the careful sifting of what goes into any knowledge system so as to understand it better and thereby ensure its advance. This surely is the more essential requirement of civilisations. The ascription of origin to a single author was not the point. Authorship was the contribution of more than one. Nor was there a desperate competition to claim that one's own civilisation had got there first.

When we start to think of the concept of civilisation not as something territorially compact and pertaining to a limited period of history, we will perhaps recognise the limitations of singularity and isolation in the current concept. We can either dispense with it or we can redefine it. Redefining it will require that some existing ideas be unpacked and rejected, some repacked and some replaced.

Civilisations as we know them now, tend to segregate rather than to integrate our information on the past. Colonial conquests, the world over, with their new and precise boundaries, ended existing inter-connections between cultures. A case in point is that of contacts between India and South-East Asia. Various regions of India had connections with various parts of South-East Asia. Colonialism split South-East Asia into colonies held by the British, French, Dutch and Spanish. This carving up terminated the earlier links.

Colonialism reformulated cultural identities with new hierarchies of status both within a society and across its frontiers. This in part accounts for what are erroneously described as civilisational clashes. What is striking about the swathes of cultures that we study from the past, is their porosity. Territories, languages, religions however stable we would like them to be, are in fact constantly taking fresh shapes. The change comes from many sources: internal pressures that alter social hierarchies; alien cultures that accrete to them and take on new identities; diversities that transform even the cultures of the frontiers; and the ensuing perceptions that those beyond the frontiers have of us.

Civilisation is a process that evolves over a long period, mutating as it goes along. We have to recognise the mutations and discover their source. In focusing on the culture of the elite the construction of civilisation overlooked its dependence on the cultures of others as participants in the same society. The essential concerns with the 'why' and the 'how' in the history of various groups along the social hierarchy, and more particularly the groups that we today call 'marginalised' did not find space in the concept.

Overlooked in earlier histories these perspectives can provide revelatory insights by forcing us to peel the layers and refrain from insisting that civilisation is a uniform entity. Cultural articulations have to incorporate the dialogue between varying social groups in the societies that constitute the players. How did the participants in a civilisation perceive themselves and their own activities, and in relation to the social hierarchy? Did they all see themselves as part of one civilisation? This is a tough question but we may find answers if we are willing to enquire.

I would like to conclude with a reference to the recent and much discussed subject among social scientists of the World System Theory and World-Systems Theory – the two not being identical. The debate rather hangs on the centrality of the rise of capitalism to the creation of a world system linking Eurasia – that some call the *oikumene* – to the Americas. Each had their systems prior to the sixteenth century, but the question is whether this constituted a world system? Was capitalism a progressive change and did it mark a departure from earlier world systems?

For some an important point in the debate was the impact of material wealth that was not at the forefront of the concept of civilisation but was essential to the economies of exchange. It also gives a place to those that labored and those that were the entrepreneurs. This extends the idea of civilisation vertically to include the substantial contribution of the non-elite to its making. Horizontally it moves from self-sufficient blocks to tracking the flow of inter connections between systems and the consequent integration of both goods and ideas.

What is of interest to me in this debate is the shift from seeing world history as a collection of autonomous civilisations to viewing the inter-connections between regions, and the degree to which such inter-connections may have modulated the forms present in these societies. In other words perhaps historians today should try and hear the dialogues among and between the systems, and their consequences.

If we choose to redefine the concept, can we think of civilisation not as a self-contained homogenous entity, valid for all time, but rather as a process of tracking cultures even those perpetually in transition? The perceptions that this may provide, can perhaps so translate the past, as to give us a new understanding of both the present and the past.

RELIGION AND CONTEMPORARY POLITICS

The Politics of Religious Communities[1]

There was a popular belief at the time of Partition in 1947, that the division of the country would end the communal tension as those in favour of a separate Muslim state would migrate to Pakistan. This in part accounts for the slogan voiced these days that all Muslims are the progeny of Pakistan and should go there. Such an attitude arises from an erroneous understanding of what the partition of India was about and, more than that, a failure to comprehend the complexities of a multi-religious society.

That the solution to communal conflict did not lie in religion-based states was evident from the rapidity with which East Pakistan broke away as Bangladesh, and by the frequency of violent confrontations between variously defined groups in Pakistan. The fact that in every case the involvement is of members belonging to the same religious community, Islam, does not reduce the tension or the violence.

---

1   First published in *Seminar*, No. 365, January 1990.

The notion of the religious community being the unit of modern political functioning has its roots in the 19th century. Not only did the British perceive Indian society in terms of religious communities, as is evident also from Indological scholarship on the subject, but this perception was projected into political representation as well with the notion of separate electorates defined by religion. The acceptance of separate electorates by Indians was an indication of the social and political disparity being by then perceived as a religious one.

For colonial purposes there were two main communities. The larger, which they referred to as the majority community, was an amorphous mass to which they applied the label of Hindu (and this included Buddhists, Jainas and Sikhs), and the others. The minority communities were the more easily defined Muslims and Christians. Included among minorities were what later came to be called the Scheduled Castes and Scheduled Tribes, a nomenclature derived from constitutional usage. The term minority community at that time referred generally to the Muslims, the largest among the minority communities. Today we have to speak of minority communities in which the Sikhs also feature.

Societies define themselves by their own perception of what they think constitute social units. In India the notion of religious communities was picked up and reinforced, and was graded into majority and minority communities. It is debatable whether what constitutes the Hindu community today was in fact a consciously recognised community in the Indian sub-continent in pre-modern times. It has been argued that the very nature of 'Hinduism' in the past, its flexibility and the identity of belief and ritual with various castes, precluded the idea of a single, closed community characteristic of Semitic religions. There were in pre-modern times a conglomerate of communities, identified by language, caste and ritual, occasionally overlapping in one or the other of these features but rarely presenting a uniform, universalising form. What is often mistaken for uniformity, namely brahmanical culture, was only the culture of the elite.

In the attempt to make inter-caste functioning more cohesive and mould social groups into larger entities, the notion of religious communities has been an acceptable alternative over the last century. The opposition to substituting caste by religious community has been a source of major ideological conflict both within the national movement and since. This is not to suggest that one should return to caste identities, but rather to understand that the notion of the religious community is not embedded in the foundations of Indian civilisation.

The posing of secularism against communalism did not at one level face the issue squarely. It was, and is, not enough to negate the emphasis of religious identity in public life; it is equally necessary to encourage other alternative identities. These can also be sought from more analytical studies of the past where the nuances and sensitivities of a variety of inter-community relationships need to be investigated and understood.

There was also a lulling of the fears aroused in the 1940s by communalism with the adoption of a constitution in the subsequent decade where secularism was given importance and by the constant reiterating of the *mantra* of secularism, particularly at the level of the state, without vigilantly ensuring that it was being put into practice.

The centrality of communalism in our lives today, is now being more widely discussed than before largely because of the political success of the BJP. Yet, for those who have been stating for some years that communalism is on the rise and who have been dismissed as alarmists in the past, this is not surprising. It has, however, required the horrific political demonstrations of its success for there to be recognition of the change that goes beyond politics.

What is really disturbing is the increasing communalisation of Indian society where various religious identities are now in confrontation, predominantly Hindu, Muslim and Sikh; where religious identities are being deliberately reiterated, irrespective of whether such a reiteration is relevant or not. The seminal period of these communalisms is not the present, for they each have roots in the immediate past. More evident on the social and political landscape are the various *shakhas, senas, parishad*s and *sammelan*s, the Leagues, the *Jamat*s and Allah's Tigers, not to mention the Damdami Taksal – each of which has at its core an aggressive, narrow, political concern which is articulated in religious terms.

The state, during the last few years, has lent itself to the politics of these groups in attempts to manipulate them, instead of exposing them. Slogans on city walls carry the messages of these groups. Where the more aggressive among them go further and appropriate state space, the state has pretended apathy, where apathy means connivance. The Congress-I is now taking a 'holier than thou' attitude in its public opposition to communalism, but it has failed to explain what it was doing during the riots in Delhi, Meerut, Bidar, Bhagalpur and other places, when it was in control of the state machinery and was unable to protect citizens. When the representatives of the state, who are supposed to be impartial protectors of the citizens, become participants in the riots, then either the state has to take action against them or else it is to be understood that they have the backing of the state.

The growth of communalism is not merely the result of governments, which at best have been unable to contain it, and at worst have tried to use it to remain in power. As an ideology, communalism has a wider appeal and it is also other situations that have given it encouragement. Communalism has to be seen for what it is: an intermeshing of ideology and power, where groups aspiring to power use a particular religious ideology to subvert a social order and replace it with an order that is based on sharp differentiations between those who accept the ideology and those who do not. It also places power in the hands of the authors of that ideology. This combination of a religious ideology and power enables such groups to define social practice and law apart from symbols and belief, all of which condition the ensuing social order.

In a multi-religious society attempts are sometimes made to introduce ascendancy through other channels, such as claims to racial superiority or civilisational continuity deliberately defined largely in terms of ritual and belief, eliminating or ignoring other aspects that go into the making of a civilisation, and thereby also marginalising those who do not observe that particular ritual and belief. Such channels are diversionary for the centrality of action remains the intertwining of the particular religious ideology and power.

The major springs of communal support are from those who are in some ways disembodied from their earlier social moorings: those sections of the growing middle class whose standard of living has risen materially and who see themselves as having to modernise, without being fully aware of the implications of this process; who see modernisation as westernisation, and, therefore, an implicit contradiction between what they have been taught to think of as 'traditional' and what they believe is modern; and who, therefore, think they are establishing a 'traditional' identity by supporting the new religious movements. In the same way, they adopt the outer trappings of western modes and assume that this makes them 'modern'.

The insistence on a dichotomy between 'traditional' and 'modern' confuses the understanding of tradition, which is, in effect, a continual process of selecting from the past, both consciously and subconsciously. Part of the flotsam and jetsam which gets carried into the communal stream are the erstwhile princelings who have lost both status and power, and who seek to find a new status as purveyors of a disappearing world. The leadership of some fundamentalist groups and communal organisations includes smugglers and drug peddlers, the kind of clientele that has also found its way into political parties. Where the religious 'cause' is highlighted, it becomes an attempt at whitewashing other activities. This in turn encourages the criminal elements already present on the political scene, who can be relied upon to start a communal riot as and when required.

Aspirations to wealth and status, whether among lower caste artisans, some of whom have improved professional prospects with new openings, or among the middle class moving into new professions, bring with them intense competition and consequent insecurity. Apprehensive of how to remain on top, as it were, of these changing prospects, it often becomes necessary to search for either a prescription or a scapegoat. The prescription seems to lie in talismans, in what is depicted even in the most elitist advertisements, the wearing of *mouli* threads and *moonga* rings to avert the evil eye; the scapegoat is often found in the numbers of the other community who are seen as competitors. In the riots in Bhagalpur, the main victims seem to have been the Muslim weavers.

Added to this, is the aspiration to political power. Secularism in India has been converted into a system by which a particular party could draw on the votes of the minority community (initially only the Muslims), and the Harijans as they were then called. In the recent elections the Sikh vote has also become part of this process. Democracy is seen as a numbers game. Mobilisation is therefore crucial and draws on religious communities. The 1980s mobilisation by the VHP through the making of bricks and *shila-pujas* linked to the building of the Rama temple, and processions where riots became an assertion of power, combined both religious and political mobilisation in a manner which had so far been unprecedented.

If the initial appeal of communal ideology is apparent among the prosperous middle class, it does not rest there; for the politicisation of religion requires mobilisation on a large scale. Unlike the RSS whose leading figures tended to be from the upper castes, the Vishva Hindu Parishad draws on a wider group for leadership, extending to what would earlier have been regarded as middle castes and professional classes. Its missionary programme of converting Dalits and tribals to Hinduism (despite 'conversion' being alien to earlier forms of Hinduism) will serve a double purpose should it succeed: it will increase the numbers of those who can be called Hindus and it will reduce the numbers involved in the policy of reservation.

This policy as applied in education and in employment for Scheduled Castes and Scheduled Tribes has been a source of considerable resentment on the part of caste Hindus who regard it a threat to their opportunities for upward mobility. Built into this kind of communalism, therefore, is the implicit factor of keeping the Dalits oppressed, for even if the policy of reservation is dropped, any concessions made to Dalits will be resented. The fear of the lower castes breaking away from the status defined for them by the upper castes, and attaining a better status is endemic to caste society. It has been recorded even in the past, in what may be called the crisis of the Kali-yuga. On repeated occasions, from the first millennium A.D. onwards, there have been descriptions of the evils of the Kali-yuga where the rise of the lower castes is seen as evidence of the world being turned upside down.

Equally implicit in communalism is the place of women, which, drawing from the conservative interpretation of ancient texts and social codes, such as the *dharmashastra*s and the *shari'a*, forecloses possibilities of independent action. The religious ideology in communalism has to be defined for contemporary times and in its representation of the universal values of ancient times it requires that women be subordinated. Such subordination, often characteristic of those in power, provided the illusion of complete authority. The reality could often be very different in other segments of society, but these realities find no place in communal ideology. Whether it is the endorsement of the ritual death of a *sati* or the denial of maintenance to a divorced Muslim woman, the underlying statement is that of subordination. That a woman must know her place and stay within its bounds is also seen as the solution to the problem of the independent woman staking new claims of status on a society in the process of change.

The projection of the past in terms of communal history, namely that the history of India is to be seen as the glory of the ancient period when Hinduism was in the ascendant, and its decline is during the medieval period when that place was taken by Islam: this continues to be the simplistic view of Hindu communal groups. The Muslim communalists see the period of Islamic dominance as the period of glory, and Sikh communalists perceive their relations with the Mughal state entirely in terms of the religious confrontation between the Muslims and the Sikhs. The appeal to history for legitimation by communal groups is in effect a red herring. The issue is not that of the historical correctness of the claim, for the claims being made are in fact political and relate to the society of today. But by reiterating a communal history, justification is sought for trying to undo the past by communal actions in the present. A communal interpretation of the past, even where clearly untenable, is useful for whipping up hysteria in mobilising a community.

If, however, history is to be brought into the controversy, then communal interpretations of history have to come to terms with the many facts that are now conveniently ignored. It has to be conceded that there has been intolerance and persecution of religious sects not just under Muslim rulers but also under Hindu rulers, and by powerful Hindu groups even in pre-Islamic times. The evidence of Shaivite persecution of Buddhists and Jainas is conveniently ignored, even though it involved the killing of monks and the destruction of temples and religious sites. The very notion of untouchability is an extreme form of intolerance and persecution. Will the Hindus of today first come to terms with their own intolerance before rushing to set right the intolerance of others from the past?

The bulk of the conversions to Islam were not by force of arms but under the influence of Sufis and other religious teachers, and these conversions were frequently by *jati* where an entire caste or professional group would convert. This raises questions about the nature of Hindu society and what might have encouraged conversions. Relations between groups in society even if identified by religious practice and belief, are never simplistically black-and-white. The evidence on such relations in the past, and the analysis of this evidence by present-day historians suggests a very different interpretation from that which was current fifty years ago. But despite historians constantly reiterating this change, the old theories still hold in the popular mind.

The refusal to recognise that historical analyses have changed our image of the past stems from the refusal on the part of the mediators of knowledge (both the educational system and the media) to first read and then pronounce. It is far easier to go on mouthing old ideas, even if these are unacceptable to historians. The old cliche of Muslim rulers being bigots, to a greater or lesser degree, continues to be repeated despite the work that has been done on their policies suggesting a far more historically complex context for such policies. This is not a question, for instance, of Hindus being more aware of Aurangzeb, but of Aurangzeb being consistently depicted only in one form.

The media is not altogether innocent in fostering communalism. The fashion for glitter and tinsel as news, and the underlining of the need for media hype, has resulted in an obsession with instant stories focusing on the view of anybody and anything, as long as it can be presented as news. Thoughtful commentaries are dismissed as too academic for the press. Doordarshan, with a few exceptions, has been largely concerned only with projecting the lowest common denominator, both in politics and in 'culture'. It is, therefore, not surprising that the definition of culture assumes that Indian society consists in the main of caste Hindus transmuting into a middle class. The success stories of Doordarshan are seemingly endless serials portraying narratives linked to Vaishnava and Shaiva worship, which are sought to be projected as the national culture of India. At least if the aesthetic qualities of the original had been sought to be conveyed, it might have mitigated the religious propaganda.

The fostering of communalism in some cases requires the issuing of *fatwas* and *hukumnamas*. Alternatively, riots are made the excuse to damage, if not destroy, the religious sites of those one is rioting against, and this ensures a continuing hostility. Frequently, such sites, or others which become the focus of dispute, are in the centre of urban areas and, therefore, as property, extremely valuable. The acquisition or control of such sites becomes an economic asset as well. But communalism can also spread in a far more subtle manner, in the gradual building up of hostile feelings against other communities that results in a subconscious discrimination. It is strange that despite the large numbers of educated Muslims, few seem to reach the upper echelons of government.

There is, of course, in addition the involvement of the Indian diaspora with some facets of communalism. The Vishva Hindu Parishad receives extensive support, financial and otherwise, from Indians settled in the United States, Canada and Britain, as indeed do Sikh communal organisations from equivalent bodies in these countries. Centres of the VHP in Britain have received hefty monetary donations from official British agencies, on the grounds that the VHP is a purely cultural organisation. Muslim communal organisations, in addition, receive support from the wealthy in west Asia.

Financial support is not, however, the only encouragement to such organisations. The question of identity is crucial to Indians in the diaspora, for in the world of Europe and north America they are the minority groups in an alien culture. Yet they have to come to terms with this insecure situation, and their solution is the attempt to assert their identity by recourse to mobilisation on the basis of a religions idiom. Their minority character in foreign lands isolates them and they frequently seek unity in religious organisations, trying to combine a western lifestyle with 'traditional' religion. Such groups become the role-model for upwardly mobile middle class Indians who, with economic improvement, are, in any case, able to maintain close contacts with segments of their families who have settled abroad.

The existence of the diaspora has implications for the growth of communalism in India. The obvious form this takes is comments from groups and organisations, and even governments outside India. When Muslims outside India and governments of Islamic states condemn riots in India where

Muslims are killed, this is objected to as outside interference. However, as long as Indian society continues to define itself only in terms of religious communities, members of such communities living outside India will comment on the situation in India. And perhaps there will be more than comment. In August 1989 a Ram Janmabhoomi *sammelan* was held in London, and bricks intended for Ayodhya were worshipped by British citizens, both white and those of Indian origin. Such activities, particularly by the former, are seen not as interference but as welcome endorsement.

The Ram Janmabhoomi issue has been in the nature of a time bomb. It has ticked since the so-called miracle of the images appearing in the mosque was fabricated, before exploding. This initial step in the drama was taken after communal tension had reached a peak with the creation of Pakistan. The revving up of the tension towards an explosive climax was encouraged by the general growth of communal identities over the years and by the closeness of the elections.

Are there other similar time bombs still ticking, which will explode in the years to come? Such explosions can only be diffused if the state takes a firm stand on the Ram Janmabhoomi issue and does not make concessions to communal politics. The BJP has already declared that, 'Such issues cannot be resolved by court verdicts' (*Times of India*, 7 December 1989). This despite the fact that the site being claimed is located on disputed land. The VHP has announced that its next campaign will be to agitate for the destruction of the mosques at Mathura and Varanasi.

It is, therefore, now possible for any group to organise itself, gain some political leverage, and proceed to occupy prime urban sites in the name of religion. Once the Muslims, the Sikhs, the Christians, the Jainas and the Neo-Buddhists get into the act, there could be pandemonium in both urban centres and at archaeological sites, not to mention those which are also places of tourist interest. This is already beginning, with Muslim groups attempting to reclaim for worship mosques which have been desanctified and which are under the protection of the Archaeological Survey. The acquisition of the Ram Janmabhoomi will be quoted as precedent and the outcome can only be violence worse than what has been witnessed so far.

If the redressal of believed wrongs of the past become the right of religious communities, then temples located at the sites sacred to other religions will also have to be destroyed; although, with the predominance of Hindu communalism, other religious communities might hesitate to make such a demand. What, for instance, is to happen to the temple at the supposed Krishna Janmabhoomi, which is built at the site of Katra in Mathura, and which, according to one authority, was the site of a Buddhist religious complex, and could therefore be claimed by the Buddhists? How far back in history will we have to go in order to satisfy the politics of religious communities?

It is not election results alone that will condition the future of communalism in India. If the reasons for the rise of communalism are understood, then it becomes clear that it is not religious sentiment that is at stake, but the exploitation of this sentiment at a moment in time when there is apprehension about the present and the future. The apprehension has to be reduced and the easy slipping into religious identities as social units has to be questioned.

Alternative identities will undoubtedly emerge with the growing strength of lower caste and Dalit movements, as also with the demands of Scheduled Tribes for greater representation and statehood. There are already movements in this direction that tend to be overshadowed by the immanence of communal violence. What Hindu communalism fails to recognise is that at the end of the road there is not going to be a dominance of the majority community because, despite its supposed uniformity at present, given that the real objective is the acquisition of power, it too will split into contending groups.

The fundamental change which is taking place in the form of Hinduism, which has been variously described as New Hinduism or, as I would prefer, Syndicated Hinduism, will eliminate the very flexibility which allowed the *sanatana dharma* to survive. From a religious form that had the openness of Upanishadic philosophy, it is now being reduced to the worship of bricks. Its aggressive militancy belies its earlier claims to tolerance and non-violence. When Hindu *mahanta*s refer to themselves as *imam*s and talk about issuing *fatwa*s, as happened recently in connection with the election of a member of the Ram Janmabhoomi Mukti Yajna Samiti, and when reference is made to ostracising non-believers, then the divorce from earlier Hinduism is complete.

The support of a religion as a form of the articulation of religious sentiments, beliefs and practices is not under question. The objection is to the manipulation of such identities for the purposes of political mobilisation, where the manipulation requires violence and aggression and destruction in order to succeed. In this latter sense, religious communities are imagined communities, and it is therefore possible to change them. In the search for identities as alternative to the notion of the religious community for purposes of political mobilisation, liberalisation in all such communities will have to proceed at the same pace. Minority insecurity underlies their conservatism and hesitancy to change. Civil codes and criminal laws will have to be common.

There is a difference between the communalism of the majority and that of the minorities. The former is often born of an aggressive assertion of power. The latter is born of fear and a sense of powerlessness in the face of the majority. In a society that sees itself as a conglomerate of religious communities, the onus for removing this fear lies with the majority community. Enhanced communalism can make communalism the only form of political dialogue. In each case, communalism suppresses the aspirations of other groups, as indeed of dissident groups within the community, since it is based on the fundamental assumption that the believers are superior to the rest – be it a Pakistan, a Khalistan or a Hindu Rashtra – and the believers are defined by those who have created the communal ideology. Its removal, therefore, becomes a necessity.

But such qualifications do not mitigate the existence of either the majority or the minority communalisms, for neither is justified. The fight is not only against the dominance of Hindu communalism asserting itself amidst a range of minority communities, but also the need within each community to marginalise its communal elements. This would be imperative if there is to be an alternative to the politics of religious communities

Justice in Gujarat[1]

In 1947, Partition was accompanied by massacres so gruesome that many said they would never allow this to happen again. But we have been through three genocides since then and the perpetrators of the violence continue to be powerful members of our society. The three I am referring to are the anti-Sikh genocide in Delhi in 1984, the anti-Muslim genocide in Gujarat in 2002, and the anti-Christian Dalit genocide in Orissa, 2007-2008. Genocide seems to follow a pattern in India post-1947. In each case, it is the majority Hindu community that targets and kills those of a minority community of a specific and different religion, and in numbers far larger than are killed in communal riots. The justification for the killings is said to be some action on the part of the non-Hindus, that is said to have angered the Hindus who then seek revenge. But, apart from the accusation being true or not, does any such action justify genocide? The actual motive often lies in the politics of

---

1   First published in *Hard News*, November 2012.

the region. Religious antagonism or conciliation is what gets discussed in the aftermath, while the political and economic motives get brushed aside.

This raises many questions. These are not irrelevant and we need to have clear answers.

Does this have to do with religion, or with the way religion is mobilised politically, with religious organisations becoming the agencies of political ideologies? Are Hindus by nature more given to killing, despite all the hype about belonging to a non-violent and tolerant culture? Or, why is it that the agencies of law and order – the police and administration – seem not to protect those attacked when they are members of a religious minority, or Dalits or women? Are they so infiltrated by religious extremist influence – Hindus in the main – that they do not bother to defend those attacked?

Or, does nationalism define 'Indian' now to mean 'Hindu', and therefore the Hindu has primacy as citizen? Does this make non-Hindus dispensable? One wonders what has happened to the earlier concept of being Indian, a category inclusive of all communities; a concept that my generation of Indians stood by? If the violence is spontaneous, and in the name of a religion, then it is a blot on the religion of the community that perpetrates the violence, be it Hindu, Muslim or Sikh. If it is orchestrated by the State, then a State resorting to genocide can hardly claim to be a well-administered State. Only an incompetent government is unable to control what turns into genocide. This negates claims of good governance.

Given the scale and type of violence, there is little doubt that in Gujarat the police and administration were ineffective, to say the least. These are agencies that, now, all over the country, see themselves not as those whose duty it is to protect citizens, but rather as primarily having to be subservient to political authority, their function being to carry out the orders of those governing. There are a few, but unfortunately too few, who still see themselves as protectors of citizens and defenders of the rights of citizens. Among these few, there have been some police officers and administrators who have suggested that the violence in Gujarat was orchestrated by those governing. Their views cannot be easily dismissed.

If the administration in Gujarat is as efficient as is projected by Narendra Modi and his supporters, then some questions still remain to be answered. Even on the specific issues linked to the genocide, there are gross inefficiencies.

Of those accused of setting fire to the coaches at Godhra, I am told that 84 are still awaiting judgement. Ten years is a long time for there to be no judgement on what is held to be a simple case of arson. Is it a simple case of arson? Why is it that almost 50 per cent of the persons said to be missing – over 200 persons – cannot be traced, and records are missing? As is usual in such incidents, the paying of full compensation has been delayed. This smacks of normal corruption in the administration from which the Gujarat administration is obviously not free.

Going beyond 2002, there is a need to understand why there was a genocide – particularly in Gujarat. The anti-Sikh and anti-Christian Dalit killings were concentrated in limited areas, but, in Gujarat, the killings were widespread. If Gujarat is a well-administered, prosperous state, why were the killings allowed? What motivated these killings?

The *patidars* lived off the rich income from their lands, there was money pouring in from Gujarati NRIs living in the West, and the corporates were investing in Gujarat. What is it that the rich Hindus feared and fear? Is it that there would be a loss of subordinated Muslim labour, employed by the *patidars*, if the standard of living of the labourer improves? The import of unskilled labour from UP and Bihar seems to point to a problem with local labour. Is there a competition for employment, making it necessary to destroy skilled Muslim artisans? Is there a fear of the upward mobility of Muslim OBCs and Dalits, also asking for quotas? Why is the Gujarat government unable to bring water to parched areas to relieve the desperation of farmers?

The enrolment of the Scheduled Tribes in the killings also needs investigation. In all tribal societies of central India, the money-lender – the *dhiku* – is the object of antagonism, and for obvious reasons. Who are the money-lenders in the tribal areas of Gujarat? Where they happen to be Muslim, the instinctive dislike could be channeled into violence. But there has to be some agency legitimising this violence. Who constituted this agency?

If the State is so well-administered, how could the Hindu extremist gangs vandalise the teaching departments in a university – the Faculty of Fine Arts in the Maharaja Sayajirao University of Baroda – manhandle the faculty, and have the department closed? All this is done in the name of one alleged action of the department having, supposedly, hurt the sentiments of some Hindus. What was once the prestigious MS University is now powerless to defend its employees and to take action against political gangs. Is this a demonstration of good administration?

The assault on women was particularly vicious in the Gujarat killings. Women are generally the most devastated victims, because the attack on them cuts both ways. It is bad enough that they are raped; the fact that they are raped by the attacking community makes them doubly unacceptable to their own community as well. This attitude has not changed since 1947. Why do we avoid acknowledging that rape is also an index of sexual perversion among men?

Where communal conflicts occur we need to know much more precisely the identity of the perpetrators of the killings and rape, and that of the victims. Categories such as 'Hindu' and 'Muslim' are, at one level, too broad. A closer look at neighbourhoods, communities, an understanding of who employs whom and what they work at, relating to both victims and the perpetrators, would tell us something about whether the antagonism is spontaneous or is rooted in other factors.

In addition to all this, there is an ideological build-up of almost a century in Gujarat, encouraging hatred between Hindus and Muslims. Two major theories have enflamed this.

There has been a historical distortion of the raid of Mahmud of Ghazni on the Somanatha temple. Through successive narratives a theory has emerged that it resulted in a trauma among the Hindus, which they have nurtured for a thousand years.

This theory was first put forward by British colonial historians, in the 19th century. Mahmud's raid on Somanatha was converted by them into an idiom of Hindu-Muslim relations. Subsequently, both Hindu and Muslim historians of the earlier 20th century continued to present it in the same way. The wider context of the event in local history, and what followed, was ignored. There was just the repetitive chorus of Hindu-Muslim antagonism.

It was taken up by K.M. Munshi and people of his ilk, who fed it into popular historical novels, eagerly read by the Gujarati middle class. Munshi left out crucial evidence in his version of the raid by Mahmud, such as major contradictions in the Persian and Turkish texts about the event, and what was attacked; as also that the Sanskrit inscriptions refer to commercial deals involving the estates of the temples in the town and their trade with Arab traders, a couple of centuries after Mahmud; or that the temple was restored by a Jain ruler and was in use for a long period before it declined. All these factors nullify the idea of a Hindu trauma.

The *rath yatra* organised by the BJP to Ayodhya was flagged off from Somanatha. It was described as a wake-up call by the Hindus avenging their trauma – even if it was late by a thousand years.

The other idea, which also had a political fall out effect in later years, was that of *asmita* – the unity of being Gujarati, or Gujarati-ness. This was based on the Hindu Gujarati culture of the upper castes. Muslims and Christians were, therefore, aliens.

This view also reflects the theories of Savarkar and Golwalkar: that only Hindus could be citizens of India, because India is their *pitri-bhumi,* the land of their ancestors, and their *punya-bhumi,* the original home of their religion.

It is also not surprising that Modi has chosen Vivekananda as his symbol, since Vivekananda's definition of Hinduism was upper-caste and exclusive. This is also linked to the definitions of Indian culture by the more influential NRI groups, which again do not include non-Hindu culture as Indian. Such groups are vocal in legitimising Modi's Gujarat.

This inevitably raises the question of secularism. Should we continue to define secularism in a specifically Indian way, to mean merely the co-existence of all religions, irrespective of the status they may have? Given that the followers of these religions in India have an unequal status, there is bound to be conflict. This was a definition specific to Indian nationalism at a time when communal politics were coming to the fore. Today, we need to return to the original meaning of secularism. As originally discussed, a secular society is one where all human rights are ensured by the State equally, and where religious organisations do not control the essentials of the social, political and economic functioning of a society.

Gujarat is not a secular state: it does not conform to either of these two definitions. It does not have religious co-existence, nor are the functions of civil society kept distinct from religious organisations, or from political organisations with a religious ideology. To that extent its system of governance negates one of the fundamental principles of the Indian Constitution.

And what about the victims of genocide?

We hear so much these days about cultivating a sense of forgetting and forgiving, and even repentance. Victims cannot forget what they have been through. The resulting fear and hatred does fester. This would also apply to others who have suffered in communal riots and terrorist attacks by a variety of religiously inspired organisations – Hindu, Muslim and Sikh – that bring death and destruction.

Apologies from the perpetrators of violence could be a prelude to the process of reconciliation, but the right conditions have to exist for this to happen. Reconciliation requires an equal parity between victimisers and victims, where the victims are no longer victims but have the power to propose and implement reconciliation. It would require an acknowledgement from the victimisers that they have victimised the victims. But would those who encouraged the victimisers to kill, in Gujarat, be willing to apologise, or even make a conciliatory gesture to the victims? That would be a confession of guilt, and guilt is what Modi is constantly denying. If this is not likely to happen, then the victims can only choose the pursuit of punitive justice.

Genocides are frightening because killing is seen as the political solution to problems. These are the beginnings of fascism, which targets a particular community as enemy. This encourages the isolation of that community, forcing it to live in ghettos. Ghettos are easy to control and easier to destroy, as we know from Gujarat, and as we also know from the extermination of Jews in Germany. To recognise the initial stages of fascism, and to confront it, it is necessary to prevent it from being seen as a political solution. To insist on justice, therefore, is, at this point, an imperative.

The Past as Present and
the Present as Past[1]

To have been asked to address the Lahore Literary Festival this year makes me feel extremely privileged. I would like to express my deep appreciation for the honor that you have done, both to me and to the discipline of history. My visits to Lahore – even though not many – have been moments of much nostalgia, entwined with memories of childhood. So thank you for giving me yet another occasion for recalling my own past.

I shall be making a few comments on the history of the subcontinent, more specifically on the way in which the past and the present have impinged on each other in our understanding of ourselves as historical societies. My focus of study has been early India, but inevitably in such studies, the shadow of the present hovers over the past. Its visibility depends on the historian's awareness of both the shadow and the substance.

---

1   Delivered as keynote address at the Lahore Literary Festival, 18 February 2015.

Let me begin with a question that we should ask ourselves but we seldom do. Are we aware of the past that is implicit in our current actions? I am not referring to the individual level where we all have pasts and keep conversing with our memories. I am referring to us as a collective – as a society, a culture, a nation. Do we stop to ask how much of what we call our tradition or our heritage is actually from the past? Or are we inventing it as we go along and then passing it off as coming from the past? We like to think that the present is different from the past but continuity suggests security.

The historian E.H. Carr maintained that history is a dialogue between the past and the present. The contradiction is that we as historians try to see the past on its own terms but our reading of it is mediated by the present. Perhaps it would be better to say that history is a dialogue between the present and the assumed past, where the assumptions do indeed come partly from the requirements of the present.

This is where historiography, that is the history of the historians writing history, becomes central. The author of a historical text is placed under scrutiny. To what degree does the historian quote evidence that is reliable and draw out logical arguments that present a reasoned explanation of past events and persons. What is the historian's intellectual framework? More recently some of us, who write on periods further back in time, have been asking the question of how societies in the past have represented their perceptions of what they saw as their own past. We are attempting to extend history beyond what is familiar.

The study of how history is written is crucial. This was recognised in discussions that emerged during the European Enlightenment. Two new ideas took shape in linking the past with the present. One was that the historian's perspective can be influential in interpreting history. The other was that the sources used by the historian have to be as complete as possible and that they have to be assessed for reliability. History is not fantasy, however attractive imagined history may be. These ideas came to India together with colonial scholars in the 19th century and they wrote the history of India starting from scratch. They conveniently claimed that Indians never had a sense of history and therefore wrote no histories of their own. This meant that the history of the subcontinent would have to be discovered and written up by colonial scholars. This they began to do.

These investigations led first to recovering records that had been forgotten, and then to interpreting them as data for histories. This first exercise was a remarkable breakthrough based on deciphering scripts, excavating ancient sites and studying ancient texts, all done in a systematic way. But the interpretation was largely tied into backing up contemporary colonial policy. It was sought to be legitimised through the colonial understanding of the Indian past.

Two basic theories emerged from this that skewed our pre-modern history and have dominated our understanding of our societies in modern times. Not that history controls our thoughts and attitudes but it becomes the bedrock of self-comprehension. One theory was that of James Mill in his History of British India in 1818, two centuries ago. Indian history was projected as that of two relatively independent nations, the Hindu and the Muslim defined by religion, and forced to live in the same territory, and this led to immense mutual hostility.

This kind of argument was appropriated by religious nationalisms, both of the Hindu and Muslim variety. The colonial view was that the British had salvaged Indian civilisation from this destructive antagonism. The Hindus, it was said, were released by British rule from the tyranny of Muslims and thereby from centuries of slavery. This is sometimes reiterated even today. It became an axiom of some aspects of colonial policy. It is surprising that more Indian historians did not seriously investigate the veracity of such statements. It reflects the nature of colonial control on the thinking of the colonised and the shackles that have not been entirely removed.

The other theory that took root in the later 19th century was the theory of Aryan race. It began with Europe searching for its ethnic origins, and the search getting entwined with ancient texts from India. It was much debated in European scholarly circles, especially in Britain, France and Germany. In Europe the debate was fueled by the search for origins, with a deliberate negation of the Semitic – hence the attraction of Aryan ancestors. The closeness of the Greek and Sanskrit languages suggested that they possibly originated from a common language. A jump was then made from ancestral language to ancestral race. Vedic Sanskrit texts described as Aryan led to Europe and India being linked through language and ethnic connection. Max Müller, a stalwart propagator of the idea, referred to both Emanuel Kant's *Critique of Pure Reason* and to the *Vedas*, as Aryan heirlooms. Keshub Chandra Sen, at a more pragmatic level, regarded the coming of the British to India as the reunion of parted cousins. This theory of Aryan origins gave added status to upper caste superiority.

Some European thinkers who did not subscribe to the theory of Aryan race, such as Hegel, emphasised the negative characteristics of Indian civilisation. A substantial number of colonial scholars thought likewise, although there were those who were more appreciative. But the Aryan foundations of Hindu civilisation became a popular theory. It is now seeded in discussions on Hindutva/Hindu-ness and in the concept of Hindu Rashtra. This requires an extension of the Aryan identity to accommodate the Harappans who were discovered a century later. So now it is being said by some that the Harappans were also Aryans.

However, not all versions of the theory were similar. There were a few alternate reconstructions that turned the theory on its head, as it were. Among them, Jotiba Phule argued that the original inhabitants of the subcontinent were the non-brahmana castes and the Dalits, and that the Aryans were alien brahmanas who through deceit and conquest became the ruling oppressors. This reading favored the lower castes as the initial legitimate inhabitants. It coincided with lower caste and Dalit movements seeking political recognition.

Those writing on the Aryans in India seldom gave a cross-reference to the debate on Aryanism in Europe. Nor was there the same degree of discussion on the origins of the non-Hindus living in India. Since caste, despite conversion, was not discarded in non-Hindu religions, the upper castes in each religion often claimed an ancestry from lands across the borders, but all the rest were given local origins.

Most historians supporting the nationalist ideology questioned some of the theories of colonial history writing. But golden ages remain necessary to nationalisms of every color. So, they maintained that kingdoms in ancient India were governed by constitutional monarchs, poverty was unknown in early times, Indians were given over to spirituality unlike the West that had succumbed to materialism, and ancient India was the golden age. As is normal in all societies, groups seeking power in the present often acquire self-confidence and legitimacy by glorifying those whom they regard as their predecessors. The golden age is preferably in the remote past so that it cannot be closely questioned. The theories of James Mill and Max Müller remained largely unchallenged.

Let me turn now to a different kind of history that my generation has been writing. Departing fundamentally from colonial interpretations, we have suggested alternate perspectives on history. We have moved away from the earlier myopic view of giving priorities to the religious identities of elite groups when explaining all events. In the process we have questioned those nationalist interpretations that still subscribe to the theories of James Mill and Max Müller. Let me just add that the issues I shall be discussing are linked to the history of the entire subcontinent. They are not just issues linked to the history of present-day India.

In periodising Indian history some historians had replaced the labels Hindu, Muslim and British with Ancient, Medieval and Modern, since the latter sounded more secular. But this was effectively a continuation of the earlier periodisation with only an alteration of the label. Recently however, new markers have replaced these older labels. They are more in keeping with the new perspectives on historical change.

The religion of rulers that had been emphasised often made little difference to society at large. And of course even within royal families, patronage to particular religious sects changed from one king to the next. Royal families, since they used marriage alliances as part of their diplomacy, also had to accommodate more than one religion. Thus some Mughal royalty and aristocracy had Hindu Rajput mothers.

Religion in the Indian past was not invariably a well-defined, precise system of belief and practice. For many it remained somewhat ambiguous. At the level of the larger society beyond just the elite, the most prevalent religious practices and beliefs were neither formal Hinduism nor formal Islam. The larger number of people followed mixed systems derived largely from Bhakti and Sufi teachings and from local folk belief and practice. There was of course no concept of majority and minority religious communities until the introduction of these categories into Indian society by the British-Indian Census. Had the Census given the option of identifying oneself by a religious sect, the Bhakti-Sufi sects may well have constituted the majority religion.

Nor were religious communities monolithic and self-contained, neatly identified as Hindu, Muslim, Sikh, Christian, and so forth. Religion was more in the nature of a mosaic of sects, shading off into a pattern most suited to local people. The identity of these sects drew on caste, language and belief. Regional differences affected belief, custom and language but were open to negotiation. The Meos of Rajasthan had little in common with the Mappilas of Kerala, but both were placed under the formal category of Muslim in the British Census. Yet the matrilineal practices of the Mappilas were unorthodox, but essential to their social functioning and nonexistent among the Meos. Laws of marriage and inheritance, constituting the structural backbone of society, when implemented, often preferred following customary law rather than the norms of religious codes. Ethnography may provide a better historical understanding of the practice of religion in the subcontinent than theology.

Tensions and conflicts among the religious sects were by no means absent, but were localised. Conflict was not projected as that of one vast religious community against another. The connection between caste and sect also influenced the degree to which a religious textual code was observed or else social identities were negotiable. This is a different pattern of interface between religion and society as compared to societies where caste is absent, as for instance in China or in Europe. One litmus test of the prevalence of caste rules was whether any religion prohibited the practice of untouchability. We know that despite rejecting it in theory, all formal religions in India observed this segregation.

As historians therefore, we searched for the more fundamental reasons for change than merely the religion of the rulers. Historical debates were initiated on changes in society and economy, on culture and on the social function of religion. As a result perceptions of the relation between the past and the present underwent spectacular change from the 1960s, when history came to be written from these perspectives.

Ancient history was no longer one long unchanging stretch of 3,000 years. Substantial variations were recognised within this time span. The Harappan cities flourished for a millennium and then declined. Yet our knowledge about their governance or their religion is, as yet, based on intelligent guesses. Their decline is attributed to environmental causes. It has also been suggested that the supply of copper and lapis lazuli to the Mesopotamians may have sustained the Harappan economy, so when the states in West Asia declined it had a negative effect on the economy of the Harappans. This might be a salutary message for us today, dependent as we want to be on a single market-economy, not of our making.

The next period was that of agro-pastoralism, as suggested by archaeological evidence and Vedic texts. Communities of village settlements in northern India, were distinctively different from the urbanism of the Harappans. This has become a period of much controversy in contemporary India, not unconnected to the identity politics of the present.

The controversy is over the origin of the Aryans. The authors of the Vedic texts were speakers of Indo-Aryan and popularly called Aryans. Did they come from Central Asia, or Eastern Iran and the borderlands, or were they indigenous to India? If they were indigenous then it meant that they were from within the borders of British India. Remember that in ancient times alien identity was determined by cultural markers rather than by political boundaries. There were no boundaries drawn on maps as maps did not exist. Borders were anyway never permanent. The argument goes that if the Aryans were indigenous to India and that the Harappans were Aryans, then the Hindus, as Aryans, have an unbroken descent of 5,000 years and can therefore claim priority in today's Indian citizenship.

If they were not indigenous then it raises more challenging questions. These are the kinds of questions that historians ask in all situations experiencing an incoming migration even in later periods. How did Indo-Aryan come to be the dominant language, given that there is evidence of other language speakers, such as Dravidian, coexisting? This would have applied to the northwest and the Punjab and other parts of northern India as well. The old idea of an Aryan invasion has long since been discarded for lack of evidence. The alternative to the indigenous origin is that there were small-scale migrations of Aryan speakers from the northwest. This led to new patterns of settlements, and possibly the use of new technologies, technology being a significant factor of change. If the language was adopted by existing inhabitants then there would presumably have also been an intermeshing of cultures? Did the populations remain separate or did they mix? The historian has now to learn about DNA analysis and genetics, since this data has recently come into the history of populations.

Another major debate in history that questioned the earlier periodisation and relates closely to the past and the present focused on the formation of states and kingdoms in the first millennium AD. By about the 7th century, society and economy underwent a substantial transformation. A category of land-owning intermediaries was visible between the king and the peasant. Some historians described it as feudalism, but others disagreed. This led to a widespread debate initially focused on the Marxist definition of feudalism. Marxism and history came in for discussion and existing colonial perspectives were further questioned. Much new evidence came from increased investigations into regional history, and as a consequence, a marked increase in questions. It was further suggested that the same basic system continued into the period of the Sultanate, although the grantees of land were more varied some having come with the Sultans.

History is now a central discipline in the social sciences. This leads to questions of a diverse kind, some of which come from other social sciences. But we haven't lost our moorings in the humanities. What this change means is that the explanation of causes becomes far more complex than it was before. It adds enormously to the intellectual excitement of what one is analysing. But this does, of course, increase the distance between the professional historian and the public – and especially from those in the public who rush to pronounce on the past, even if they lack both information and the ability to analyse.

History has to rise beyond the politico-religious contentions that clouded the gaze of some historians a century ago. Historical writing now has to address itself to understanding and explaining the past. Testing the reliability of evidence is more exact. Historical investigation is based on a recognised method of critical enquiry. This is a necessary step before making a statement of fact.

Given this change in the orientation of historical studies, some of us took time off from research and wrote history textbooks for middle and high schools. We maintained that history was not like a multiplication table and that dates and events were not merely to be memorised. The student has to be encouraged to see the past from various aspects; and has to be taught that the past, going back to the earliest times, can be investigated. This helps in understanding its relevance. It teaches the young that learning how to constructively question existing knowledge is essential to being educated. The historian then becomes something of a detective working with limited clues.

Our textbooks were effectively questioning the mythology that accrues to popular historical narrative. The books were used for four decades up to 2005. Attempts were made to have them proscribed and we fought back. Fundamentalists of various hues were obviously unhappy with secular history that disallowed their mythologies.

When history starts interrogating the sources then the questioning becomes incisive. Let me illustrate what I am saying by referring to the familiar history of a monument, the temple at Somanatha. A monument is a physical fact, whether it is a temple, mosque, palace, or whatever. It becomes history when we know who built it and why, at what cost and labor, what determined its location, whom did it empower and legitimise, who bestowed wealth on it, and additionally in terms of its history, did its role change from past times to the present? As I went deeper into the history of this temple, the narrative became curiouser and curiouser, and I began to feel just like Alice in Wonderland.

The temple at Somanatha in Gujarat is embedded in layers of history and in modern myth-making. It is a great example of the past speaking to the past, and then the recent past speaking to the earlier pasts. In this case the historical perceptions of the monument became larger than life especially when its history was subjected to popular political perceptions as well. We all know the story that we grew up on. Mahmud of Ghazni desecrated the temple at Somanatha about a thousand years ago and destroyed the icon. Colonial writers claimed that this act created a trauma among Hindus and that it was the initial reason for Hindu-Muslim antagonism. This is another example of our accepting the colonial version of our history without investigating it.

What I did not know is that the history of the event and subsequent events is immensely complex with many perspectives and nuances. These are drawn from an array of sources some of which obviously contradict each other. It is not the simple story that is popularly accepted. So let me give you a small taste of the complexity.

The event is celebrated in a series of chronicles written by chroniclers to the Sultans and visitors from the Islamic world. In these, Mahmud is held up as an exemplar of an Islamic ruler. This imagery has been much embroidered both by medieval chroniclers and modern commentators. His marauding was confined to only one region of the subcontinent and beyond that he was unknown. Plundering wealth was not an extraordinary achievement, however much the chroniclers and some Persian texts eulogised it as a triumph over idolatry. The wealth after all was used to ensure further plunder.

It remains quite unclear as to what he destroyed at Somanatha. The object said to be destroyed strangely enough changes from one chronicle to the next. This naturally alters the historical explanation for the attack. The range of what may have been the destroyed object is vast. Some accounts say it was a *lingam*, either with a face or sometimes without one; or it is said to be the Arabian goddess Manat, either aniconic or in female shape, ordered to be destroyed by the Prophet; or there are stone figures of deities with jewels cascading out of their stone bellies; or a stone image but with arms that moved; or even more intriguingly, a metal *lingam* suspended in midair by a huge magnet placed in the ceiling of the shrine, arousing the curiosity of those who saw it. This last contraption is also described in an entirely different context in another part of the subcontinent and had obviously captured the popular imagination. Surely these contradictory descriptions cannot be taken seriously by us? Could they be a competition in fantasy? Clearly none of these authors knew quite what Mahmud had destroyed, nor was there a consensus about what had happened. The interesting question is: Why are the chroniclers inventing stories and fantasising the event? Was it just to glorify its reading as a religious act celebrating what they thought was a triumph of Islam? Should we not be asking what is actually implied in the connection between the temple, the object, the fantasy, the purpose of the chroniclers, and Mahmud?

And then there are stories of what happened to the temple. One chronicle tells us that Mahmud burnt the temple to ashes. Others write that subsequent to Mahmud's raid the temple was converted into a mosque. But strangely, every Sultan that came to the area, and there were many in the early centuries of the second millennium AD, each claimed in turn to have destroyed the structure. Why would Sultans be attacking a mosque and then taking credit even if the mosque was a converted temple? This somehow echoes the stories of Mahmud desecrating the Shia mosques in Multan and Mansura, although the reasons were different and did not apply to Somanatha. The texts of others who were not chroniclers continue to refer to it as still being a temple and much visited for worship. And we know it remained a temple at least until the 16th century when Akbar is said to have given it a grant as a temple. So the dome built over a part of it in an attempt to convert it into a mosque may have been later.

And there are many other sources too. An interesting bilingual inscription in Sanskrit and Arabic from Somanatha is a legal document recording the grant of land from the local political and civic authorities for the building of a new mosque at Somanatha by Nur-ud-din, a Persian trader. It dates to a couple of centuries after Mahmud and tells an entirely different story.

The administrators of the town and the management of this and other temples in the vicinity were active participants in the trade with the Arabs and Persians. They also made a grant from the Somanatha temple estate towards the building of this mosque. The relationship is cordial, the mosque is referred to as a *dharmasthana*, a sacred place, and there is no mention of the Somanatha temple being converted into a mosque.

A Jaina chronicle of the 14th century mentions the Chaulukya king, Kumarapala, rebuilding the temple at Somanatha as an impressive Shaiva temple. It is said to have fallen into disrepair because of neglect by its uncaring management and by intensive weathering of the stone, brought on by the spray from the sea beating against its walls – the temple being located on the shore of the sea. The remains of the earlier temples at this site were excavated in 1951. They confirm that some sculptures appear to have been deliberately mutilated but many suffered weathering by sea spray.

So how does the idea of the trauma of the Hindus and the hostility of the Hindus and Muslims first get currency? The story of events at Somanatha continues. A discussion takes place in the British Parliament, in the House of Commons, in 1843 on the action of the Governor-General in which Mahmud's raid on Somanatha is referred to. The Governor-General had issued the famous Proclamation of the Gates, asking his commander in Afghanistan to bring back the wooden gates from Mahmud's mausoleum said to have been taken by Mahmud from the Somanatha temple. The gates when brought back turned out to be from some other part of West Asia and not in the least bit Indian. In the course of a debate on whether the Governor-General acted rightly or wrongly, a member of the House of Commons mentioned for the first time that the Hindus are likely to have suffered a trauma because of Mahmud's raid, which event had led to hostility between Hindus and Muslims. The suggestion became a historical statement in colonial discourse, and subsequently in various nationalist discourses. The trauma was thus established without recourse to contemporary evidence. Avenging the raid of Mahmud, held responsible for creating this trauma, became a part of 20th century politics.

Those who worshipped in temples would not have relished such places being looted, but their reaction in this case seems not to have been a continuing trauma as has been projected in earlier reconstructions of the narrative. This is yet another instance of not questioning even the premise of the historical reconstruction, quite apart from recognising its impact on the modern politics of the subcontinent. We have here an example of an event of the 11th century being converted by later medieval chroniclers in various contradictory ways for legitimising their patrons, the sultans, and their religious affiliations and for political purposes; and now people in our time are using those very versions to legitimise current political activities. The event is so enveloped in these perceptions that it becomes difficult to assess it for what it was. This echoes the Roshomon presentation where each person gives his or her version of an event as each perceived it. We take the versions at face value and ignore the intensive investigation of the entire range of sources that should always be a prelude to statements about the past. It is difficult to ascertain what might have been the perceptions at that time of those who experienced or remembered the event, whether they were Hindu or Muslim, because the event has been overlaid by the politics of subsequent times.

How do we look at it now? Mahmud undoubtedly desecrated the temple of Somanatha. What actually followed, if we put all the sources together, is a far more complicated story than the one we are familiar with. It has multiple ramifications, involving trading arrangements, grants of land, the rebuilding of the temple, and the fascinating way in which these fragmentary narratives became entwined in folk narratives (an aspect of the narrative that I do not have time to go into here). It is necessary to locate and consider all the sources in narrating the event and the context of the period. It is these that the historian has to investigate in wishing to understand the past and to hear the dialogue between the past and the present.

The past then can become an agency in the construction and legitimising of current ideologies. Eric Hobsbawm had a memorable comment on this when he said, "For history is the raw material for nationalist or ethnic or fundamentalist ideologies, as poppies are the raw material for heroin addiction. The past is an essential element, perhaps the essential element, in these ideologies. If there is no suitable past it can always be invented."

Ideologies that were intended to encourage the creation of nation-states in the subcontinent now are in need of reassessment. Our nations have come into existence. Our concerns should be with re-examining the colonial stereotypes that still color our perceptions of who we are and where we are going. The colonial readings should be viewed for what they gave birth to. They need to be replaced by nurturing a sensitivity as to how we listen to the dialogue between the past and the present; how we determine the authenticity of the past; and how we recognise when a past is being configured only for use in the present, rather than for an understanding of itself.

And, as I have tried to suggest, it is not just the recent past that needs to be looked at afresh. We have to remember that even the events of today have elements of a long gestation of centuries. Perhaps what we need to understand is how, in the relationship between the past and the present, each impinges on the other. Such an insight is crucial, not only for itself but even more, for how we move towards our future.

Index